FAKE MEAT

REAL FOOD FOR VEGAN APPETITES

ISA CHANDRA MOSKOWITZ

ABRAMS, NEW YORK

Editor: Holly Dolce
Designer: Headcase Design, www.headcasedesign.com
Design Manager: Heesang Lee
Managing Editor: Lisa Silverman
Production Manager: Sarah Masterson Hally

Library of Congress Control Number: 2022933607

ISBN: 978-1-4197-4745-8
eISBN: 978-1-64700-861-1

Printed and bound in the United States

10 9 8 7 6 5 4 3 2 1

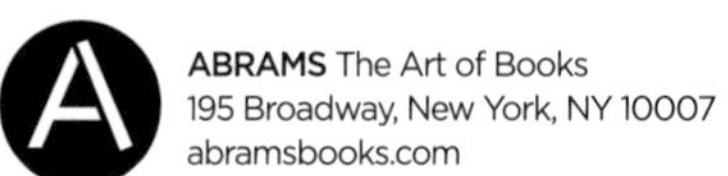

ABRAMS The Art of Books
195 Broadway, New York, NY 10007
abramsbooks.com

CONTENTS

INTRODUCTION

WHY FAKE MEAT?

How boring would life be if we didn't try new things? I am speaking about "we" as a civilization, and "we" as individuals who make breakfast.

Thousands of years ago, in the volcanic ash of the Andes, someone found a knobby clump and figured out a way to eat it.

"What could this be?"

She turned the clump over in her hands. It sprouted vines and small flowers and those vines led to more vines which led to more clumps. She smashed one with a rock. It split. She bit into it. She probably died.

But the community kept the seeds from the ones that didn't kill anyone. Again and again, year after year, seed after seed. That clump became a potato, or at least potato-ish. They kept at it. Cross-pollinating it in different soils, on reverse sides of the mountain, identifying the insects that did damage, and the ones that helped. The potatoes that survived, they thought, let's keep those.

Years passed. Thousands of years passed.

Today, we have french fries. We don't even think about how lucky we are, or how close we came to never having them. Both the fries, and us, may never have existed, had no one moved some poisonous vines just a few feet higher.

"What could this be?"

Food evolves.

Take meat. It wasn't until the Middle Ages—a time period when Europeans talked real weird—that "meat" even meant capital *M* "MEAT." "Mete" simply meant "food." So, when one serf asked another if he wanted some mete, no one started tweeting furiously that mete wasn't really mete. The mete industry didn't sue anyone. We simply ate it without question, probably without really caring what the word meant.

Because words evolve.

Both of these things, language and dinner, have held hands down a grassy path since the dawn of civilization.

I use the term "fake meat" in part because as a child I went to Jewish sleepaway camp in the Catskills, making me a natural comedian. This description is tongue in cheek, yes, but it's also true. Although it may not be true forever.

"OK, thanks for the history lesson, now how do I make vegan chicken nuggets?" I hear you, we are getting there.

Before that, a little story.

The first time I tried mock meat, as we called it back then, I was on a bus in Brooklyn, straphanging with a friend after watching *Indiana Jones and the Last Crusade*. He was pissed because I talked through the whole movie, a trait that I find charming but everyone else finds annoying.

I had recently joined a Buddhist temple. The congregation was kind, and it necessitated that I build a shrine in my bedroom filled with kumquats, cool art, and scarves that smelled like an incense shop.

He was making fun of me about that, and I was making fun of him because that's what teenagers do on public buses.

I wasn't vegetarian yet, but I had thought about it. To be honest, I wasn't sure the meat I was eating even contained that much meat (remember Steak-umms?) Still, I was dissing him for being vegetarian. And he said I should be, too, if I was going to be Buddhist.

And this is where the story gets weird. He pulled a little zip-top bag out of his ripped jeans pocket.

Inside were saucy, mahogany bits of food, which I learned to be wheat gluten. I refer to it, still to this day, as the "pocket seitan." He asked me to just try it, and I never turn down a dare.

Days later he took me to the origin of the pocket seitan: a restaurant in Chinatown called House of Vegetarian. On the menu, Hot Steak Kew. Much better warm on a plate. Chewy morsels covered in savory gravy that I still can't crack the code on.

It was there, dipping my dumplings into the leftover sauce, that I decided to give up meat.

Do I miss it? I don't, which is ironic, maybe, since I am hell-bent on re-creating it. But I didn't give up meat because I didn't like it. I just realized that I could never look a cow in the eye, her big, beautiful eye, with the gorgeous eyelashes, and cause harm to her. And why can't my eyelashes look like that?

As a child, I cried at *Bambi*. I tried to save every dog I found. I talked to my cat like he was my personal therapist.

I'm an animal lover and that love doesn't end when I get hungry.

But here's what I do miss: Aromas. Experiences. Methods. Traditions. And as for that last one, traditions, I've been creating new ones for over thirty years.

My brain must be a gravy boat because I remember all the tastes and sensations from my meat-eating days, even though they were so long ago. My grandmother's meatballs, burnt on one side. Stuffed clams at a café along the bay, crusty on top, my teeth scraping against the hard shell. My favorite pizza burger from a diner underneath a midtown office building, the feel of the vinyl seat as I bounced with excitement at the sight of the melty mozz arriving at the table. Reaching for spareribs from the Chinese restaurant, in a white foil bag, each one smothered in caramelized sauce that you sucked off your fingers.

These are the moments I guess you could say I miss. But I don't have to.

The point isn't always to completely re-create the inspiration. Often, it's an invocation, a rough translation. Some are more realistic than others. Could a vegan Philly Cheesesteak trick anyone? Most likely. But will someone mistake a cauliflower wing for a piece of chicken? Probably not. Instead it suggests, hey, a cauliflower wing is its own delicious thing. And I'm going to call it a wing because it invokes a wing. And you can't stop me.

"What could this be?"

In a hundred years will a new generation be discussing how a "wing" once came from an actual animal? No one would ever possibly believe it.

Needless to say, fake meat has been around a lot longer than me. By the time I put my chopsticks down and savored the very last of my very first fake meat experience, it had already existed for hundreds, maybe thousands, of years. Recipes for fake lamb appear in a Chinese cookbook from 900 CE. Mostly it was tofu.

Throughout history human beings have thrown themselves into the food-making process, come what may. And it's with that spirit that we leap into fake meat.

Not everything is quick and easy, but it won't take a millennium, either.

While thinking all this over I texted my friend, the one from the bus. I asked if he remembered anything at all about that day. He responded, "I only remember you being terrible to go to the movies with."

So I'm still vegan, and still annoying. But I promise those are totally unrelated.

INGREDIENTS

There are two main ways that I translate meat into vegan versions. Let's break it down into: literally and symbolically. My goal is to reach a nice balance between these two approaches in this book. To that end, you'll find common whole foods and relatively obscure specialty items, aka "weirdo ingredients."

1) Literally: Trying to mimic the taste and texture of familiar meats. Creating a very literal fake meat that is aimed at making people ask, "Is this real?" Yes, it's *real*, you'll say with a wink. *But it's vegan*. A few examples: flaky chicken nuggets, juicy meatballs, and veal Parmesan. Unless you have a gluten allergy, it might escape you that these yummy bites are vegan. A lot of these types of recipes are made with wheat gluten.

2) Symbolically: Translating vegetables and legumes into meaty facsimiles. This is a more creative approach to using conventional whole foods and a fun project for me, personally. Sometimes it's about visual appeal, as in the case of Root Marrow (page 227). It's inspired by bone marrow, created from roasted parsnips filled with a savory pâté. One bite and you know it's not a bone, but it's playful and delicious. Another, more familiar, example is cauliflower wings (page 211). Their organic shape has made them a mainstream darling of the fake meat world, but I don't think most people will mistake them for chicken.

THE VEGGIE BURGER DILEMMA

Sometimes you have a recipe that fits neatly into both categories. This is called the Veggie Burger Dilemma. Well, just by me. It's something that is both symbolic and literal and has been accepted into society. No one questions veggie burgers anymore. They are their own beautiful thing.

THE FAKE MEAT PANTRY

FLAVOR BOMBS

Nutritional Yeast
Aka nooch, a yellow pixie dust that floats around your kitchen, turning everything it touches vegan. We use it in cheeses for both taste and texture; it's nutty and savory! But we also use it in fake meats. With the touch of a tablespoon, you can cut into the meat to play with texture, making it flakier or chewier while also imparting an umami punch.

Kala Namak
Egg salt is a thing! These recipes call for it in its fine, powdery form. It's also known as Indian Black Salt, but when ground, it's actually a beautiful shade of light pink that deserves to be Pantone color of the year, every year. That flavor is something else, though. Sulfuric and yolky, adding eggy flavor primarily to omelets, salads, and dressings, but it's also a nice addition to fake meats at times, when you wanna little intrigue.

Citric Acid
This isn't a total necessity here; it's found in only a few recipes for cheese and seasoning. But it is a fun ingredient to play with if you want that lip-puckering punch. You won't find it in most stores, so this is one you'll want to special-order online.

Miso
What would we do without miso! So much flavor, zero fuss. Miso is a fermented bean paste that originated in Japan more than two millennia ago. With all its nuance and umami notes, miso is doing half the cooking for you. The two kinds I use in this book are chickpea miso and red miso. Chickpea miso is the milder of the two; it has a cheesy flavor with a pleasant bitterness (like Swiss cheese, for example) and a hint of sweetness. I use it primarily in sauces and cheeses, but also in meats that are lighter in color. It's soy-free, so I use it when I'm keeping allergens in mind as well. Red miso kicks up the funk! It's rich and salty with a red wine aroma. Its meaty flavor is a key ingredient when making red meats, like steaks and other beef dishes.

Dried Porcini Mushrooms
If you take all the mushroom flavor in the universe and pack it into one small little morsel, then you have a dried porcini. Porcinis taste like a magical meaty forest after the rain—like black truffles, sourdough, and steak all at once. When concentrated, that flavor is turned up to eleven. I use dried porcini in anything I want to call "beefy." Beyond the flavor, when rehydrated, they become sink-your-teeth-into-it chewy. Sometimes they're used whole and sometimes blended smooth with other ingredients. You can also process them into a powder to use as a seasoning, or purchase them in powder form.

Truffle Oil
If you use truffle oil on the TV show *Chopped*, you're essentially digging your own grave and are definitely the next to go. However, in the fake meat universe, you'll have a seat at the head of the table. I use it sparingly with other seasonings to enhance umami overall. In cheeses (like Swiss especially), it lends a je ne sais quoi flavor that no one identifies immediately as truffle.

Liquid Smoke
Don't do as I did as a young and wild vegan; use this stuff sparingly or prepare to have everything taste like a campfire. I used to be addicted to it but have learned with age and wisdom that a little bit really does go a long way. But when you want smoky bacon and don't want to break out the smoker, nothing beats a dewy drop or two.

Tomato Paste
There're a million different permutations for tomato products at the grocery store, but this is the only one that is pure, concentrated tomato goodness. Thick, rich, and full of umami, it adds both color and scads of flavor to all sorts of meats. Even if you don't want an overtly tomato-tasting dish, just a little dab of this stuff will do wonders to create depth and nuance. I buy it in tube form that can be refrigerated for nonwasteful ease and convenience.

Sun-Dried (and Smoked Sun-Dried) Tomatoes

There are sexier ingredients stealing the headlines, but tomatoes are high in natural glutamates, which are what's responsible for umami flavor. Drying them further concentrates their umami quotient, turning each tiny, shriveled fruit into an absolute flavor bomb. Sun-dried tomatoes packed in oil are more meat-like than those that are simply dried, thanks to all that fatty goodness. Some recipes call for smoked sun-dried tomatoes, which come in packages. They can be hard to find, so get thee to the internet.

Sauerkraut Juice

Whatever you do, don't dump that brine! That stuff is valuable culinary currency. In Germany, and on the internet, they even sell it separately, no cabbage involved. Definitely purchase some juice if you plan on making lots of cheese. Otherwise, just use the leftover kraut juice from your hot dog party. This liquid adds funky, stinky flavors to cheese like nothing else, and don't forget those built-in probiotics for a natural fermentation assist.

Vegetable Broth

Lots of these recipes call for vegetable broth, and although I offer recipes for every style—beefy, chicken-y, and ocean-y—you can't always make your own. There are so many options on the market, too! I always recommend bouillon cubes or concentrate for flavor, but also because packages of broth are so expensive. As far as brands, you can find beef-style and unchicken versions of Better Than Bouillon, and those are great concentrates. Beyond that, choose those with high-quality ingredients, avoiding the words "natural ingredients" and "palm oil" on the label.

LET'S GET NUTS

Cashews

Some people might look at cashews and see bar snacks, but vegans see plant-based dairy. Butter, milk, cheese, ice cream, heavy cream—you name it, cashews can make it. Most of the recipes in this book call for a high-speed blender; however, if you don't have one you can get those same results by soaking. Place cashews in enough water to submerge the nuts by a few inches and soak them overnight. If you're impatient or don't plan it out in advance, you can always boil them gently for 20 minutes instead. Then cool them and use as directed in the recipe.

Walnuts

They don't call the shelled morsels "nut meat" for nothing. Chopped finely, they turn toothsome, rich, and perfect for adding texture and flavor to burgers, loaves, and ground meats. Go for raw walnuts, not toasted, for a more neutral flavor.

I'M SOY EXCITED

Extra-Firm Tofu

Bean curd, the original meat substitute, the *real* white meat, is still a staple. Here we use it whole to form all manner of chick'ny business. But it's also used blended into gluten for a springier wheat meat, or pureed into a custard for eggy things.

Extra-Firm Silken Tofu

Though it sounds like an oxymoron, tofu *can* be both extra firm and silken at the same time! This is only possible with the aseptic packages that are shelf stable, not the water-packed, refrigerated variety. They have the heft and density of conventional extra-firm tofu but can be blended to a silky-smooth consistency without a hint of grit. Mori-Nu is the most popular brand, and my favorite one.

Tempeh

Tempeh is its own food group. My passion for it only grows as I cook with it and discover its versatility. Basically, it's a fermented bean cake. But it is anything but basic. From vegan classics to tempeh bacon, to ground up and seasoned like sausage in Cacio e Pepe (page 190), tempeh's nutty flavor and succulent texture is a fake meat treasure box.

Yuba

The luxurious skin that forms in a pot of cooking tofu. It has a legacy almost as impressive as its tofu parent, but I didn't work with it very much before writing this book. I quickly came to realize that it's convenient AF and no more complicated than boiling pasta. It turns into a highly versatile "skin" that crisps up beautifully and soaks up flavor like nobody's business. Here, I use only the dried variety, for ease and consistent results, but separately from these recipes I urge you to seek out fresh yuba if you've never used it. So simple and yummy for stir-fries and wrapping stuff in.

Textured Vegetable Protein

TVP has entered the chat. It's dehydrated soy protein, to be precise, which is why some label it as TSP; same difference. TVP comes in many shapes and sizes, but we use it in granule form here. The granules are tiny pea-size pieces that are chewy and springy. On their own, they offer a nice meaty bite, perfect for making ground meat and tuna or chicken salads. We also add them to seitan to create flakiness and something akin to gristle. Brands I recommend: Bob's Red Mill, Anthony's, and NOW.

FLOURS, BINDERS, AND SUCH

Vital Wheat Gluten

Vegans have been making "hail seitan" jokes for years. This book really takes it to an extreme. The flour made from pure wheat protein is the building block for many a fake meat. There is no substitute for it. It is truly wheat meat! Depending on what it's blended with, it can create any texture imaginable. There's only one problem: The protein content from brand to brand can vary A LOT. Some contain 60 percent protein, while others have 75 percent. For the most consistent results, don't find a no-name brand that seems a lot cheaper. I used either Bob's Red Mill or Arrowhead Mills wheat gluten to develop these recipes.

Breadcrumbs

Maybe you're a homemaker who likes to make your own breadcrumbs from homemade sourdough. Well, stop it. Or don't blame me if the recipe doesn't come out as stated. Store-bought breadcrumbs yield consistent results in meatloaves and meatballs. Just be careful to read labels and avoid anything with added cheese or other mysterious, unpronounceable ingredients. If you must make your own, just make sure they are as fine and dry and as close as possible to the kind you find in a store. If you're looking for gluten-free, might I recommend gluten-free panko. If the recipe calls for fine breadcrumbs, just give them a whirr in a blender.

Chickpea Flour

The chickpea is the Giving Tree of the vegan pantry. We use it in every way, shape, and form. Have you tried chickpeas ground up into a fine, powdery flour? We mix it into fake meats to play with flavor and texture, but also into crispy batters, eggy fillings, and for gluten-free fake meatiness.

Pea Protein

Spoiler alert: It's protein from split peas! Shocking, right? You may know it as a smoothie booster, but we use it in seitan recipes to play with the texture, creating flakiness in chick'n and tenderness in sausages. You can use chickpea flour instead, but the bean flavor will be more pronounced.

REAL WEIRD STUFF—GELS AND STARCHES

Tapioca Flour

Answering the question: What if cornstarch and chewing gum had a baby? Also described as tapioca starch, it's a bright white powder derived from cassava root, and it creates a uniquely stretchy texture when cooked with liquid. That means it's perfect for making gooey cheese sauces and creamy, sliceable blocks.

Carrageenan

Carrageenan is simply seaweed that's dried and ground into powder, frequently seen in products from salad dressing to soy milk. Here, we use it most often in cheeses. It's different from other gels, because you see the results immediately. Add some water and watch it bloom into a luxuriously gloopy mess! Its big magic trick is that it can melt again and again after it's set, which makes it ideal for making meltable cheeses. Occasionally, it's handy when thrown into a meat or two, if you want a springier, chewier bite.

Agar-Agar

It's vegan gelatin from the sea! This book uses powdered agar exclusively, for ease and simplicity—ignore the agar flakes, and a hex upon the agar bricks. Although agar-agar is not a direct substitute for gelatin, it can be used in similar ways: to gel, set, thicken, and make it bounce.

SPICE RACK

Poultry Seasoning

We use poultry seasoning like it's going out of business in, you guessed it, the chick'n chapter! Check out page 89 for a DIY poultry seasoning and other suggestions.

Kelp Powder

There aren't plenty of fish in the sea anymore, but there is an abundance of seaweed! Kelp packs in that same oceanic, briny flavor for making excellent vegan seafood. It comes in cute convenient shakers, too, usually with a picture of a wave on them so you get a little art for your spice rack. You can also replace it with ground nori. Just make sure the nori sheets are lightly toasted and completely dry so they don't gunk up your food processor.

Turmeric

Called "poor man's saffron" by some, a little pinch of this ground tuber will give everything a gorgeous golden glow. Painting everything varying shades of yellow—from cheeses to fake meats to eggy stuff—it's indispensable for creating a more convincing vegan version of our favorite foods.

Smoked Paprika

Smoked paprika is the MVP of your spice rack, bearing the gentle warmth of punchy, sharp Hungarian paprika with a soulful depth of smoky flavor. If there was any one spice to buy in bulk, this is it. I have yet to taste a recipe where I thought, "This is good, but maybe there's too much smoked paprika." I don't think it's possible to overdo it, and you'll easily blow through your first bottle once you start putting it on everything.

A LEAGUE OF THEIR OWN

Beet Powder

OK, so I joke about calling this *The Beet Powder Cookbook*. It dominates my pantry triumphantly, in its snazzy fuchsia packaging, because color is important. Whether turning tofu pink for tuna or adding a deep red hue to pastrami, beet powder is the ROOT of all fake meat. It does have an earthy flavor, but in the amounts we use, your taste buds probably won't pick up on it.

Jackfruit

Jackfruit became the talk of the vegan town in the 2000s, and with good reason. It's got a flaky texture, perfect for pull-apart shredded pork. But, because it lacks fat and flavor, it was never my darling. However, I'm not one to completely cast aside vegan ingredients! I found that I love it marinated and grilled until smoky, or as part of a stew that has body and flavor from other ingredients. Plus, when combined with seitan, it creates a really great gristle that works wonders for the overall texture. This book calls for canned, young jackfruit that's packed in water. Make sure it's not canned in juice or syrup, or else your meats will taste like a confusing tropical smoothie. I always rinse it first to get rid of any tinny taste from the can and prepare it to soak up some real flavor.

SPECIALTY EQUIPMENT AND ACCOUTREMENTS

High-Speed Blender

I resisted a high-speed blender for so long, because I wanted to be one with the people. But I came to realize that time is money! A Vitamix or Blendtec will be the last blender you will ever buy, and the amount of time you save will add up to eternity. Basically, you'll be a vampire. If you have a regular old blender, you can get by, but make sure to read the recipe thoroughly. If it contains cashews that need to be blended, you can boil the cashews for about 20 minutes in plenty of water, or soak the cashews overnight. Drain them and they're ready to use!

Steamer

Have your steamer ready before busting out any ingredients. This could be anything from a wire rack in a large pot with an inch or two of water at the bottom to a fancy, stand-alone unit. My preferred steamer is a large pasta pot with a deep steamer basket that fits right inside.

No matter the vessel, keep it covered with more foil across the top to trap the heat and steam inside. Watch the heat, since you don't want all the water to evaporate. That might be unavoidable, depending on your pan, so keep a close eye and top it off with more water if needed. Just like you would never walk away from an open flame, don't let the long periods of inactivity convince you that it's safe to go doomscrolling on Facebook for an hour. I mean, you can, but stay in the kitchen and glance up at the food every now and then to make sure it's not going awry.

Cast-Iron Pan

No kitchen is complete without a cast-iron pan. It's incredibly versatile, capable of withstanding intense heat from the oven or grill, while still looking highly Instagrammable right on the table. Once seasoned, it has a naturally nonstick coating and will last a lifetime with the proper care. Love your cast-iron pan and it will love you back, if a skillet was capable of such deep emotion.

Cast-Iron Wok

Sometimes the pan is just not big enough! A cast-iron wok is perfect for large batches of pasta or noodles that have lots of ingredients you need to toss around without making a mess.

Cast-Iron Grill

Something about dark, evenly spaced grill marks makes everyone want to drop their drinks and bust out their camera phones. Beyond the obvious curb appeal, a solid sear is incredibly satisfying to sink your teeth into. This is my solution, in lieu of a charcoal grill.

Too Many Mixing Bowls

Yes, you need too many mixing bowls. Trust me.

Dry Measuring Cups

I used dry measures to test all the recipes. Even for the liquids, as long as they're not over 4 cups. You should do the same for the most consistent results.

Granny Spatch™

I trademarked the granny spatula. Fine, I didn't. But I should. What it is, is a very flexible, thin metal spatula and I am constantly calling for one to flip, sauté, and generally move your food around without losing the gorgeous browning and grill marks you just worked for. Do not waste your time trying to keep a sear with a rubber spatula; they work about as well as a flip-flop.

Smoker

While you don't need to run out and buy a $400 Bluetooth digital electric smoker, it would be pretty cool, right? Okay, most of my smoking happens in a cheap roasting pan. Just scatter some wood chips in the bottom, put your meats on a rack positioned right above it, loosely cover the pan with foil, and apply heat. You'll know it's working its magic when you start seeing ominous wisps of smoke emerge. Side note: You might want to temporarily take the batteries out of your smoke detector before getting started.

Cheesecloth

Cheesecloth: It's not just for cheese anymore. We do use this gauzy fabric for some vegan cheeses, but also for wrapping up seitan that needs more room to breathe. Once you have it on hand, you'll find a million uses for it. Buy it by the yard if you can.

Masher

Crush, smush, and pulverize your food the old-fashioned way. If you have unaddressed anger issues, this should be one of your favorite tools. You can probably find a vintage one at a yard sale for a buck, or ask a neighbor and they might just give you theirs for free. A proper potato masher is essential but also ridiculously cheap, so don't waste your money on a purported "deluxe" model. Because we use it to mash more than potatoes, find a masher that can really get the small stuff, like chickpeas and tempeh. Find one that is just a circular piece of metal with holes in it, instead of a zigzaggy one.

Fine-Mesh Strainer or Sieve

Sieve? Strainer? It's all the same thing. Leave your pasta colander out of this because those holes are too big and spread out to be helpful right now. Get something with solid construction that won't buckle under pressure, since you'll have to apply force from time to time.

Parchment Paper and Aluminum Foil

These two sheets will help wrap up any job in the kitchen, big or small. For parchment, opt for unbleached when possible and NEVER waxed. It's perfect for creating a smooth surface on tube meats, like hot dogs. Aluminum (aka tin) foil molds to any odd shape and holds tight, but tends to get wrinkly very quickly. Sometimes one is better suited for a recipe than the other, and sometimes they work harmoniously together, like practiced partners in crime.

Smoke Chips

The most flavorful wood chips for smoking come from deciduous trees, such as hickory, applewood, pecan, and mesquite. Some are more mild while others are super assertive. Each one imparts a unique taste, so try them out and see which you like best. You can often find a decent selection at hardware stores, near the grills.

ICONIC SANDWICHES

If your eyes always wander over to the sandwich section on a menu, you're not alone. What is more satisfying than meat and bread? Exactly. And that is why sandwiches are the perfect starting point for the fake meat journey we are about to embark on.

The convenience. The comfort. The customization. The condiments! Sandwiches have it all and, to keep up the words beginning with C theme, there is nothing more craveable.

I aimed to cover the gamut here to meet all your needs. Whether you are bringing a few sammies to a picnic or sitting in front of the TV (watching a historical documentary, of course), you will find a sandwich for every occasion.

It's all about combining flavors and textures. Creaminess and crunchiness. Balancing warm and cold items. And don't forget the pickles! Some of the recipes here are seitan, to mimic the taste and appearance of meat. Or tofu thinly sliced and marinated to make everyone say "tastes like chicken." And some are vegetable stunt doubles, to evoke and play with the idea of meat. Roasted parsnips are lobster. Smoky beets are ham. Because it's fun and because I said so.

There is some debate on what exactly the definition of a sandwich is. Like, are burgers and hot dogs sandwiches? My philosophy: If it comes on bread, it's in this chapter and then it's in your mouth. Case closed. Also, there's a taco in the sandwich section. So sue me.

This chapter will provide you not only with heaven on bread, but also with meaty recipes that you can use anywhere meat is needed. So if you're just looking for some fake meat to use elsewhere, this is the spot! You don't have to make the whole sandwich. That roast beef would be great in a salad. That pulled pork would be an excellent accompaniment to some rice and beans, no? And you can use the lunch meats however you like. Let's do this thing!

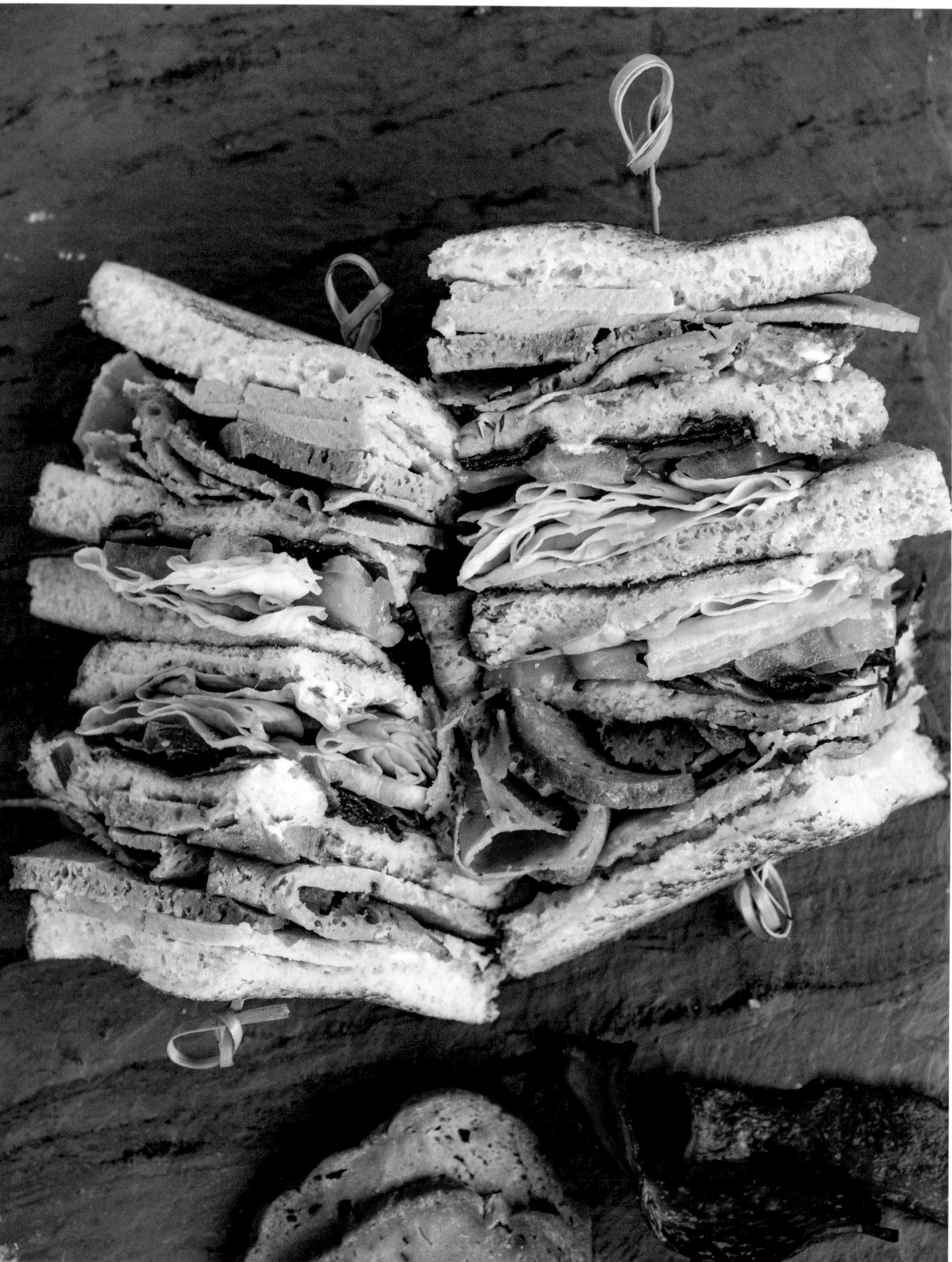

JOIN THE CLUB TURKI SANDWICHES

Makes 4 sandwiches

Let's start with the classic club! Juicy turkey piled high with crisp lettuce, heirloom tomato—or use regular tomato, I can't stop you—and smoky bacon. Add some cheddar to the mix and you've got yourself a sandwich that Dagwood would be proud of. And if you're too young to know who the hell Dagwood is, how about swapping in a real stoner like Pete Davidson? He'd absolutely murder this sandwich.

So how to make vegan turki slices? The alchemy is simple. A blend of pureed tofu for flexibility, a little textured vegetable protein pulsed in for gristle, and agar seals the deal with a nice chewy bite that slices beautifully.

If you don't feel like stacking, the turki slices are perfectly happy being tucked between two slices of whole wheat bread for a wholesome lunch instead. Pete Davidson would still absolutely destroy it.

- 1 loaf Roast Turki (recipe follows)
- 1 large heirloom tomato
- 12 slices soft but sturdy white bread
- Vegan mayo, prepared or homemade (page 309)
- 12 crispy romaine lettuce leaves
- Salt and freshly ground black pepper
- 1 recipe Trumpet Mushroom Bacon (page 167), or bacon of your choice
- 8 slices vegan cheddar, prepared or homemade (page 291)
- 16 long toothpicks

1. Use a steak knife to thinly slice the turkey on a bias, about ⅛ inch (3 mm) thick. Slice the tomato about ⅛ inch (3 mm) thick as well, and lightly blot with a paper towel so it doesn't make the sandwich too wet and slippery.
2. Toast the bread. Dry off the cutting board and place eight slices of the toast in a single layer. Have the other four slices at the ready. Spread mayo on the eight slices.
3. Top four of the slices with the lettuce and tomato. Sprinkle on a little salt and pepper. Layer four slices of bacon on top of each stack.
4. Spread mayo on both sides of the four remaining slices of toast and place them on top of the bacon layer.
5. Layer a good amount of folded turki slices on each sandwich. Then add the cheddar slices. Top with the last four pieces of bread, mayo side down.
6. Place a toothpick in each quadrant of a sandwich, and use a serrated knife to carefully slice it into four triangles. Repeat with the other sandwiches. Serve a few triangles on their sides, so diners can see how much work went into this!

HOT TAKE

If you choose not to make or buy vegan cheddar, there is no shame in an avocado club sandwich! Just replace the cheese with thinly sliced avocado.

ROAST TURKI

Makes 2 turki loaves

Turki is probably one of the first fake meats people try, thanks to the ubiquitousness of tofu turkey, which has been the punch line in many a Sunday comic strip since the Reagan administration. But the eighties are over, and no one reads the Sunday comics! Turki has performed a heroic 180 from ironic gag to national treasure. Drape it into a sandwich slathered with mayo or mustard, or even both. You can also use it cooked in Turki Pot Pie (page 259) or Turki Tetrazzini (page 203). It comes together quickly, and is baked in parchment for that beautiful crusty skin and roasty flavor.

- ½ cup (35 g) textured vegetable protein (TVP)
- 7 ounces (half a block/ 200 g) extra-firm tofu
- 2 teaspoons apple cider vinegar
- ¼ cup (15 g) nutritional yeast flakes
- 3 tablespoons tamari
- 2 tablespoons olive oil
- 1 teaspoon salt
- 1 teaspoon granulated sugar
- 1 teaspoon agar powder
- 2¼ cups (270 g) vital wheat gluten
- 2 teaspoons poultry seasoning, store-bought or homemade (page 89)
- 1 teaspoon onion powder

1 First, prepare the TVP. Submerge it in a pot of water, bring to a low simmer, and cook for about 10 minutes. Turn the heat off and let rest for 10 minutes. Strain into a mesh strainer and let cool completely in the strainer while you get everything else ready. Once cool enough to handle, push the TVP against the strainer to squeeze out as much liquid as possible. If you don't squeeze enough it will mess up the water/gluten ratio and the world will end.

2 In a blender, puree the tofu, 1¼ cups (300 ml) water, the apple cider vinegar, nutritional yeast, tamari, olive oil, salt, and sugar until smooth. This will take less than a minute in a high-speed blender, and about 3 minutes in a standard blender. Add the agar and blend briefly (make sure the mixture doesn't get hot so you don't activate the agar). Pulse in the cooked and cooled TVP. Don't blend it until smooth, just 10 pulses or so to get it incorporated while retaining some texture.

3 Prepare two 14-inch (36 cm) pieces each of aluminum foil and parchment paper. Place a 14-inch sheet of parchment on top of each sheet of foil. Preheat the oven to 350°F (175°C).

4 In a large bowl, sift together the vital wheat gluten, poultry seasoning, and onion powder. Make a well in the center. Mix in the wet stuff from the blender. Knead for 5 minutes or so until it's stringy and springy.

5 Divide the dough in half. Form two fat loaves that are roughly 8 inches (20 cm) long. Wrap each one in a piece of parchment-lined foil and secure the edges by twisting. Make it snug but not too tight as the loaves will expand in the oven.

6 Place the loaves directly on an oven rack and bake for about 50 minutes, using tongs to turn them every 15 to 20 minutes or so.

7 Let the turki loaves cool completely in the wrappers, for about an hour.

HOT TAKE

If you're putting in the effort of making your own turki, you might as well make enough for leftovers! The recipe makes double what you'll need. Save the other half for snacking, or try Turki Pot Pie (page 259) or Leftover Turki Salad (page 80).

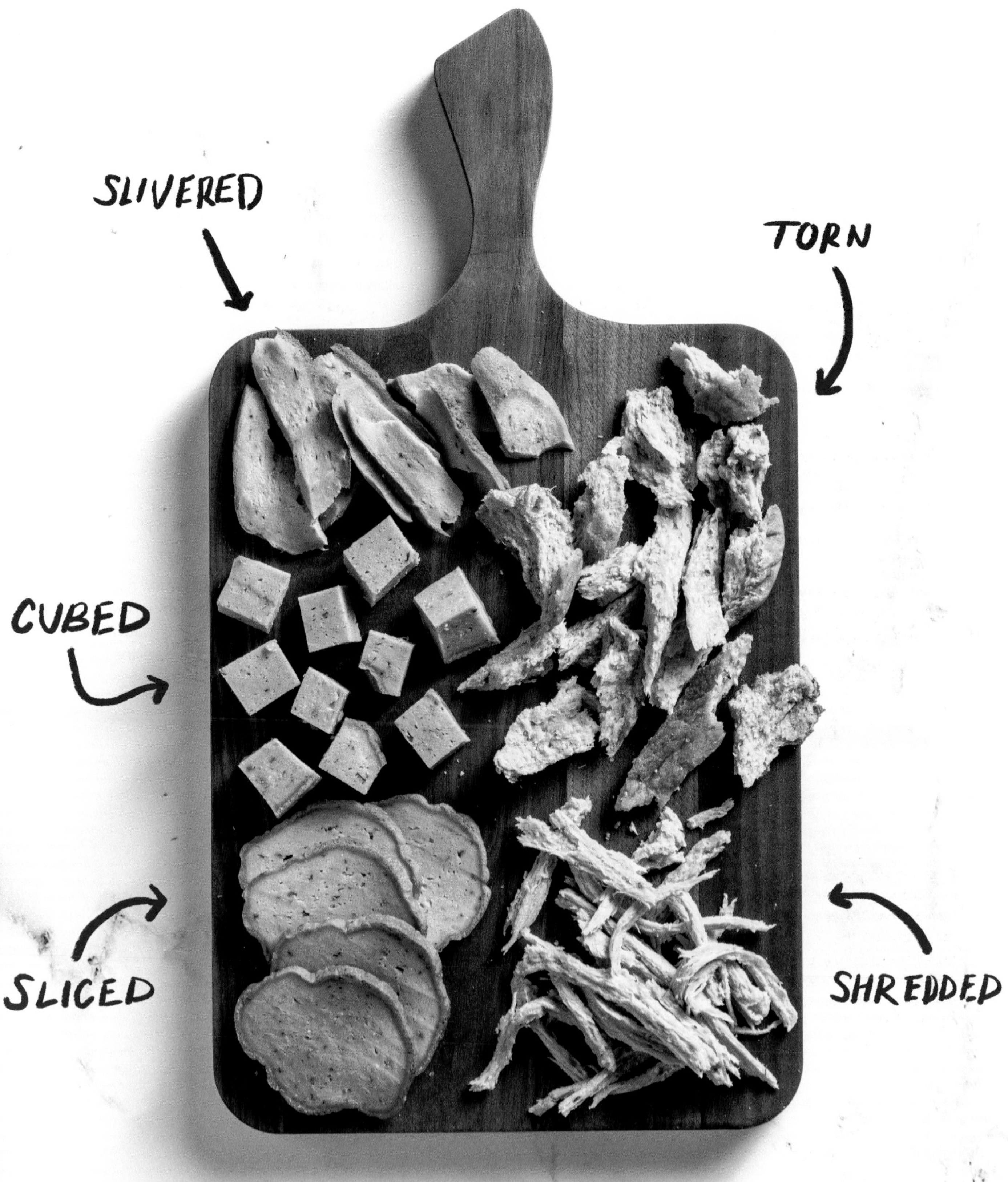
SLIVERED
TORN
CUBED
SLICED
SHREDDED

NOSHVILLE HOT HONEES

Makes 4 sandwiches

Confession: I've only been to Nashville once and it was lovely. I bought some Carl Sagan records at Jack White's record store, but I didn't get to have any vegan Nashville hot honey chicken! So I went ahead and made my own. Introducing Noshville Hot Honee, because you're gonna wanna nosh. A spicy, buttery glaze over a crisp, breaded tofu cutlet. What I think separates this from the pack is the fresh minced garlic instead of powdered. It really upgrades the flavor here, bringing everything together—sweet, spicy, pungent, and salty. Ugh, so good. I use FTAP tofu (page 89) to soak up loads of chicken-y essence, and lend a chewy texture. You can easily make it gluten free with some gluten-free panko. If you want the sauce even hotter, add a little cayenne to taste. I left the breading mild so that you can adjust the heat to your liking via the sauce.

- 5 cups (1.2 liters) Chick'n Broth (page 299) or prepared vegetable broth
- 2 tablespoons olive oil
- 2 tablespoons fresh lemon juice
- 2 tablespoons tamari
- 1 tablespoon poultry seasoning, prepared or homemade (page 89)
- 1 (14-ounce/400 g) block FTAP tofu (page 89)
- ¼ cup (30 g) all-purpose flour
- 1 tablespoon cornstarch
- 2 cups (200 g) dry breadcrumbs
- ½ teaspoon ground black pepper
- 1 teaspoon salt
- Oil, for sautéeing

1 In a wide rimmed bowl, mix together 3 cups (720 ml) of the vegetable broth, the olive oil, lemon juice, tamari, and poultry seasoning. Slice the FTAP tofu the long way into 4 rectangular planks. The long way means if the block of tofu is sitting flat on the counter, imagine it's a book and make the cuts in the direction of the pages. Marinate the tofu in the bowl for about an hour, flipping occasionally.

2 Make the slurry and breading. In a wide shallow bowl, use a fork to mix together the flour and cornstarch. Add 1 cup (240 ml) broth and stir well until it's a thick smooth paste. Mix the remaining cup of broth into the slurry. On a large rimmed plate, mix together the breadcrumbs, pepper, and salt.

3 Now form an assembly line, from left to right: the marinated tofu, the slurry, the breadcrumbs mixture, and lastly a piece of parchment to put the prepared cutlets on.

4 Lift the tofu out of the marinade. Dip the cutlets one by one into the slurry, letting the excess drip off. Transfer to the breadcrumbs bowl and use the other hand to sprinkle a handful of breadcrumbs over the tofu to coat completely. Transfer to the parchment and repeat with remaining slices. Make sure you use one hand for the wet batter and the other for the dry batter, or you'll end up with a breadcrumb glove on your hand.

CONTINUED →

FOR THE HOT HONEE SAUCE:

- ¼ cup (60 ml) refined coconut oil
- 4 cloves minced garlic
- ¼ cup (60 ml) Vegan for My Honee (page 306) or agave syrup
- ¼ cup (60 ml) Louisiana-style cayenne hot sauce, such as Tabasco
- ½ teaspoon sweet paprika
- ½ teaspoon salt

FOR ASSEMBLY:

- 4 potato buns
- Vegan mayo, prepared or homemade (page 309)
- Pickles
- Super Simple Slaw (page 312)

5 Preheat a large cast-iron skillet over medium heat. Spray the pan with oil. Cook the cutlets for about 6 minutes on each side, spraying the pan with more oil as needed. Remove the pan from heat.

6 Preheat the oven to 350°F (175°C). This will be for toasting bread. In the meantime, make the hot honee sauce: Melt 2 tablespoons of the coconut oil in a small saucepan over medium heat. Add the garlic and lightly cook it for about 30 seconds. Transfer the garlicky oil to a mixing bowl while still hot. Add the remaining 2 tablespoons oil to melt. Then mix in the honee, hot sauce, paprika, and salt.

7 Now form the things! Slice the buns and place them in the oven for 5 minutes. Remove from oven when toasted and have them lined up on plates, ready to go. Spread the bottom buns with mayo. Layer on some pickles.

8 Dunk each cutlet into the hot honee sauce to completely coat it. Place on a prepared bun. Drizzle with some extra sauce. Top with coleslaw. Close bun. Repeat and eat!

HOT PASTRAMI SANDWICHES

Makes 4 sandwiches

The stuff of your Jewish deli dreams. Imagine piles and piles of briny meat, sizzling in a hot skillet, then stacked up even higher on toasted pumpernickel bread with a healthy smear of mustard and a crunchy layer of fresh coleslaw. Drool much? We take the Roast Be'ef recipe, slice it up, and douse it in a tangy marinade seasoned like pastrami with smoked paprika, coriander, mustard seed, and a touch of cinnamon. Serve a whole dill pickle on the side, like a real New Yorker. Naturally, beet powder adds that bright red color for a picture-perfect finish. And as an added bonus, this recipe calls for pickle juice! What better way to use that jar in your fridge with one pickle floating in it. Now, sit back, enjoy, and transport yourself to the Lower East Side a hundred years ago, but completely gentrified and vegan.

- 1 recipe Beefy Seitan (page 28)
- ¾ cup (180 ml) Beefy Broth (page 302) or prepared vegetable broth, slightly warm
- 2 tablespoons beet powder
- 3 tablespoons olive oil
- ¼ cup (60 ml) pickle juice (from a jar of dill pickles)
- 1 tablespoon brown sugar
- 2 teaspoons coriander seeds, crushed
- 2 teaspoons yellow mustard seeds, crushed
- ½ teaspoon salt
- ½ teaspoon ground black pepper
- ⅛ teaspoon ground cloves
- 2 cinnamon sticks

1 Slice the Beefy Seitan the long way about ⅛ inch thick, or as thin as you can get it.

2 In a 9 by 13-inch (23 by 33 cm) baking pan, mix together the vegetable broth and beet powder. Add the olive oil, pickle juice, brown sugar, coriander seeds, mustard seeds, salt, pepper, cloves, and cinnamon sticks. Mix well.

3 Add the sliced seitan to the marinade, flipping to get it nicely smothered. Cover and marinate for about 1 hour, flipping occasionally.

HOT TAKES

If you want to make this a Rachel, the cousin of Reuben, use Russian dressing instead of mustard, add a slice of Swizz Cheeze (page 294) and some sliced pickles, and grill the sandwich instead of toasting.

To crush the seeds needed for the marinade, place them under a piece of parchment and roll a rolling pin firmly over them until they break apart.

CONTINUED →

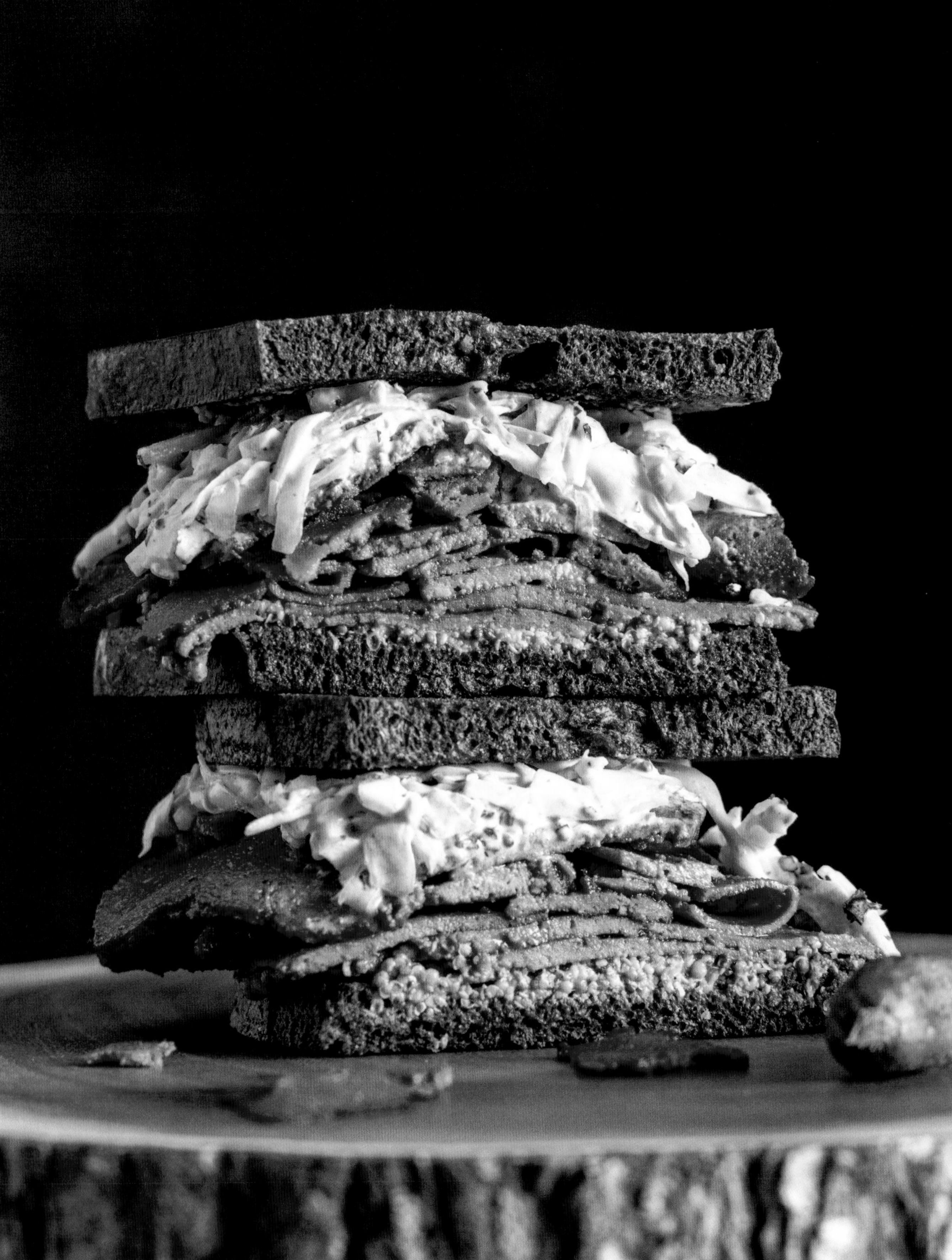

4 Make the coleslaw: In a mixing bowl, stir together the mayo, pickle juice, mustard, parsley, salt, and pepper. Mix in the carrot. Mix in the cabbage and let it wilt for 20 minutes or so, then give the slaw a stir again. Refrigerate until ready to use.

5 Time to cook the seitan! Preheat a large cast-iron pan over medium-high heat. When the pan is hot, spray with cooking oil or add a thin layer of olive oil. Too oily and it will stick.

6 Remove the seitan from the marinade and shake off the excess. Toss the slices into the pan in as much of a single layer as possible. You may have to do this in separate batches depending on the size of your pan. Use a thin metal spatula to flip every few minutes for about 5 to 8 minutes total. The pastrami is done when it is nicely browned in some spots. Turn the heat off.

7 To assemble the sandwiches, toast the pumpernickel. Spread the amount of mustard you desire on the bread. Layer the pastrami on four slices of toast. Place a few spoonfuls of coleslaw on top and close the sandwiches with the remaining toast. Slice in half and serve each sandwich with a pickle on the side.

FOR THE DELI COLESLAW:

- ½ cup (120 ml) vegan mayo, prepared or homemade (page 309)
- 2 tablespoons pickle juice
- 2 teaspoons whole grain Dijon mustard
- ¼ cup (60 ml) finely chopped fresh parsley
- ½ teaspoon salt
- ¼ teaspoon ground black pepper
- ½ cup (55 g) shredded carrot
- 3 cups (450 g) finely shredded green cabbage (about ½ a small head of cabbage)

FOR EVERYTHING ELSE:

- Olive oil or cooking spray, for sautéeing
- 8 slices pumpernickel bread
- Whole grain Dijon mustard
- Whole dill pickles

BEEFY SEITAN

Makes 2 pounds (910 g)

FOR THE BROTH:

- 6 cloves garlic, peeled and smashed
- 8 bay leaves
- ¼ cup (60 ml) tamari
- ¼ cup (65 g) red miso

FOR THE SEITAN:

- 2 cups (240 g) vital wheat gluten
- ¼ cup (15 g) nutritional yeast flakes
- ¼ cup (25 g) chickpea flour
- 2 teaspoons onion powder
- ½ teaspoon salt
- ¼ cup (60 ml) tamari
- 1 tablespoon olive oil
- 1 tablespoon tomato paste

This is an excellent starter seitan. It's simmered and simple, the ingredients list isn't too long or obscure, and it's relatively hard to mess up. It's also incredibly versatile, a jack-of-all-trades, ideal for shredding, breading, slicing, and dicing. I use it throughout the book wherever a nice meaty bite is required, especially in the Comforting Beef Stews chapter (page 118). The neutral flavors make this seitan a go-to for any type of cuisine, from Southeast Asian to Southeast Philly!

1 Make the broth: Pour 2 quarts (2 L) water into a stockpot. Add the smashed garlic, bay leaves, tamari, and miso. Cover and bring to a boil.

2 In a large bowl, mix together the vital wheat gluten, nutritional yeast, chickpea flour, onion powder and salt. Make a well in the center and add 1¼ cups water, the tamari, olive oil, and tomato paste. Mix with a fork and then use your hands to knead for about 3 minutes, until it's a firm dough and everything looks well incorporated.

3 Divide into 4 equal pieces. Stretch each piece into a loaf that's about 6 inches long and 4 inches wide, rolling it on the counter to smooth the surface. Let rest until the broth has come to a full boil.

4 Once boiling, lower the heat to a simmer. This is important; the broth should not be at a rolling boil or you risk the seitan getting waterlogged. Add the gluten loaves and partially cover the pot so that steam can escape. Let simmer for 45 to 55 minutes, turning occasionally. Make sure to keep an eye on the heat, because it may start to boil again, in which case, just turn it down a notch to keep it at a slow, steady simmer. The seitan should feel firm when you squeeze it with tongs.

5 When the seitan is done, you can let it cool right in the broth, or remove a portion to use right away. Once cooled, keep stored in a tightly covered storage container, submerged in broth.

HOT TAKE

The number-one mistake new seitan-makers make is boiling the wheat gluten too high, too fast. Pay attention to the directions and lower the heat before adding the gluten. It should be steaming hot, but not boiling. As the temperature comes up to a simmer and the seitan cooks, it develops a "skin." Once that has happened, it's safe to bring the heat to a low boil so the seitan cooks through.

PARSNIP LOBSTER ROLLS

Makes 6 sandwiches

FOR THE ROASTED PARSNIPS:

- 2 tablespoons olive oil
- 1 teaspoon salt
- ½ teaspoon ground black pepper
- 2 pounds (910 g) parsnips, peeled, cut into 1½-inch (4 cm) chunks (see Hot Takes)

FOR THE DRESSING:

- ½ cup (120 ml) vegan mayo, prepared or homemade (page 309)
- 2 tablespoons fresh lemon juice
- 1 teaspoon kelp powder
- 3 tablespoons capers, drained and rinsed
- ⅓ cup (15 g) thinly sliced chives, plus extra for garnish
- ½ teaspoon salt
- 2 ribs celery, thinly sliced

FOR ASSEMBLY:

- 6 large split-top hot dog buns
- Vegan butter, softened
- Sweet paprika
- ¼ cup (11 g) thickly sliced chives

Don't tell this sandwich, but it was an accident. One summer, at the restaurant, I made some parsnip potato salad. It turned out delicious but the title was misleading; it wasn't simply potato salad with parsnips. It was something more. Trying to put our finger on it, we had a eureka moment: "Lobster roll!" We studded it with capers for brininess and a dash of kelp powder for fishiness and the Parsnip Lobster Roll was born. The parsnips are roasted, but not overcooked, so you get a nice snappy bite. It's all tossed together with mayo and fresh lemon juice, then served in buttered, toasted hot dog buns and sprinkled with a little paprika for that lobster color. How would this version play out in Maine? Queue a Stephen King miniseries and let me know!

1 Roast the parsnips: Preheat the oven to 425°F (220°C). Line a large baking sheet with parchment paper.

2 Drizzle the olive oil, salt, and pepper on the baking pan. Toss the parsnips in the oil to coat. Bake for about 20 minutes, flipping occasionally, until the parsnips are tender inside and golden brown in some spots. Let cool.

3 Make the dressing and assemble the salad: In a large mixing bowl, stir together the mayo, lemon juice, kelp powder, capers, chives, and salt. Fold in the celery and the cooled parsnips. Chill the salad for about 20 minutes.

4 Preheat a large skillet, preferably cast-iron, over medium heat. Butter the outside of each hot dog bun. Place them in the skillet and toast until golden brown, about 2 minutes for each side.

5 Fill the buns with salad. Sprinkle with paprika and additional chives. Serve with plenty of napkins.

HOT TAKES

Parsnips can vary in size and have thin, spindly bottoms, so don't expect to make perfectly even cuts. As for the spindly end, just slice it off where the thicker part begins. If your parsnip is about 1 inch (2.5 cm) in circumference, simply slice it on a bias into 1½-inch (4 cm) chunks. If it's much thicker than that, slice it in half lengthwise, then on a bias.

Split-top hot dog buns can be hard to find, so if you have to use regular hot dogs buns, I'm not mad at you.

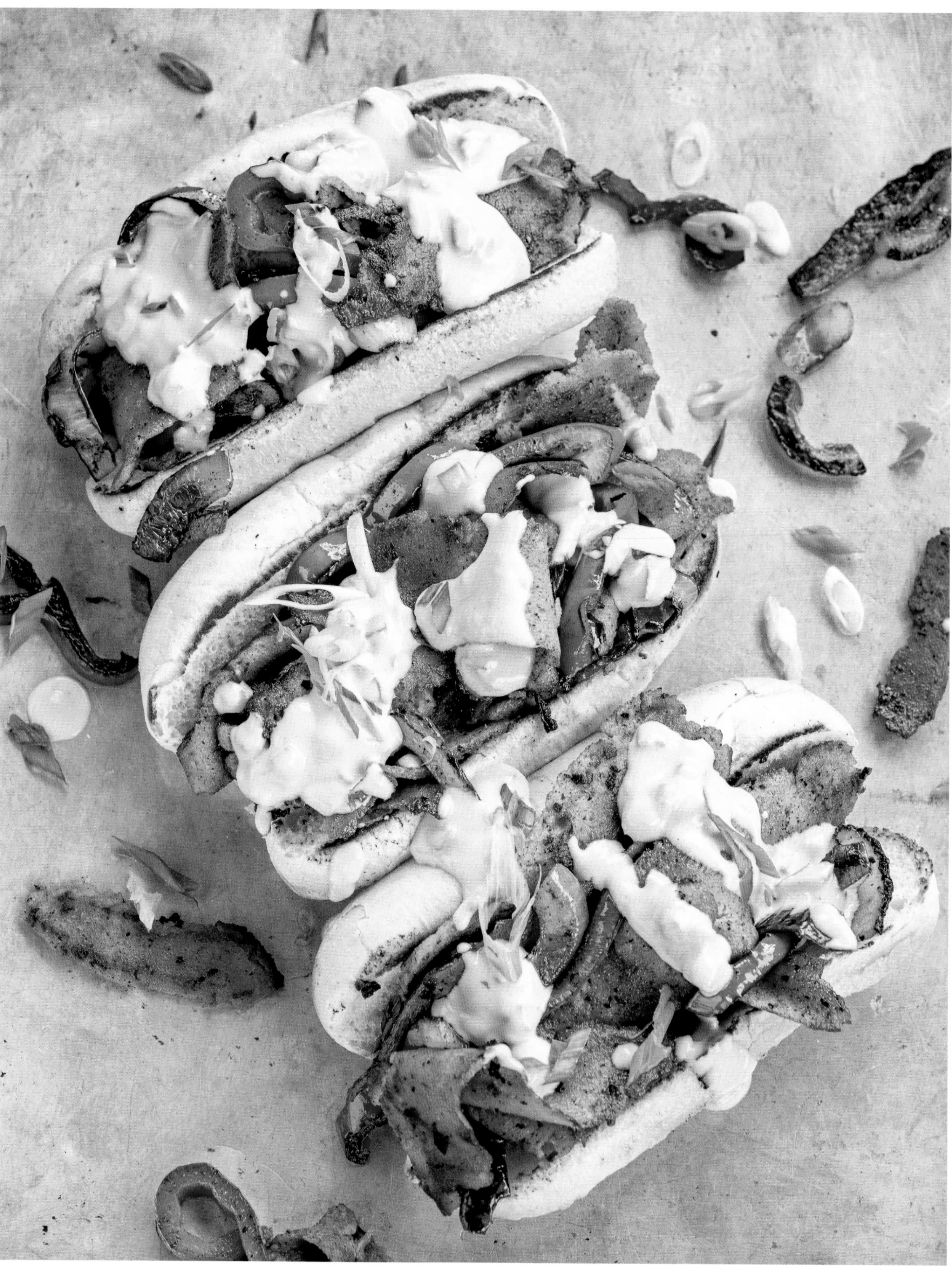

PEPPERJACK CHEESESTEAKS

Makes 4 sandwiches

Phillies are great, no one is denying that. But have you tried a Pepperjack Cheesesteak? Shaved seitan sautéed with all the spicy yums: jalapeño, red bell peppers, and red onion. Then it's stuffed into a toasted hoagie and topped with a snap-to-prepare pepperjack cheese sauce. The recipe is more weeknight friendly than you'd think, if you've got some seitan around, and you do, because you've listened to me and have seitan around at all times. I sear the peppers and onions first, then set them aside while I sear the seitan. This way, all the ingredients are cooked perfectly, with just the right amount of smoky blistering. The seitan ends up soaking up some of the great flavor the veggies leave behind in the pan. It's just win after win. Like Rocky! Who is from Philly. And I hope he doesn't fight me over these cheesesteaks.

- 4 tablespoons olive oil, divided
- 1 red bell pepper, sliced in ¼-inch strips
- 1 medium red onion, sliced into ¼-inch half-moons
- 6 jalapeños, seeded and sliced in long thin strips
- Pinch salt
- 1 pound (455 g) Beefy Seitan (page 28), thinly sliced
- 4 hoagie rolls
- ½ cup (120 ml) vegetable broth or Beefy Broth (page 302)
- Pepperjack Cheese Sauce (recipe follows)
- ⅓ cup (30 g) thinly sliced scallions

1 Preheat a large skillet, preferably cast-iron, over medium-high heat. Add 1 tablespoon olive oil to the pan and sauté the bell pepper, onion, and jalapeños with a pinch of salt, until nicely seared but still snappy. Transfer to a plate and set aside.

2 Do not rinse out the skillet because you're going to sear the seitan in it. Add the remaining 3 tablespoons olive oil to the pan. Scatter the seitan in as much of a single layer as you can. Let cook for about 4 minutes, until lightly browned and charred in some spots. Use a thin metal spatula to flip. It doesn't have to be perfect, just as long as you get some sear on each piece. Cook for 5 more minutes, flipping occasionally.

3 In the meantime, preheat the oven to 350°F (175°C) to toast the hoagies. Split the rolls open (but not pulled apart) and place them facedown on a baking sheet. Bake for about 5 minutes.

4 Pour the vegetable broth into the pan and deglaze the bottom, scraping up any yummy bits. Let the broth cook for 2 minutes. Add the pepper mixture back to the pan and toss to combine. Cook 3 more minutes.

5 Assemble the cheesesteaks. Use tongs to fill each hoagie roll with the beefy seitan and place them so that they're standing straight up with the meat exposed on top. Drizzle with plenty of Pepperjack Cheese Sauce. Garnish with scallions and serve!

HOT TAKE

The best way to toast the hoagie rolls is in the oven, so they're all ready at once. Preheat the oven to 350°F (175°C). Split them open (but don't them pull apart) and put facedown on a baking sheet. Bake for about 5 minutes. Pull out some toasty rolls!

CONTINUED →

PEPPERJACK CHEESE SAUCE

Makes 2 cups (480 ml)

This is a lush, spicy cheese sauce for cheesesteaks, but don't stop there. Use as you would queso, to dip chips and whatnot. And it also makes a wonderful mac and cheese.

FOR THE CHEESE SAUCE:

- 2 tablespoons refined coconut oil
- 1 red bell pepper, cut into tiny dice
- 5 average-size jalapeños, seeded and cut into tiny dice
- 4 cloves garlic, minced
- ¼ teaspoon salt, plus a pinch
- 1 cup (120 g) whole unroasted cashews
- 2 cups (480 ml) vegetable broth
- 2 tablespoons white miso
- 2 tablespoons nutritional yeast flakes
- 1 tablespoon fresh lemon juice
- 2 teaspoons cornstarch

1 Melt the coconut oil in a 4-quart (3.8 liter) pot over medium heat. Sauté the bell pepper, jalapeño, and garlic in the oil with a pinch of salt, just until soft, about 3 minutes. Turn off the heat and set the pot aside (do not remove the aromatics).

2 In a high-speed blender, combine the cashews, broth, miso, nutritional yeast, lemon juice, cornstarch, and the ¼ teaspoon salt. Blend for about 1 minute or until completely smooth, using a rubber spatula to scrape down the sides every 20 seconds or so.

3 In the meantime, bring the pot with the pepper mixture in it up to medium heat again. Pour the cashew mixture into the pot. Turn the heat up a bit and whisk often until the sauce comes to a slow rolling boil. Lower the heat so that it doesn't burn and cook for about 15 minutes until nicely thickened and pourable. Taste for salt and seasoning. Keep warm to serve.

TWENTY-FIRST-CENTURY SEITAN BURGERS

Makes 4 burgers

At some point in time, veggie burgers became not so veggie. They transformed into something downright MEATY with nary a carrot or pea in sight. These are the burgers you want to throw on the grill. And you literally can throw them—they are not the fragile veggie burger of yesteryear. Seitan is the base here, combined with savory elements like sautéed onions, and umami flavors like miso, tomato, and porcini powder. Mashed pinto beans create a texture similar to ground meat while mayo keeps things juicy. A little fennel adds a pop of "Mmm, what what?" flavor. And everything becomes even more meatily delicious when cooked over an open grill. That being said, a cast-iron grill or pan-frying is just great, too.

- **1 cup (125 g) finely diced onion**
- **3 tablespoons olive oil**
- **½ teaspoon salt, plus a pinch**
- **3 cloves minced garlic**
- **½ teaspoon chopped fennel seed**
- **2 tablespoons red miso**
- **2 tablespoons tomato paste**
- **¾ cup (130 g) canned pinto beans, rinsed and drained**
- **2 tablespoons porcini powder**
- **¾ cup water**
- **1 teaspoon smoked paprika**
- **½ teaspoon lemon pepper**
- **¼ cup (60 ml) vegan mayo, prepared or homemade (page 309)**
- **2 teaspoons apple cider vinegar**
- **¼ cup (15 g) nutritional yeast flakes**
- **1¼ cups (150 g) vital wheat gluten**

1 Have your steaming setup ready to go (see page 14). Have ready four 10-inch (25 cm) squares of aluminum foil and parchment for wrapping and steaming.

2 Preheat a heavy pan over medium heat. Sauté the onion in the oil with a pinch of salt until translucent, 3 to 5 minutes. Add the garlic and fennel seed and sauté for another minute. Add the miso and tomato paste. Mix them in, letting them warm and dissolve into the onions. Remove from heat.

3 In a mixing bowl, mash the pintos with the onion mixture and the porcini powder. There should be some texture but no whole beans left. Work in ¾ cup (180 ml) water. Make sure the mixture is totally cooled before proceeding.

4 Mix in the smoked paprika, ½ teaspoon salt, lemon pepper, mayo, apple cider vinegar, and nutritional yeast. Add the gluten and knead with your hands for about 4 minutes until gluten strands appear.

5 Break into 4 even pieces and form into large patties about 4 inches (10 cm) in diameter. Flatten and make them as circular as you can but they don't have to be perfect.

6 Steam the patties: Wrap each patty in a square of parchment and then an aluminum foil square. Take care to reshape the burgers once wrapped. Steam with a tight-fitting lid for about 45 minutes, flipping once.

7 Cool completely before using. Once cool, preheat your grill over high heat. Brush burgers with oil and grill just until grill marks appear, about 4 minutes each side. If pan frying, preheat pan over medium. Cook for about 5 minutes on each side, until lightly charred.

CONTINUED →

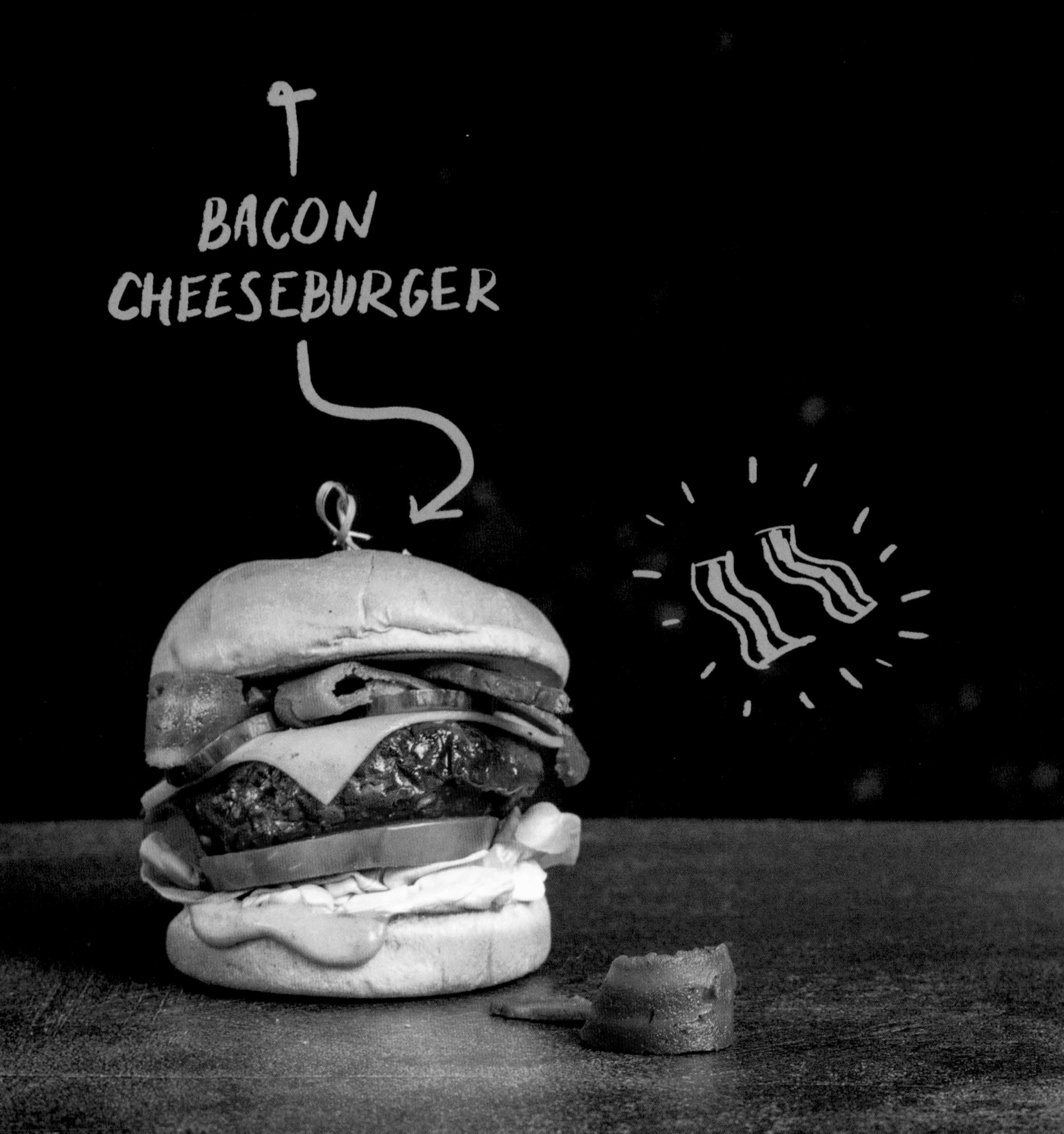
BACON
CHEESEBURGER

MUSHROOM SWISS BURGER

PIZZA BURGER

BURGER NIGHT!

Obviously, burgers are a popular food item. Food empires have sprung up serving nothing but burgers, and veggie burgers were arguably the first fake meat to really take off. At my restaurants, even though there are dozens of other options, the burger remains the top seller. There's definitely appeal in the classic toppings: pickles, mayo, lettuce, tomato, onion. But when we put specials on the menu, that is when people really go wild. I'm going to share a few of my favorites here. But I encourage you to create your own signature burger!

MUSHROOM SWISS BURGERS

Makes 4 burgers

- 2 tablespoons olive oil
- 2 cups thinly sliced shallots
- 8 ounces cremini mushrooms, thinly sliced
- ¼ teaspoon salt
- Freshly ground black pepper
- 4 burgers
- 4 slices Swizz Cheeze (page 294) or store-bought vegan swiss cheese
- 4 burger buns
- Garlic Mayo (page 309)
- 4 small handfuls baby arugula

1. Preheat a large skillet over medium-high heat and add the olive oil. Cook the shallots in the oil for about 3 minutes. Add the mushrooms, salt, and a few dashes freshly ground black pepper. Sauté until the mushrooms are lightly browned, about 7 minutes. Turn heat off.
2. Brush the burgers with oil and grill just until grill marks appear. Flip the burgers and immediately add a slice of Swizz Cheeze to each. Cover the pan and let the cheese melt, about 4 more minutes.
3. Toast the burger buns. Spread mayo on each side of the buns. Place a handful of arugula on each bottom bun. Add the burger. Top with a healthy amount of the shallot and mushroom mixture. Close the burger bun and enjoy!

PIZZA BURGERS

Makes 4 burgers

- 4 burgers
- Olive oil, for brushing
- 4 burger buns
- Pesto Mayo (page 309)
- 1 cup marinara
- 1 ball Fresh Mozz-Shew-Rella (page 286)
- Fresh basil leaves

1 Preheat a grill over medium-high heat. Brush the burgers with oil and grill just until grill marks appear, about 4 minutes. Flip and grill the other side another 4 minutes.

2 Toast the burger buns. Spread pesto mayo on each bottom bun. Place a burger on each bun. Top with marinara. Break the mozzarella ball up into 3 clumps and place on top. Scatter basil over the mozzarella and close the bun.

BACON CHEESEBURGERS

Makes 4 burgers

- Cooking oil for sautéeing
- 8 strips Ribbony Seitan Bacon (page 171)
- 4 burgers
- Olive oil, for brushing
- 4 slices Shreddy Cheddy (page 291) or store-bought vegan cheddar cheese
- 4 burger buns
- Dippy Sauce (page 222)
- 4 crisp romaine leaves
- 4 slices of tomato
- ¼ cup sliced dill pickles
- ¼ cup finely minced yellow onion

1 Preheat a large skillet over low heat. Cook the bacon with a light spray of oil for about 1 minute each side. Immediately lift the bacon and lightly fold and twist to give it shape.

2 Preheat a grill over medium-high heat. Brush the burgers with olive oil and grill just until grill marks appear. Flip the burgers and immediately top each with a slice of Shreddy Cheddy. Cover the pan and let the cheese melt, about 4 more minutes.

3 Toast the burger buns. Spread Dippy Sauce on each bottom bun. Place romaine and tomato on the bottom bun. Add the burger. Top with the pickles, minced onion, and bacon. Close the burger bun and enjoy!

CLASSIC LENTIL-BEET BURGERS

Makes 4 burgers

Before the vegan burger was Impossible, before it was Beyond, it was . . . lentils. And we didn't just like it, we loved it. Honestly, we still do. Sometimes you just want a veggie burger with actual veggies in it, ya know? This one is beautifully bright red thanks to the power of shredded beets. It really does look like meat at a glance if you're just scrolling through your feed. The lentils are ground up like beef and mashed up with walnuts and sturdy brown rice for extra texture. Almond butter is wonderful as a binder while adding greater depth of flavor. Granted, it's the kind of veggie burger that might mush out the side of the bun if you squeeze it, but that just might be the best bite in the world!

- 6 ounces (170 g) beets, peeled and quartered
- 1¼ cups (245 g) cooked, cooled brown rice (see Hot Take)
- 1 cup (190 g) canned lentils, rinsed and drained
- ¼ teaspoon salt
- ½ teaspoon ground black pepper
- 1½ teaspoons Italian or pizza seasoning, rubbed between your fingers
- 1 teaspoon onion powder
- 1 teaspoon dry mustard powder
- 3 tablespoons very finely chopped onion
- 2 cloves garlic, minced
- 2 tablespoons smooth almond butter
- 1 tablespoon red miso
- ½ cup (50 g) walnuts, chopped
- ½ cup (50 g) very fine dry breadcrumbs
- Olive oil, for cooking
- 4 burger buns
- Suggested fixings: lettuce, tomato, onion, ketchup, mustard, Swizz Cheeze (page 294)

1 Shred the beets with the shredder attachment of your food processor.

2 Change the attachment to the metal blade, but don't remove the shredded beets. Add the rice and lentils to the beets and pulse about 15 to 20 times, until the mixture comes together but still has texture. It should resemble ground meat.

3 Transfer the beet mixture to a large mixing bowl and add the salt, pepper, Italian seasoning, onion powder, dry mustard, onion, garlic, almond butter, miso, walnuts, and breadcrumbs. Use your hands to mix very well. Everything should be well incorporated, so get in there and take your time; it could take a minute or two. Place the mixture in the fridge for a half hour to chill.

4 Preheat a large cast-iron pan over medium high. To form each patty, take a heaping ½ cup of the burger mixture and form it into a 3½-inch (9 cm) patty to make four patties in all. You can use a 3½-inch (9 cm) ring mold to make them perfect.

5 Pour a thin layer of olive oil into the hot cast-iron pan. Add the patties and cook for about 12 minutes, flipping occasionally. You may have to do this in batches to avoid crowding the pan; drizzle in a little more oil if needed. When ready, the burgers should be charred at the edges and heated through the center. Serve immediately on toasted burger buns with the fixings of your choice!

HOT TAKE

I like to use thawed frozen rice here to save a cooking step! Just place the frozen bag in the fridge a day ahead, or you can follow the microwaving directions on the bag and let cool. Brown rice works best because it's chewier, but in a pinch, you can use white rice instead.

SMOKY BEET CUBANS

Makes 4 sandwiches

Beet lovers rejoice, your favorite root veggie is getting the Cuban treatment. See them in a whole new light—sliced, roasted until tender, and smoked. Then they're stuffed into a roll with flavors that will make your eyes pop: mustard, pickles, and Swizz Cheeze! And next, dear reader, the whole thing is buttered, pressed, and grilled. Start freaking out now. The beet brings this classic to new heights with its smoky, sweet flavor offsetting the earthiness.

If you have a panini press or something similar, it will totally work here. But assuming that you do not, I'm giving instructions for a cast-iron grill. You simply use another heavy skillet to press it. Voilà, a panini press. I should add, even if you don't have a cast-iron grill (but why don't you?), you can make this in a regular pan, it just won't have cool grill marks. It will be more like a grilled cheese. In other words, still totally delicious.

- 6 medium beets (about tennis ball size), peeled and sliced ¼ inch thick
- 3 tablespoons olive oil
- ¼ teaspoon salt
- ⅓ cup dill pickle slices
- 4 Cuban rolls or soft seedless Italian rolls
- Whole grain mustard
- 8 slices Swizz Cheeze (page 294), about ⅛ inch thick, or store-bought vegan Swiss slices
- Vegan butter, for grilling
- Stovetop smoker (see Hot Takes)
- Panini press or cast-iron grill plus a heavy skillet (see headnote)
- Applewood smoke chips, soaked in water for an hour

1 Preheat the oven to 425°F (220°C). Have ready two baking sheets lined with parchment paper.

2 In a large bowl, toss the beets with the olive oil and salt until well coated. Use gloves unless you want to stain your fingers.

3 Spread the beet slices into an even layer on the pans. Bake for 20 to 25 minutes until lightly browned on the edges and tender.

4 Have your stovetop smoker ready, smoking and on low heat. Place the beets in the smoker. It's OK if they are not in a single layer. Cover the smoker and smoke for 5 minutes. Turn the heat off completely and continue to smoke for 10 minutes.

5 Prepare the sandwich. Slice the dill pickles lengthwise into 8 sandwich-appropriate slices.

6 Preheat a cast-iron grill over medium high.

7 Cut the rolls in half lengthwise. Spread both halves of the rolls with mustard. Place a slice of Swizz on both the top and bottom halves of the rolls. Place a big pile of beets in the center of the bottom halves. Place two pickle slices per sandwich across the beets. Place the top roll onto the sandwiches.

8 Spread a good amount of vegan butter onto the top and bottom of each sandwich. Place a sandwich on the grill. Press down on the sandwich with another heavy skillet. Toast for 2 to 3 minutes on each side. Repeat with the other sandwiches and serve immediately.

HOT TAKES

Don't have a stovetop smoker but still desperately want to try this? Make the recipe as directed, but add 1 teaspoon smoked salt to the beets. Sprinkle additional smoked salt on the beets when assembling the sandwiches to be pressed.

If you can't find Cuban bread, use a soft Italian roll with no seeds. Crusty bread doesn't press well so don't even try it.

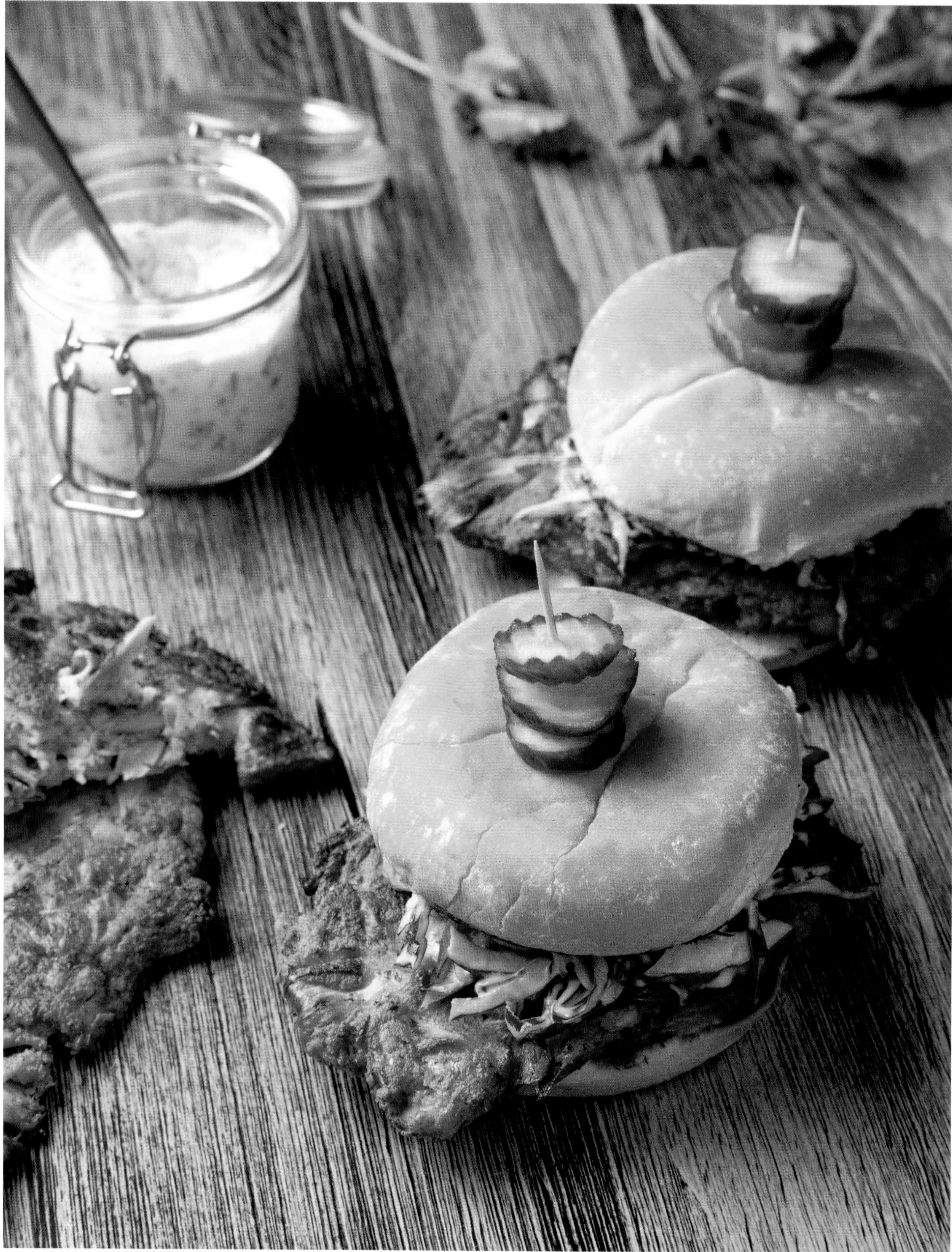

ARTICHOKE FISHWICHES

Makes 6 sandwiches

Artichokes create a golden, flaky fillet that is a dream vehicle for tartar sauce and coleslaw, making this fish sandwich the bomb dot com. I know no one says that anymore, but after trying this sandwich, it will make a comeback. Flavors like fresh dill and Old Bay complete the fishy package. Tofu creates a binder that, when combined with panko, holds the whole shebang together, while retaining a tender texture that is still crispy when fried. I love how these look on a potato bun, with the cute little ends poking out, just begging to be bitten into. Serve with some pickles, either in the sandwich or skewered onto a toothpick on top of the bun for some added drama.

- 2 (14-ounce/395 g) cans whole artichoke hearts packed in water, drained
- ½ pack extra-firm tofu (7 ounces)
- ½ cup Bay Broth (page 303) or prepared vegetable broth
- 1 teaspoon kelp powder
- ¼ teaspoon ground black pepper
- 2 tablespoons fresh chopped dill
- 1 teaspoon onion powder
- 2 teaspoons Old Bay Seasoning
- ½ teaspoon salt
- 1 cup panko breadcrumbs
- Safflower oil, for frying

FOR ASSEMBLY:

- 6 burger buns
- Super Simple Slaw (page 312)
- Crinkle-cut dill pickles
- Jimmy Carter Tartar Sauce (page 310)

1. Rinse the artichokes and pat dry with a paper towel. Slice them in half and fan out the halves to create fish-like layers.
2. In a blender, combine the tofu and broth and blend until smooth. Transfer to a mixing bowl.
3. Add the artichokes, kelp powder, black pepper, dill, onion powder, Old Bay, and salt and mix well. Add the breadcrumbs and mix again, using your hands, until the mixture holds together.
4. Now deep-fry! Preheat a large cast-iron pan over medium heat. Add about ½ inch (1.5 cm) of oil. Test the oil by dropping in a little piece of dough. Bubbles should form quickly around it.
5. In the meantime, create six relatively equal-size balls of dough, then flatten on a cutting board to a fillet shape that's about 5 inches (13 cm) long and 3 inches (8 cm) across.
6. Have ready paper towels or paper bags to drain the oil. Fry the fillets three at a time until golden brown, about 3 minutes each side. Use more oil as needed.
7. Drain and serve on toasted burger buns with slaw, pickles, and tartar sauce.

FIVE-SPICE BURNT ENDS TEMPEH TACOS

Makes 6 tacos

Burnt ends are typically the leftover pieces from barbecued meats. They're crispy, sweet, and charred. Here, tempeh and mushrooms get the burnt ends treatment. They're cooked on high heat in an easy to throw together sauce that is smoky, sweet (but not too sweet), and a little spicy. Some slaw to cool it down and lend some fresh crunch, some sliced avocado for creaminess and because avocado on everything always. I love the Asian-Mexican vibe. Now you've got yourself a taco Tuesday on a Friday because you don't know what day it is!

- 3 tablespoons tamari
- 1 tablespoon sriracha
- 1 tablespoon sesame oil
- 1 tablespoon canola oil plus additional for cooking
- 1 tablespoon brown sugar
- 1 tablespoon smoked paprika
- ½ teaspoon five-spice powder
- 1 (8-ounce/225 g) package tempeh, diced
- 8 ounces (225 g) cremini mushrooms, thinly sliced

FOR ASSEMBLY:

- 6 (8-inch/20 cm) tortillas
- 1 recipe Super Simple Slaw (page 312)
- 1 avocado, thinly sliced
- Juice of 1 lime (optional)
- Salt (optional)
- Fresh cilantro sprigs

1. In a bowl large enough to hold the tempeh, vigorously mix the tamari, sriracha, both oils, brown sugar, paprika, and five-spice powder. Add the tempeh and toss to coat. Let marinate for 15 minutes to an hour. When you're ready to make the tacos, preheat the oven to 350°F (175°C).
2. Preheat a large skillet over medium heat. When good and hot, cook the mushrooms in canola oil until their moisture is released and they've browned a bit, about 7 minutes.
3. Add the tempeh, reserving some marinade. Cook for about 10 minutes, flipping often, until caramelized on the edges. Add more marinade to coat as needed.
4. Wrap the tortillas in foil and heat in the oven for about 10 minutes. Or use your preferred way of warming up tortillas!
5. To assemble the tacos, lay out a warm tortilla, put some slaw in the middle, then some tempeh, then tuck in some sliced avocado. Sprinkle the avo with a little lime juice and salt if you like. Top with cilantro and repeat. Serve asap!

HOT DOG SUMMER
WITH HOT DOG ONIONS

Makes 8 hot dogs

You can't have a fake meat cookbook without a hot dog recipe, now come on. And this one is perfection adorned in hot dog onions! Sweet, smoky, almost BBQ-ish dollops of these onions will complete your NYC hot dog experience. I put them on knishes, too. But this is not a knish cookbook so you don't need to worry about that. The key to perfect onions is to cook them low and slow! Obviously, you can also skip all that and serve these the old-fashioned way, with mustard and sauerkraut. Steaming the dogs creates a skin that really pops, and grilling them to order adds another layer of meatiness. This recipe is modified from one in *The Superfun Times Vegan Holiday Cookbook*.

- 6 ounces (170 g) extra-firm silken tofu, such as vacuum-packed Mori-Nu brand
- ¼ cup ketchup (60 ml)
- 1 cup (240 ml) vegetable broth
- 1 tablespoon olive oil
- 2 tablespoons soy sauce
- 1½ cups (180 g) plus 2 tablespoons vital wheat gluten
- ¼ cup (15 g) nutritional yeast flakes
- 1 tablespoon smoked paprika
- 1 tablespoon onion powder
- 1 teaspoon garlic powder
- ¾ teaspoon salt
- ¼ teaspoon ground white pepper
- 8 hot dog buns
- Hot Dog Onions (page 311)

1. Make the hot dogs: In a food processor fitted with a metal blade, puree the tofu, ketchup, broth, olive oil, and soy sauce until completely smooth, scraping down the sides with a rubber spatula to make sure you get everything.
2. In a large bowl, mix together the vital wheat gluten, nutritional yeast, smoked paprika, onion powder, garlic powder, salt, and white pepper. Make a well in the center and add the tofu mixture. Use the rubber spatula to mix until well combined, and then use your hands to further knead the mixture until it's a well-formed dough with a little spring to it.
3. Prepare your steaming apparatus. Have ready eight 10-inch (25 cm) squares of parchment and eight 10-inch (25 cm) sheets of aluminum foil.
4. Divide the dough into 8 equal pieces. Roll each piece into a hot dog shape. Place a dog at the bottom of a square of parchment and roll it up. Then place it in a piece of foil and roll it up, this time, tightly sealing the ends like a Tootsie Roll. Repeat with the remaining dogs.
5. Steam the hot dogs for about 40 minutes, until very firm. Let them cool completely before unwrapping. Then preheat a grill pan over medium high. Unwrap the cooled dogs and grill for about 3 minutes, turning them once, until grill marks appear.
6. Serve in toasted hot dog buns with hot dog onions.

POR QUE PULLED PORQ TORTAS

Makes 4 sandwiches

In seventh grade I had a Spanish teacher who had a Burt Reynolds mustache and an arsenal of dad jokes. One of his favorite things to say was "Por que? Por que? Por que pig?" Get it, like Porky Pig? Unfortunately, these words are stuck in my head more than the actual language I was supposed to be learning. But it turns out Mr. L. was predicting this very sandwich. Por Que Pulled Porq Torta! A smoky, shreddy, and spicy pulled seitan porq, piled onto a fluffy bolilla bun with a smear of refried beans, layers of avocado, tangy pickled jalapeños, and a crunchy bright slaw to balance out the heat. Now you've got yourself one satisfyingly sloppy torta.

The pulled porq itself will knock your socks off. To get the beautiful shreddiness, the dough is rolled out into a snake and then coiled and wrapped into a little bundle. Steam it, cool it, shred it, and NOM. You'll have some left over to make a nice big burrito bowl, if you like.

FOR THE PULLED PORQ:

- 1 (15-ounce/430 g) can lentils, rinsed and drained (or 1½ cups/285 g home-cooked lentils; see Hot Take, page 262)
- 2 tablespoons olive oil
- 2 tablespoons tomato paste
- 1 teaspoon pure maple syrup
- 1 teaspoon apple cider vinegar
- 1 tablespoon beet powder
- 1 tablespoon onion powder
- 2 teaspoons salt
- 1 tablespoon smoked paprika
- ½ teaspoon chipotle powder
- 3 tablespoons nutritional yeast flakes
- 1¾ cups (210 g) vital wheat gluten

FOR THE REFRIED BEANS:

- 2 tablespoons refined coconut oil
- 1 small yellow onion, finely chopped
- 3 cloves garlic, minced
- ¼ cup (10 g) finely chopped fresh cilantro
- 2 teaspoons ground cumin
- 1 teaspoon dried oregano
- ½ teaspoon salt
- 1 (24-ounce/680 g) can pinto beans, drained and rinsed

MAKE THE PULLED PORQ

1 Have a steamer at the ready.

2 In a food processor fitted with a metal blade, blend together the lentils, 1 cup (235 ml) water, oil, tomato paste, maple syrup, vinegar, beet powder, onion powder, salt, paprika, chipotle powder, and nutritional yeast. Add the vital wheat gluten and pulse it in. Once it is all incorporated, process the mixture on low for about 5 minutes. It will be very stretchy, stringy, and pliable. Give the motor a break once in a while if your processor can't handle it.

3 Divide the dough into 2 pieces. Roll one out into about a 12-inch (30 cm) snake. Fold the snake in half, give it a twist, then roll again so it's about an 8-inch (20 cm) bundle. This creates the layers.

4 Wrap the dough in parchment then a piece of aluminum foil, making it snug but not too tight. Steam it for at least an hour, turning every 20 minutes. The porq is done when it feels really really firm.

5 Cool completely before proceeding with the recipe.

CONTINUED →

- ½ cup (120 ml) vegetable broth, plus extra for thinning if needed
- 3 tablespoons tomato paste
- 3 tablespoons medium hot sauce

FOR THE SPICY PURPLE SLAW:

- ½ cup (120 ml) vegan mayo, prepared or homemade (page 309)
- 2 tablespoons medium hot sauce
- 2 tablespoons fresh lemon juice
- ¼ cup (10 g) finely chopped fresh cilantro
- ½ teaspoon salt
- 4 cups (380 g) finely shredded purple cabbage (about half a head)

FOR ASSEMBLY:

- ½ recipe Por Que Pulled Porq (see below)
- 2 tablespoons olive oil
- 1 recipe Super Simple Slaw (page 312)
- 4 bolillo buns (see Hot Takes)
- 2 avocados, thinly sliced
- 1 handful pickled jalapeños
- ½ cup (15 g) loosely packed fresh cilantro sprigs
- Spicy mayo (optional; see Hot Take)

MAKE THE REFRIED BEANS

1 Heat the coconut oil in a 2-quart (2 liter) pot over medium heat. Sauté the onion in the oil for 3 to 5 minutes, until translucent. Add the garlic, cilantro, cumin, oregano, and salt. Sauté for another minute or so, stirring frequently, until the cilantro is wilted and the garlic is fragrant.

2 Add the pinto beans and vegetable broth. Let the beans heat up for a few minutes, then mash them with a mini potato masher or whatever you use to mash. There should be some texture left, so don't puree, just mash them.

3 Add the tomato paste and hot sauce. Cook to heat through, adding splashes of broth to thin as needed. You may need up to ½ cup (120 ml) additional broth. Cook for about 10 more minutes for the flavors to marry.

MEANWHILE, MAKE THE SLAW:

1 Mix together the mayo, hot sauce, lemon juice, cilantro, and salt. Toss in the cabbage and use tongs (or your hands) to combine.

ASSEMBLE THE SANDWICHES:

1 You only need one-half of the pulled pork; wrap and refrigerate the rest. Preheat a cast-iron grill over medium heat. Use your fingers to tear the pork into shreds. Sauté the meat in the olive oil until lightly browned and charred in some spots, about 7 minutes. Remove from heat. Split open and toast the buns.

2 Spread about 3 tablespoons of the refried beans onto the bottom buns. Layer on the avocado. Portion the pulled porq onto each sandwich. Top with slaw and scatter on the pickled jalapenos. Add cilantro sprigs. Spread spicy mayo on top bun if using. Close the sandwiches and enjoy!

HOT TAKES

Bolilla buns have a crunchy crust but they are still light and squishy. If you can't find them, then use a French or Italian roll, or even a ciabatta roll will work. Don't use anything rustic here: nothing "artisan" and no heritage sourdough.

You'll often find spicy mayo on a torta, but this one has a nice creamy slaw, so I don't think it's totally necessary. However! If you are a mayo fiend like me, go for it. To make spicy mayo, simply mix a little mayo in with hot sauce. You don't need a recipe for that, right?

SPICY ITALIAN ROAST BE'EF SUBS

Makes 4 subs

In grade school, your lunch box was your social status. My mom packed sandwiches in used Wonder Bread bags. Needless to say, I was not popular. If I could go back in time with this sandwich and a Wonder Woman lunch box, it would save me many years of therapy and have made me prom queen—if we had prom queens in elementary school. It boasts the meatiest cold cuts, creamy provolone cheese, Italian dressing with shredded lettuce, hot pepperoncini, and olives sprinkled with red pepper flakes and layered on crusty Italian bread. It's kind of like a lazy muffaletta, now that I think about it. The trick is to scoop out some of the bread from the inside, leaving more room for meat and cheese! The mayo is optional, but if you're a mayo freak like me, go for it!

- 4 Italian sesame seed hoagie rolls
- Vegan mayo, prepared or homemade (page 309; optional)
- 4 cups (220 g) shredded romaine lettuce
- ¼ cup (60 ml) Italian Herb Dressing (page 314)
- 2 beefsteak tomatoes, cut into 8 slices
- Salt and freshly ground black pepper
- 1 cup (140 g) thinly sliced pepperoncini
- ½ cup (75 g) sliced kalamata olives
- ½ recipe Roast Be'ef (recipe follows), sliced ⅛ inch thick
- ½ recipe Prove-Me-Wrong Provolone (page 292), sliced ⅛ inch thick

1 Slice the hoagie rolls in half and scoop out some of the bread from the inside of the bottom roll. Just pull five or six fingerfuls out, working down the center; you don't have to be too precise about it. Spread mayo on each side, if using.

2 Place lettuce on the bottom rolls, stuffing it in, and drizzle with Italian herb dressing. Then layer on the tomatoes and sprinkle them with a little salt and fresh black pepper. Scatter on the pepperocini and olives. Layer roast beef on top, then a few slices of provolone. Put some mayo on top if you want, close the sandwich, and enjoy!

HOT TAKE

If you can't find hoagie rolls, that's OK. Use any nice doughy roll, preferably with sesame seeds, and make sure it's 6 to 8 inches (15 to 20 cm) long to contain this behemoth.

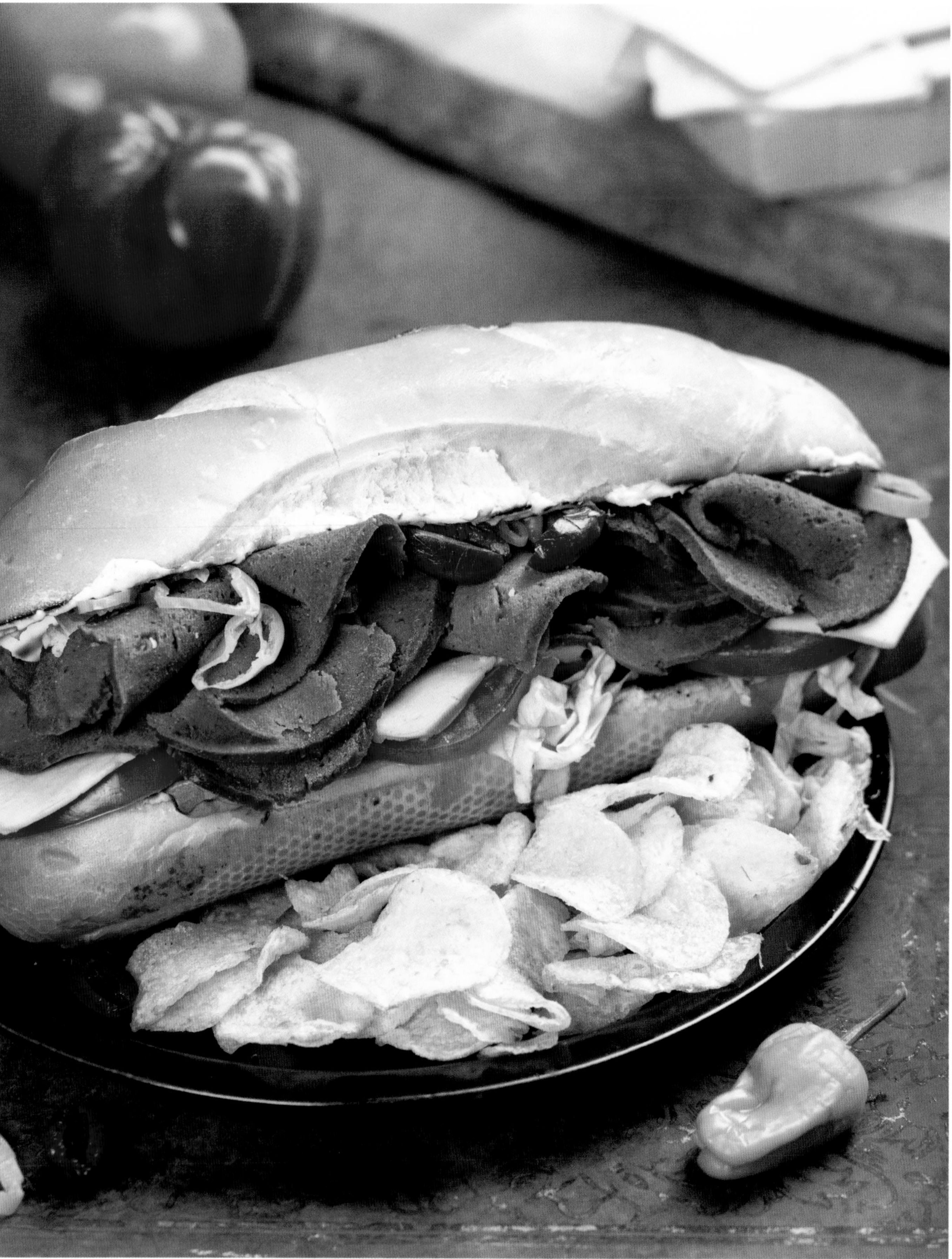

ROAST BE'EF

Makes 1 large loaf

This roast be'ef is equally amazing sliced up for a sandwich or sautéed for . . . a different sandwich! You can also serve it warm as its own thing, and carve it up at the table with gravy and mashed potatoes on the side.

- 1½ cups (285 g) overcooked lentils (from one 15-ounce/430 g can, rinsed and drained)
- 3 tablespoons olive oil
- 3 tablespoons tomato paste
- 2 tablespoons red miso
- 1 teaspoon balsamic vinegar
- 3 tablespoons nutritional yeast flakes
- 2 teaspoons granulated sugar
- 2 tablespoons beet powder
- 1 tablespoon onion powder
- 2 teaspoons garlic powder
- 1 teaspoon sweet paprika
- 1 teaspoon salt
- 1¾ cups (210 g) vital wheat gluten
- 1 teaspoon ground black pepper

1 In a blender, puree the lentils, ¾ cup (180 ml) water, the olive oil, tomato paste, miso, balsamic vinegar, nutritional yeast, sugar, beet powder, onion powder, garlic powder, paprika, and salt until smooth. This will take less than 1 minute in a high-speed blender, and about 3 minutes in a standard blender.

2 Prepare two 14-inch (36 cm) pieces of aluminum foil and parchment paper. Place the parchment on top of the foil. Preheat the oven to 350°F (175°C).

3 In a large bowl, sift together the vital wheat gluten and black pepper. Make a well in the center. Mix in the wet stuff from the blender. Knead for 5 minutes or so until it's stringy and springy.

4 Divide the dough in half. Form two fat loaves that are roughly 8 inches (20 cm) long. Wrap each loaf in parchment-lined foil and secure the ends by twisting. Make it snug but not too tight as the loaves will expand in the oven.

5 Bake for about 50 minutes, using tongs to turn every 15 to 20 minutes or so. The loaves should feel firm. Remove from the oven and let cool completely in the wrappers. To store, wrap tightly in plastic wrap and refrigerate.

FRIED-EGG BAGELS WITH CARROT LOX CREAM CHEESE

Makes 4 sandwiches

Bagels are life, death, and everything in between. It sounds a little too contemplative for the morning, but we are actually just getting warmed up. Prepare yourself for tofu that looks and tastes more like an egg than it has any right to. This sandwich is an homage to my fave breakfast bagel! Smoky, creamy carrot lox topped with a perfectly fried, crisp on the edges, over-easy egg.

FOR ASSEMBLY:

- 4 eggs (recipe follows)
- 4 everything bagels
- 1 cup (260 g) Carrot Lox cream cheese (page 282)
- Vegan butter
- Freshly ground black pepper

FOR THE EGG WHITES:

- 1 (14-ounce/400 g) package extra-firm silken tofu (I use vacuum-packed Mori Nu brand)
- 1 tablespoon melted refined coconut oil
- ½ cup (60 g) white rice flour
- 1 tablespoon cornstarch
- ½ teaspoon kala namak
- ½ cup (120 ml) cold water
- 1/16 teaspoon agar powder (eyeball one-half of an ⅛ teaspoon measure)

FOR THE YOLKS:

- ½ cup (120 ml) egg white mixture (see above)
- 2 tablespoons nutritional yeast flakes
- ¼ teaspoon ground turmeric
- ⅛ teaspoon paprika
- ½ teaspoon kala namak
- 1½ teaspoons melted refined coconut oil
- 1 teaspoon tomato paste

1 To assemble the sandwiches, slice the bagels in half and toast them. Spread the bottom of each with cream cheese and the top with butter. Place an egg on each bagel, sprinkle with pepper, close the bagel, and devour. Make the egg whites: In a blender, combine all of the egg white ingredients and blend until smooth. Transfer to a medium bowl using a rubber spatula to scrape the sides.

2 Now on to the yolks: Scoop up ½ cup of the egg white mixture and return it to the blender. Add the nutritional yeast, turmeric, paprika, kala namak, coconut oil, and the tomato paste. Blend until smooth. Transfer mixture to a smaller bowl.

3 Preheat a well-seasoned cast-iron pan over medium heat. Spray a small area with cooking spray (I like coconut). Do a tablespoon test of the egg white. It should cook in about 2 minutes and be matte on top, golden underneath. If it burns, lower the heat; if it takes too long, raise it a little.

4 OK, now make the eggs. Have a piece of parchment ready on the counter. Spray the bottom of the pan with cooking spray. Fill a ¼ cup (60 ml) measuring cup about three-fourths (45 ml) of the way with the egg mixture and pour it into the pan in a circle, leaving a hole in the middle. Fill the hole with about a tablespoon of the yolk mixture. Depending on the size of the pan, you can do 3 to 5 eggs per round.

5 Let the eggs cook for 2 to 3 minutes, until matte on top. Spray the tops with more cooking spray and, using a thin metal spatula, flip and cook them on the other side for 30 seconds to a minute. Transfer to the parchment paper as you continue with the others.

SALADS, SPREADS, AND COLD STUFF

In a restaurant, the garde manger oversees all things cold. And, if you're American, that gets shortened to "garmo" because that is what Americans do: ruin perfectly good French things. In this chapter, you will become your own garde manger!

In our modern world, salad is dinner and lunch and everything in between. Long gone are the days when you have to explain why salad isn't just lettuce and tomatoes; there are in fact empires built around the whole concept of arugula tossed with some other stuff. Let's start with the classics, like Caesar and Niçoise. Fresh, simple components along with cooked meats come together to satisfy a craving that is more than the sum of its parts. Hearty composed meals that happen to have lettuce.

But cold doesn't mean just salads. This chapter contains light and refreshing cold plates. Meaty "salads" that double as sandwich fillings. And the reason we are all really here: charcuterie!

So strike a balance of indulgent and filling while still getting some greens in!

SUPER CLASSIC CHICK'N CAESAR SALAD

Serves 4

I have a LOT of Caesar recipes out in the world. For this one, I chose to stick to the script as much as possible. No funny business here; no tempeh croutons, no quinoa, no kale. Just rich, garlicky, anchovy-esque dressing smothering crisp romaine hearts and garlicky croutons—don't forget the Parmesan, and plenty of lemon, too! Since there are a lot of separate components to contend with, I kept the chick'n relatively simple by using some breaded chicken-y tofu. Fresh cracked pepper is integral to the recipe. At many fancy restaurants during the twentieth century, servers tossed Caesar salad tableside. I suggest trying that to freak your date right out.

FOR THE CAESAR DRESSING:

- 6 cloves garlic, minced
- 2 tablespoons olive oil
- ⅔ cup (165 ml) vegan mayo, prepared or homemade (page 309)
- 2 tablespoons capers, brine included
- ¼ cup (60 ml) unsweetened soy milk
- 3 tablespoons fresh lemon juice
- 2 tablespoons nutritional yeast flakes
- ¼ teaspoon ground black pepper
- Salt

FOR THE SALAD:

- 1 (16-ounce/455 g) package romaine hearts
- 1 recipe Rustic Garlicky Croutons (recipe follows)
- Freshly ground black pepper
- 1 recipe DAD Chicken-y Tofu (recipe follows)
- 1 recipe Pantry Mushroom Bacon (page 173)
- It's Great Parmesan (page 285) or store-bought vegan Parmesan
- Finely chopped fresh parsley

MAKE THE DRESSING

1 Preheat a small pan over low heat. Be careful! The garlic needs to be cooked low and slow so don't let the pan get too hot. Add the garlic and drizzle the olive oil over it. Cook for about 2 minutes, using a rubber spatula to stir it occasionally. You don't want it to brown or toast, just be aromatic and gorgeous.

2 Immediately transfer the garlic and oil to a small blender. Add the mayo, capers, soy milk, lemon juice, nutritional yeast, and pepper. Blend until smooth. The dressing might be salty enough from the capers. But make sure it's plenty salty and add some salt if needed.

ASSEMBLE THE SALAD

1 Pour half the dressing into a 9 by 13-inch baking dish. Since the romaine leaves are large and you want to keep them whole, it works better than a bowl. So, add the leaves now and smother them in the reserved dressing, flipping and rubbing them with your hands. Toss in the croutons.

2 Divide the dressed lettuce and croutons among shallow serving bowls. Sprinkle with plenty of fresh black pepper. Slice the DAD Chicken-y Tofu on a bias and place on top, along with the Pantry Mushroom Bacon. Grate a ton of Parmesan over each salad and sprinkle with the parsley.

HOT TAKE

I use Pantry Mushroom Bacon here because it's the easiest of the bacon recipes. But you can use any vegan bacon you prefer, or, honestly, just leave it out!

CONTINUED →

RUSTIC GARLICKY CROUTONS

- 4 cups soft rustic white bread, crust removed, torn into 1-inch (2.5 cm) pieces
- 2 tablespoons garlic oil, prepared or homemade
- ¼ teaspoon salt

Makes 4 cups (170 g)

It's the little things that matter. Small details like tearing croutons into big, organic chunks instead of cubes make all the difference in the world. Don't we have enough square cubes in our lives? Slice the crusts off and go to town creating gorgeous, rustic bites.

1 Preheat the oven to 350°F (175°C). Line a large baking sheet with parchment paper.

2 Place the bread in a large bowl with enough space to toss stuff around. Drizzle with the garlic oil and salt, tossing to coat.

3 Spread onto the prepared baking sheet and bake for 12 to 15 minutes, tossing once. The croutons should be golden and crunchy.

DAD CHICKEN-Y TOFU

- ¾ cup (75 g) fine dry breadcrumbs
- 1 tablespoon poultry seasoning, prepared or homemade (page 89)
- ½ teaspoon freshly ground black pepper
- 3 tablespoons tamari or soy sauce
- 1 (14-ounce/400 g) block extra-firm tofu, sliced widthwise into 8 slabs
- Olive oil, for frying

Serves 2 to 4

I call this DAD Chicken-y Tofu, not because your dad loves it (although he might), but because it's an acronym for "down and dirty." This is a really simple way to make some chicken-y tofu with as few ingredients and in as little time as possible. It's perfect for salads (like we are doing here) but also completely awesome in a sandwich or on top of pasta. If you are a dad, as a bonus, your kids might like it because it tastes like a chicken nugget!

1 On a dinner plate, use your fingertips to mix together the breadcrumbs, poultry seasoning, and pepper. On a separate plate, pour the soy sauce.

2 Place a tofu slab in the soy sauce and toss to coat. Then dredge the tofu in the breadcrumbs, tossing to coat as well as you can. Try to leave no naked spot. Use your dry hand to handle the tofu in the breadcrumbs, otherwise you'll get a crumb mitten on your hand. Put the breaded slabs off to the side of the plate and continue until all the tofu is coated.

3 Preheat a large nonstick pan, preferably cast-iron, over medium-high heat. Drizzle a thin layer of olive oil in the pan. Don't use too much oil or the breading won't stick to the cutlets—2 tablespoons should do it.

4 Transfer the tofu slabs to the pan. Let them cook for about 5 minutes, until golden. Spray the tops of the tofu with a little cooking oil. Flip the tofu slabs, using a thin metal spatula so that you don't scrape off the breading. Cook for about 5 more minutes. Once browned, remove from the pan and use on top of salads or in sandwiches or just as a snack!

I've come to lean on pre-ground black pepper more often than I used to. But not here, my fellow Caesar Stans! Fresh cracked pepper is integral to the recipe. So dust off that pepper grinder.

To get this done in record time, make the tofu before you prepare the rest of the salad. Also have ready the croutons. And the Parmesan, of course.

SHREDDED BEEF AND CABBAGE SALAD
WITH PEANUT AND LIME

Serves 6

When you want a meal that is BURSTING with flavor, look no further. Inspired by some of my favorite Vietnamese ingredients, including peanuts, lime, fresh mint, cilantro, and a little spice, this one has it all. It's crunchy, spicy, and mouth-wateringly savory. The beef is sautéed with garlic and red pepper flakes, then cooled before joining the party. This salad travels well, too, making it a great packed lunch, but keep the dressing separate until you're ready to eat.

FOR THE SPICY LIME MISO DRESSING:

- 2 tablespoons red miso
- 2 tablespoons rice vinegar
- 2 tablespoons fresh lime juice
- 1 tablespoon grapeseed oil or other neutral-flavored oil
- 1 tablespoon siracha
- 2 teaspoons agave syrup
- 2 teaspoons minced fresh ginger

FOR THE SEITAN:

- 3 tablespoons refined coconut oil
- 1 pound (455 g) (½ a recipe) Beefy Seitan (page 28), sliced into long thin matchstick-like strips
- ¼ teaspoon salt
- ½ teaspoon red pepper flakes
- 3 cloves garlic, minced

FOR ASSEMBLY:

- 6 cups (570 g) shredded green cabbage (about 1 pound/455 g)
- 1 cup shredded carrots
- ½ cup (75 g) very thinly sliced red radish
- 1 cup (140 g) lightly chopped roasted salted peanuts
- ½ cup (15 g) loosely packed fresh mint leaves (see Hot Take)
- 1 cup (30 g) loosely packed fresh cilantro sprigs

1. Make the dressing: Add all the ingredients plus 2 tablespoons water to a small blender and blend until smooth and incorporated. Refrigerate in a tightly sealed container until ready to use. It will keep for 5 days.
2. Prepare the seitan: Preheat a large cast-iron pan over medium heat. Sauté the seitan in 2 tablespoons of the coconut oil, seasoning with the salt and red pepper flakes, for about 5 minutes, until lightly browned. Add the garlic with the remaining tablespoon oil and cook for 3 more minutes, flipping the seitan often. Taste for salt. Set aside to cool.
3. Assemble the salad: Pour the dressing into a large bowl. Toss in the cabbage, carrot, and seitan and mix with tongs (or your hands) to coat. Taste and adjust for salt and seasoning.
4. When ready to serve, top individual bowls (or a serving tray) of salad with the radishes, peanuts, mint, and cilantro.

HOT TAKE

Try to use the tiniest leaves of mint to top the salad. If you have only large leaves, roll them up and cut into thin ribbons, know as a chiffonade in chefspeak.

SALADE NIÇOISE

Serves 4

I was introduced to the Niçoise while waitressing in Soho in the late nineties. Every table I brought it to would be impressed, from the record execs on their cell phones, which were the size of a shoe back then, to the models, who were also the size of a shoe. Even Alanis Morissette marveled at its beauty (now I'm just bragging that I waited on her once). It's a little warm, a little cold, and a lot French. My version is a feast of a salad, with tender tofu tuna, flaky and grilled. In place of an egg from a chicken (what! who eats those?) we use a chickpea egg salad. And since all the other elements are already vegan, we are good to go. Tender baby potatoes roasted and warm, crunchy grilled green beans with hints of smoke (or haricot verts, since we are in France). An herby zesty dressing completes the scene! Serve on a large platter to dazzle diners or, if you can, just arrange it in big individual bowls, if you don't trust common folk to serve themselves without destroying your masterpiece.

- 8 ounces (225 g) baby potatoes
- 3 tablespoons olive oil, divided
- Fine sea salt to taste
- Fresh black pepper
- 3 Tuna Steaks (page 256)
- 1 recipe Dilly Chickpea Egg Salad (page 75)
- 8 ounces (225 g) haricots verts, trimmed
- ½ cup pitted mixed olives
- ½ cup radishes, quartered
- 1 ripe avocado, sliced
- ¼ teaspoon flaky sea salt (like Maldon)
- 1 tablespoon chopped fresh parsley

1 Roast the potatoes: Preheat the oven to 425°F (220°C). Toss the potatoes in a 9 by 13-inch (23 by 33 cm) baking dish and drizzle with 2 tablespoons olive oil. Sprinkle with a big pinch of salt and several dashes of fresh ground black pepper. Toss to coat. Bake for 20 to 25 minutes, tossing once, until fork tender.

2 Warm the tofu tuna in a pan, if it's not warm already: Preheat a pan over medium low with a bit of cooking spray. Place the tuna in the pan and warm through slowly, 10 to 15 minutes, flipping occasionally.

3 Preheat a grill pan over medium-high heat. In a small bowl, toss the haricot verts with 1 tablespoon olive oil and a big pinch of sea salt. Grill for about 5 minutes, tossing every minute or so. You want them to be charred in spots but still have snap. Remove them from the pan immediately and place back in the mixing bowl.

4 Assemble the salad. A bit of artistic license is permitted here (and maybe even demanded). Please refer to the pic but also let your creativity flow. Scatter a cup of greens onto a large platter. Use an ice cream scoop to scoop the chickpea salad into one corner of the platter. Tear the tofu tuna into bite-size pieces with a fork and place it in the opposite corner.

5 Place the potatoes between the tuna and the chickpea salad. Use tongs to place the haricot vert in the space next to the tuna. Now scatter the radishes across the plate, starting wherever looks most empty. Same with the olives. Tuck the avocado slices in empty-looking spots.

6 Drizzle everything with vinaigrette, leaving some on the side. Sprinkle the avocado slices with flaky sea salt and garnish everything with fresh chopped parsley. Serve with big serving spoons and tongs.

STEAK SALAD WITH GREEN GORGONZOLA

Serves 4

A lip-smacking balsamic vin, complemented by peppery arugula and a succulent steak, all brought together with what is lovingly referred to as a "stinky" cheese. This is my dream combo. The cheese melts in your mouth, the arugula is fresh and clean, and the meat gives you plenty to chew on. The dressing couldn't get any simpler! A bright and tangy number that is also thick and creamy. The secret? Blending to emulsify! Even though you think you can stir all the ingredients together, you really need to blend them, which whips air into the oil, bringing everything together. The whole-grain Dijon mustard is important, too. When you destroy those seeds in the blender something magical seems to happen. If you can find sunflower sprouts, they are a wonderful fresh and crunchy addition! You will need to have ready Cast-Iron Steaks, cooked and cooled, and Green Gorgonzola.

FOR THE BALSAMIC VINAIGRETTE:

- 1 clove garlic
- ½ cup (120 ml) balsamic vinegar
- 2 tablespoons whole-grain Dijon mustard
- 1 teaspoon granulated sugar
- 1 teaspoon salt
- ½ teaspoon ground black pepper
- 1 cup (240 ml) extra-virgin olive oil

FOR THE SALAD:

- 1 recipe Cast-Iron Steak and Onions (page 247)
- 12 ounces (340 g) baby arugula
- ½ recipe Green Gorgonzola Cheeze (page 289)
- 2 cups (240 ml) sunflower sprouts or sprouts of your choice

FOR THE VARIATION:

- 4 portobello mushroom caps, stems removed
- ¼ cup olive oil
- ½ teaspoon salt
- Fresh black pepper

1. Make the dressing. Place the garlic in a small blender and pulse to chop. Add the vinegar, mustard, sugar, salt, pepper, and olive oil and blend on low until thick and creamy, about 2 minutes. Transfer to a container, seal, and refrigerate until ready to use.
2. In a cast-iron pan, reheat the steaks with just 1 cup of their sauce. Reserve the rest of the sauce for another use (gravy or soup?). Slice the steaks into ½-inch (12 mm) strips.
3. Serve family-style on a big salad platter: Scatter the arugula leaves. Place the warm steak strips over the greens. Crumble on the gorgonzola and top with the sprouts. Serve the balsamic vinegar in a lipped jar for drizzling.

VARIATION:

1. Portobellos can be steak! The secret is to treat them with as few ingredients as possible, letting the natural, juicy steakiness shine. So try this recipe with a roasted mushroom instead. Preheat the oven to 450°F (230°C). Line a rimmed baking sheet with parchment. Toss the portobellos with olive oil, then sprinkle with salt and pepper. Arrange on the baking sheet with the trimmed side up. Place in the oven and roast until tender and juicy, 18 to 22 minutes. Use a fork and steak knife to slice the mushrooms on a bias and place them on the salad.

PINEAPPLE CEVICHE

Serves 6

A few fishy ingredients—chickpeas and oyster mushrooms—create a toothsome ceviche, which is typically seafood "cooked" in an acid. Here, the chickpeas provide a shrimp-like bite, while the oyster mushrooms add a fishy texture and hint of salinity. It's a really nice summery lunch but could also be bulked up and poured over some rice and baked tofu. And if you're partying, serve with tortilla chips and guacamole. It's tasty, tropical, and beachy. Get ready to spread out your towel and relax because it requires very little effort.

- ½ cup (120 ml) pineapple juice
- ½ cup (120 ml) fresh lime juice
- ¼ teaspoon salt
- 2 cloves garlic, minced
- 2 tablespoons finely chopped fresh cilantro
- 2 tablespoons olive oil
- 8 ounces (225 g) oyster mushrooms, cut into bite-size pieces
- 1½ cups (240 g) cooked chickpeas (from one 15-ounce can)
- 1 cup (165 g) diced fresh pineapple
- ½ cup (95 g) cherry tomatoes, sliced in half
- 1 jalapeño, seeded and thinly sliced
- 1 small red onion, cut into small dice (about ¼ cup/ 35 g)
- ½ cup (20 g) chopped fresh cilantro

FOR SERVING:

- Additional fresh lime juice
- Fresh cilantro sprigs
- Tortilla chips (optional)
- Guacamole (optional)

1. In a huge bowl, whisk together both juices, the salt, garlic, cilantro, and olive oil. Add the mushrooms and chickpeas and let marinate for about 30 minutes.
2. Add the pineapple, tomatoes, jalapeño, onion, and cilantro to the bowl. Let marinate for another 30 minutes, stirring occasionally.
3. Place in a serving bowl, or divide into cute serving cups and serve!

WHAT AM I, VEGETARIAN CHOPPED LIVER?

Makes 4 cups (960 ml)

- ½ cup (50 g) walnuts
- 1 cup (115 g) sliced shallots
- 2 tablespoons refined coconut oil
- 1 teaspoon salt plus a pinch
- 8 cloves garlic, minced
- 1 teaspoon dried thyme
- ½ teaspoon ground black pepper
- 8 ounces (225 g) cremini mushrooms
- ¼ cup (60 ml) dry sherry
- 1½ cups (285 g) cooked lentils (from one 15-ounce/435 g can, rinsed and drained)
- 1 tablespoon beet powder
- ¼ cup (13 g) finely chopped fresh parsley

FOR SERVING (OPTIONAL):

- Matzoh or crackers
- Seedless grapes
- Additional toasted walnuts

Jewish kids already know, vegetarian chopped liver is a thing. Long before we even had Unturkey, we had this spread. And we loved it. Right there on the table with the matzoh balls and brisket, all brown and weird, it held some inexplicable attraction. Toasted walnuts, caramelized shallots, and browned mushrooms, plus lentils and a little sherry to appease the refined palate. It's manna from meatless heaven. Classically, it's served with matzoh for dipping and spreading. If you don't want to live the vegetarian chopped liver life, just think of it as pâté and serve with garlic toast and crudités. Boom; it's a whole new concept.

1 Preheat a cast-iron pan over medium-low. Toast the walnuts for about 5 minutes, flipping them occasionally. Place them in a food processor fitted with a metal blade and set aside.

2 Turn the heat up to medium. In the same pan, sauté the shallots in the coconut oil with a pinch of salt until caramelized and browned, about 10 minutes. Add the garlic, thyme, and pepper to the shallots and continue cooking for another 2 minutes while stirring often. Add the mushrooms and cook for 10 more minutes, until the mushrooms are browned and juicy.

3 Pour in the sherry and turn the heat up to high to reduce some of the moisture, about 5 more minutes. Remove from heat.

4 Pulse the walnuts in the food processor into fine crumbs. Add the lentils, beet powder, 1 teaspoon salt, and the mushroom mixture to the food processor. Puree with the toasted walnuts for about 1 minute to create a pâté. It should have some texture, not be completely smooth.

5 Taste for salt and seasoning. Transfer to a bowl and fold in the parsley. Chill for about an hour before serving.

DILLY CHICKPEA EGG SALAD

Makes 3 cups (510 g)

Never underestimate the power of chickpeas. When mashed up just so, they transform into the most deli-perfect egg salad. Kala namak brings the eggy flavor, turmeric brings the eggy color, some sweet pickle relish and dill bring the point home. This egg salad is grand for a sandwich, obviously, but also stuffed into an avocado (as pictured here and described in the box on page 76), scooped onto a salad, such as the Niçoise (page 67), or anywhere you need a stunt egg. I'm also a big fan of open-faced egg salad toast instead of—or in addition to—avocado toast, with some sliced radishes, olive oil, and flaky salt. Kala namak's saltiness can range from brand to brand, so definitely taste and adjust as you go. This may need a little bit more.

- 3 cups (480 g) cooked chickpeas (two 15-ounce/430 g cans, rinsed and drained)
- ⅓ cup (75 ml) vegan mayo, prepared or homemade (page 309)
- 2 tablespoons smooth Dijon mustard
- 2 tablespoons sweet pickle relish
- 2 teaspoons kala namak, or more if needed
- 1 teaspoon ground turmeric
- ½ teaspoon ground black pepper
- 2 ribs celery, finely diced
- ¼ cup (13 g) chopped fresh dill
- Additional dill for garnish

1. In a medium-size bowl, use an avocado masher or a strong fork to mash the chickpeas well. They should retain some of their texture and not appear pureed. A few whole ones left are OK.
2. Mix in the mayo, mustard, pickle relish, kala namak, turmeric, and black pepper. Mash a little bit more. Fold in the celery and dill. Taste for kala namak.
3. Store in a covered container in the refrigerator until ready to use.

HOT TAKE

If you don't have sweet pickle relish, you can chop up some bread and butter pickles! Or even dill pickles would work. Basically, whatever pickles you've got in the fridge.

SPICY TEMPEH TUNA SALAD

Makes 4 cups

- 2 (8-ounce/225 g) packages tempeh
- 2 tablespoons tamari
- ½ cup (120 ml) vegan mayo, prepared or homemade (page 309)
- 1 tablespoon fresh lemon juice
- 1 small carrot, peeled and finely chopped
- 2 ribs celery, finely chopped
- 1 teaspoon kelp powder
- ¼ cup (13 g) finely chopped parsley
- ¼ teaspoon freshly ground black pepper
- ½ teaspoon salt, plus more if needed

It's tempeh of the sea! Tempeh is poached with a little tamari, which seasons the tempeh, makes it succulent, and "opens its pores." Now it's ready for all the flavor we are going to throw its way. Kelp powder lends ocean flavors, and you can't have tuna without mayo, now can you? With a hint of lemon and your classic crunchy elements: carrots and celery. It's fun. It's fresh. It's fishy, And it's infinitely as yummers as the ocean is blue.

1 Tear the tempeh into bite-size pieces and place them in a small saucepan. Submerge in about 1 quart (960 ml) water and add the tamari. Cover the pot and bring to a boil, then reduce the heat and simmer for 15 minutes. Drain and transfer the tempeh to a bowl to cool.

2 Add the mayo, lemon juice, carrot, celery, kelp, parsley, pepper, and salt. Stir with a fork, mashing the tempeh as you go. Taste for salt and seasoning. Store in a covered container in the refrigerator until ready to use.

Level up your salad! Obviously these salads all work as sandwiches as well. All of them would be welcome with open arms in any lunch box, on some whole-wheat bread with lettuce and tomato. But don't stop there!

STUFFED INTO AVOCADOS

First chill the ripe avocados. This will enable them to slide easily out of their skins. Slice each avo in half as evenly as you can. Pluck out the pit. Gently peel away the skin. Season with lemon juice and salt. Use an ice cream scoop to put a scoop of salad into each avocado half. Garnish with pretty green things.

STUFFED INTO TOMATOES

If avocado is for millennials, stuffed tomato is for boomers. I love and respect both of those generations and their fruits that are considered vegetables. Choose hothouse tomatoes. Hollow out the cores with a paring knife. I don't know what to do with the stuff you hollow out. Feed it to your dog? But now you can fill tomatoes to the brim with salad!

LET US CUPS! LETTUCE CUPS

Choose boaty-shaped lettuce leaves, like butter, Bib, radicchio, or endive. Yes, radicchio and endive are technically in the chicory family, but "let us" not get into all that. Sometimes romaine will let us turn it into a canoe. Scoop salad into the leaves.

CURRY CHICK'N SALAD

Makes 5 cups

Fragrant, warmly spiced, and studded with juicy grapes and crunchy toasted almonds. This chick'n salad just feels special. I wouldn't hesitate to serve it in lettuce cups for a dinner party or stuffed into a pita to eat over the kitchen sink. There's no real secret to it, all the flavors fit seamlessly together, but if there IS a secret, it's to sear the chick'n in coconut oil before adding it to the mix. It gives it a mysteriously delicious, slightly smoky flavor and a little crunch to the skin.

- ½ cup (55 g) slivered almonds
- 4 cups Pull-Apart Seitan Chick'n (page 115), torn into bite-size pieces
- 2 tablespoons refined coconut oil
- ½ teaspoon salt plus a pinch
- 1 tablespoon mild curry powder
- ¼ teaspoon garam masala
- ¼ teaspoon ground turmeric
- 2 tablespoons very hot water
- 2 tablespoons fresh lime juice
- 1 tablespoon agave syrup
- 1 tablespoon sriracha
- ¾ cup (180 ml) vegan mayo, prepared or homemade (page 309)
- 1½ cups (225 g) red seedless grapes, cut in half
- 1 cup (55 g) thinly sliced scallions (white and light green parts only)
- ¼ cup (10 g) finely chopped fresh cilantro, plus extra for garnish

1. First, dry toast the almonds. Preheat a cast-iron pan over medium heat. Add the almonds and toast for about 5 minutes, flipping often, until lightly browned and aromatic. Remove from the pan and set aside to cool.

2. Give the seitan a light squeeze over the sink to remove any excess broth. Keep the pan on the heat. Add the coconut oil to melt, then add the seitan along with a pinch of salt. Sauté for about 7 minutes, flipping to sear and brown the chick'n.

3. In the meantime, in a large bowl, mix together curry powder, garam masala, and turmeric. Add the hot water and use a fork to mix the spices together into a loose paste. This will help them incorporate into the dressing.

4. Add the lime juice, agave, sriracha, ½ teaspoon salt, and the mayo to the spice paste. Mix well. Add the grapes, scallions, and cilantro to the dressing and let the mixture hang out to blend for about 5 minutes.

5. Fold in the almonds and chick'n. It's OK if the chick'n is still a little warm. Seal in an air-tight container and chill in the fridge or eat it right away!

LEFTOVER TURKI SALAD

- 1 small yellow onion, thinly sliced
- 3 ribs celery, thinly sliced
- 2 tablespoons olive oil
- ½ teaspoon salt plus a pinch
- 1 teaspoon dried thyme
- 1 teaspoon dry rubbed sage
- ¼ teaspoon freshly ground black pepper
- 1 loaf Roast Turki (page 20), shredded (about 4 cups)
- ¾ cup (180 ml) vegan mayo, prepared or homemade (page 309)
- 2 teaspoons whole grain mustard
- 1 tablespoon champagne vinegar
- ½ cup dried currants

Makes 5 cups

Thanksgiving leftovers, any time of the year! This salad gives big holiday vibes. The celery and sage are reminiscent of stuffing, while the currants add sweet, tart bites throughout, just like cranberry sauce. Do not be afraid to stuff this on a pretzel bun or any big, hearty hunk of bread. It's all gravy. Shredding the turki with your fingers is so fun! Just keep pulling the long way until it becomes long, thin slivers. See page 21 for reference.

1. Preheat a cast-iron pan over medium heat. Sauté the onions and celery in the olive oil and a pinch of salt for about 7 minutes. The onions should be lightly browned and the celery a bit softened.
2. Add the thyme, sage, and pepper to the pan and toss to coat. Add the turki and lightly brown it, about 7 more minutes.
3. In the meantime, in a large bowl, mix together the mayo, mustard, salt, vinegar, and currants.
4. Add the turki mix to the dressing while it's still warm. Let the salad cool a bit, then seal and refrigerate until ready to eat.

PICNIC PERFECT CHICK'N SALAD

Makes 3 cups

- 1¼ cups (85 g) textured vegetable protein (TVP)
- 2 tablespoons apple cider vinegar
- 2 tablespoons tamari
- 1 medium carrot, peeled and roughly chopped
- 2 ribs celery, roughly chopped
- ¼ cup (13 g) chopped fresh dill
- ⅔ cup (165 ml) vegan mayo, prepared or homemade (page 309)
- 2 tablespoons fresh lemon juice
- ½ teaspoon salt
- ¼ teaspoon ground black pepper

Picture it: NYC in the nineties, when Snoop Dogg and Nirvana ruled the airwaves, and unchicken salad lined the shelves of every corner store. It was sort of a counterculture version of heaven, looking back on it. Those little plastic containers of unchicken salad could easily fit in your fanny pack to bring to the park with a hunk of bread, or a fork, or, sometimes you had none of that and had to create a makeshift spoon out of the lid. You'd set yourself up in Prospect Park, watch a game of cricket, and have the best lunch. Supposedly, each 8-ounce (225 g) container served six, but we know it just served one. Now this unchicken salad is gone, and we're still grieving. But turn that frown upside-down, because this recipe comes as close to it as I can remember. Break out your Discman, get to a park, and enjoy.

1 Place the TVP in a saucepot and submerge in water by about 6 inches (15 cm). Add the apple cider vinegar and tamari. Cover and bring to a boil. Lower the heat, uncover, and simmer for 15 minutes.

2 Drain the TVP in a fine-mesh strainer and let cool. When cool enough to handle, press out as much water as you can by firmly pressing the TVP against the strainer with your hands.

3 While the TVP is cooling, start prepping the veggies. Place the carrot and celery in a food processor fitted with a metal blade. Pulse about 15 times untili finely chopped. Add the dill and pulse a few more times. The veggies should be fine but not pureed and the dill well dispersed.

4 Use a rubber spatula to transfer the veggies to a medium bowl. It's OK if some are left in the processor.

5 Put the cooled TVP, mayo, lemon juice, salt, and pepper in the food processor. Pulse about 15 times. The TVP should be fine and a bit creamy but still chunky.

6 Transfer everything to the bowl with the veggies. Mix well. Adjust the seasoning and mayo, transfer to a covered container, and refrigerate until ready to use.

The fastest way to do this is in a food processor. If you don't have one or would rather chop, that's fine, too! But it will come out a bit more crumbly and not quite as nineties-like as possible.

The trick to getting that "health food" flavor out of TVP is adding some apple cider vinegar and tamari to the boiling liquid.

CARROT LOX

Makes a 12-inch "fillet"

Carrots are by far the top choice for making fish-free lox at home. The color is spot on, and the layered texture really tricks people into thinking it's lox! Strips of carrot are soaked in a briny, smoky concoction and then layered and baked. Aquafaba holds the parcel together, and in the end you have a beautiful, fishy slab to use on bagels, in omelets, and at your Passover seder. Look for the biggest, freshest carrots you can find. You'll be using a peeler to make the ribbons, and the chunkier the carrot, the easier this will be.

- 1 pound carrots, preferably large (at least 1 inch thick)
- 3 tablespoons organic sugar
- 2 tablespoons rice vinegar
- 1 teaspoon kelp powder
- 1 tablespoon smoked salt
- ½ teaspoon smoked paprika
- ⅓ cup (80 ml) aquafaba (chickpea cooking liquid)
- 1 tablespoon olive oil, plus additional for oiling parchment paper

FOR GARNISH:

- Sprigs of fresh dill
- Paper-thin lemon slices

1 Thoroughly scrub carrots and trim off any stems. Use a peeler to make ribbons that are long as you can manage.

2 In a 9 by 11-inch (23 by 28 cm) pan, mix together the carrot ribbons, sugar, rice vinegar, kelp powder, smoked salt, and smoked paprika. Toss to coat with spices and set aside for 30 minutes, tossing occasionally.

3 Preheat the oven to 350°F (175°C) and line a sheet pan with parchment paper; lightly grease the paper with olive oil.

4 Stir the aquafaba and olive oil into the carrot ribbons, coating them completely.

5 Neatly layer the carrot ribbons over the parchment paper. Arrange the ribbons in the same direction, with strips overlapping one another. Ideally, the longer strips will be in the middle and the shorter ones at the ends, so they taper into a diamond shape (see photo). Brush the top with any remaining aquafaba mixture.

6 Tightly cover the pan with foil and bake for 30 minutes, until the carrots are tender. Transfer the pan to a cooling rack and keep covered until cool enough to handle.

7 Transfer the cooled lox, still on the parchment, to a small cutting board or something that will fit in the fridge. Wrap with plastic wrap and refrigerate for at least 30 minutes before using.

CUTIE CHARCUTERIE

Vegan charcuterie is all the rage, and you simply can't have a fake-meat cookbook without it. But this isn't so much a recipe as it is a guide.

Charcuterie is meat. Cured, pâté-d, smoked . . . its literal definition would send shivers down a vegan's spine, so I'm not even going to put it in print. What I will put in print is this: Vegan charcuterie will make everyone happy!

As charcuterie became popularized in the 2000s, it took on a new meaning, vegan or not. Instead of just meat, the idea evolved to include crackers, breads, cheeses, fruits, and pickles. You'll also want some wine. Huzzah.

The first step, though, is getting a really cool board. You don't have to spend a lot of money. Like I said, charcuterie is all the rage, and boards are easy to come by. Visit an off-price retailer and you will be able to find something affordable that everyone will assume costs a hundo.

HOW TO PLATE:

1 Scatter some pretty field greens or arugula over the board. This isn't a "bed of lettuce." You just want a few pops of green.

2 Now let the magic begin. Meat first! Lay your meat out, and don't overthink it. Just make a pile or two of each meat. The meats can even touch each other; it's a free country. A few fun ones:

- Proper Pepperoni (page 149), slice it lengthwise and then into bite-size pieces.
- Roast Turki (page 20), sliced so that it that will fit nicely on a cracker.
- Ribbony Seitan Bacon (page 171), cooked and folded into a twirly pile.
- Sun-dried Tomato Chorizo (page 177), portioned into a cute little bowl. Heart-shaped, preferably.

3 Next, some cheeses. Use a nice variety, and slice them in different shapes. Here we have cubes of Shreddy Cheddy (page 291), Faux Feta balls (page 290), and little Swizz Cheezes (page 294).

4 It's time for crackers! Go to the nearest expensive grocery store and raid the cracker aisle. This is your calling. Get round, buttery ones. Rustic wheat ones. Thin ones, thick ones, ones with rosemary. Leave no cracker unturned.

5 Now to add freshness. Slice strawberries into fans. Place clusters of juicy grapes everywhere, like you're about to feed a Greek god.

6 And finally, pickle-y and briny stuff. Use different kinds of olives. Attack the pickle bar and pick out whatever looks pretty. And make your own very simple Pickled Red Onions (page 311).

7 Nuts are nice, too, but in my opinion not wholly necessary. I did go ahead and use some walnuts here, and you can, too.

CHICK'N DINNERS

FOR WEEKNIGHTS AND WEEKENDS

You know how everyone's like "I can't live without bacon"? Well, first of all, yes, you can. But no one really says that about chicken. And when offered a chewy, juicy alternative they tend to be unable to tell the difference. It's probably the first fake meat we reach for and the simplest to replace. And to turn chicken vegan all you have to do is remove the *e*: chick'n. See how easy that was?

These recipes are great for weeknights, if you make the chick'n in advance or use a cheater chick'n. But they're here to demonstrate how much seasoning plays a part in how much "we" enjoy chicken.

Several methods and ingredients are used, each with its own unique flair. Tofu, often frozen, thawed, and pressed ("FTAP" tofu, as I call it), makes the chick'n chewy and also readies it for marinades. Seitan is a no-brainer, and my main go-to for chick'ny-ness. And different cooking methods yield various chick'ny results. Frying, grilling, searing.

But seasoning is key. You will see many of these chick'ns call for "poultry seasoning." There are so many different brands of this spice mix and they really do vary. Some contain ginger and rosemary. Some contain thyme and pepper. The two brands of poultry seasoning I enjoy most are luckily widely available and hopefully companies that will be around for as long as this book is: Frontier Co-op and Penzey's Spices. They're different, but you can't go wrong with either. They are both unsalted, so make sure whatever blend you choose contains no salt, or you may have to adjust the recipes.

For your convenience, here is a DIY poultry seasoning blend if you'd like to make your own.

- 2 tablespoons dried sage
- 1 tablespoon dried thyme
- 1 tablespoon onion powder
- 2 teaspoons celery seed
- 2 teaspoons dried marjoram
- 2 teaspoons dried rosemary
- 2 teaspoons lemon pepper
- 1 teaspoon ground white pepper
- 1 teaspoon ground ginger

1 Add all ingredients to a small blender (I use a Magic Bullet) and pulse them together for about 15 seconds. It shouldn't quite be a total powder, but everything should be coarsely ground. Store in an airtight container. Used, empty spice jars work great!

SHEETPAN TANDOORI CHICK'N

Serves 6 to 8

Spicy, blistered chick'n with its signature red skin always makes me salivate, but I never found a vegan version at any Indian restaurant. That's why I set about creating one! It's undoubtedly inauthentic, but it's what satisfies my taste buds after studying millions of cookbooks. The chick'n is marinated in a rich, peppery coconut yogurt sauce and baked to high heaven so that it's caramelized and smoky, but tender and juicy inside, and a real pleasure to slice your steak knife into. Dress this up or down! Serve with basmati rice for simplicity. And if you're feeling ambitious, you can also add some simple homemade elements to make it really pop! Pickled Red Onions (page 311) and cooling Coconut Raita (page 122) are super-delish accompaniments. If you're not feeling like a Top Chef, then prepared mango chutney is a perfectly adequate condiment on its own.

- 1 cup (240 ml) coconut yogurt
- 1 tablespoon tomato paste
- 1 cup (110 g) chopped yellow onion
- 6 cloves garlic, peeled and smashed
- 3 tablespoons peeled, roughly chopped fresh ginger
- 2 tablespoons mild paprika
- 2 teaspoons mild curry powder
- 1 teaspoon garam masala
- ½ teaspoon ground cayenne (use less if you're scared of spice)
- 3 tablespoons olive oil, plus extra for the baking sheet
- 3 tablespoons fresh lime juice
- 1 recipe Pull-Apart Seitan Chick'n (page 115)
- Cooked basmati rice, for serving
- Chopped fresh cilantro, for garnish

1 In a blender, combine the yogurt, tomato paste, onion, garlic, ginger, paprika, curry powder, garam masala, cayenne, olive oil, and lime juice. Puree until relatively smooth. There should be some remaining texture from the onion.

2 You should have 4 big bundles of chick'n. Tear each in half so that you have 8 big pieces. Give each a light squeeze to drain excess broth. Score small slivers all over the seitan chicken, just deep enough to pierce the skin, about 10 times per piece. This way, the flavor soaks in. Place in a baking dish and pour in the marinade. Using your hands, rub the marinade all over the chick'n pieces to make sure they are well coated and submerged. Let marinate for at least 1 hour, flipping occasionally.

3 Preheat the oven to 425°F (220°C). Line a large baking sheet with parchment paper. Place each piece of chick'n on the baking sheet with space between them. Cook for about 25 minutes, flipping and basting with more marinade three times, every 8 minutes or so. The chick'n should be charred in spots but not burnt.

4 Serve with basmati rice and cilantro, plus any other fixings you like. See the headnote for ideas.

SPANISH CHICK'N AND RICE

Serves 6 to 8

ME: Goes to Barcelona once, craves these flavors forever.

I had the most delightfully touristy time. In fact, for the first and last time in my life, I took a double-decker tour bus in order to view the work of Gaudí throughout the city. It was a high Gothic moment for me. And, beyond the art and architecture, the vegan food was SO GOOD. Simple but bold flavors—paprika, garlic, wine, lemon, and olives suddenly hit different.

I saw versions of chicken and rice on many menus and couldn't wait to make my own! One of my favorite ways to cook rice is in a cast-iron skillet, with all the flavor baked right in. The chick'n is lightly seared and then placed on top to cook the rest of the way, resulting in a stunning presentation, but also sublime textures, where the top of the chick'n is crispy and underneath it's flavor-soaked and juicy. Definitely showstopping, but also easy enough to pull off on a weeknight if you have the chick'n made ahead and a little bit of energy to spare. Just think of all the work Gaudí put into that cathedral; this is NOTHING compared to that.

HOT TAKE

If you don't have a 12-inch (30 cm) cast-iron pan, you can start this in a pan and then transfer into a 11 by 13-inch (28 by 33 cm) casserole before baking.

FOR THE CHICK'N:

- ½ recipe Pull-Apart Seitan Chick'n (page 115), pulled into 3-inch (7.5 cm) chunks
- 2 tablespoons olive oil
- 1 tablespoon fresh lemon juice
- 1 teaspoon sweet paprika
- ¼ teaspoon salt

PREPARE THE CHICK'N

1 Preheat a large cast-iron pan over medium heat. In a bowl, toss the chick'n with 1 tablespoon of the olive oil, the lemon juice, sweet paprika, and salt. Cook the chick'n in the hot pan for 7 minutes, flipping occasionally and drizzling in the remaining tablespoon olive oil, until it's lightly browned. Transfer back to the bowl. Do not clean the pan.

CONTINUED →

FOR THE RICE:

- 2 tablespoons olive oil
- 1 small yellow onion, finely diced
- 1 red bell pepper, finely diced
- Pinch plus ½ teaspoon salt
- 6 cloves garlic, minced
- 1 pint (300 g) cherry tomatoes, cut in half
- 3 bay leaves
- ½ cup (120 ml) dry white wine
- 2 teaspoons sweet paprika
- 1 teaspoon smoked paprika
- ½ teaspoon red pepper flakes
- 2 tablespoons tomato paste
- 3 cups (720 ml) vegetable broth
- 2 tablespoons fresh lemon juice
- 1½ cups (270 g) uncooked white jasmine rice, rinsed

FOR GARNISH:

- ½ cup loosely packed fresh parsley leaves and stems, finely chopped
- 1 cup (155 g) sliced green olives

MAKE THE RICE

1. Preheat the oven to 350°F (175°C). In the same cast-iron pan over medium heat, sauté the onion and red bell pepper in the 2 tablespoons olive oil with a pinch of salt for 7 to 10 minutes, until lightly browned. Add the garlic and sauté for 1 minute.
2. Add the cherry tomatoes and bay leaves and cook until the tomatoes are juicy and soft, about 7 minutes. Pour in the white wine and turn the heat up to reduce it, about 3 minutes.
3. Mix in the paprikas, salt, red pepper flakes, and tomato paste. When the tomato paste is dispersed, add the broth, lemon juice, and rice. Place the chick'n pieces on top of the rice, leaving some room at the edges.
4. Cover the cast-iron pan and place in the oven for 25 to 30 minutes, until the rice is cooked. If you don't have an oven-safe lid, tightly sealed aluminum foil will work.
5. Remove the cover and cook uncovered for another 7 to 10 minutes to get the chicken a little crispy. The cast-iron will be very hot, so use oven mitts and be careful when you remove it from the oven. Uncover carefully, as there will be lots of hot steam.
6. Scatter the olives over the top and sprinkle with the parsley. Let rest for a few minutes before serving. Tell guests to watch out for bay leaves!

SWEET-ISH AND SOUR CHICK'N

Serves 4 to 6

OK, this is sweet and sour, but just not AS sweet as you might get at your fave Chinese takeout spot. Yes, it's sweet, don't get me wrong, but the other flavors are permitted to shine through, too. Crispy chicken with an exterior that the sauce just loves to cling to. Bright, crisp, pepper and onions and juicy, tart pineapple. I don't want to break out a deep-fryer for an everyday meal like this, so I simply coat the chicken in cornstarch and then use a hot wok, with a combination of spray oil and a little peanut oil to get the job done. Serve with jasmine rice for maximum flavor!

HOT TAKE

You can use canned, diced pineapple in this and reserve the juice for the sauce. That's just fine! But if you don't have fresh pineapple around, my preference is for frozen pineapple chunks and unsweetened pineapple juice. Just thaw the pineapple first.

FOR THE SAUCE:

- 1 cup (240 ml) cold pineapple juice
- 1 tablespoon cornstarch
- ¼ cup (60 ml) rice vinegar
- 2 tablespoons tamari
- 3 tablespoons tomato paste
- 1 tablespoon sriracha
- ½ cup (100 g) granulated sugar
- 1 teaspoon onion powder

MAKE THE SAUCE

1 In a small saucepan, use a fork to mix together the pineapple juice and cornstarch. When no big clumps are left, mix in the vinegar, tamari, tomato paste, sriracha, sugar, and onion powder.

2 Place the pan on medium-low heat and let the sauce simmer for about 10 minutes, stirring often, until thickened, caramelized, and gorgeous. Turn the heat off and let it hang out.

CONTINUED →

FOR THE VEGGIES:

- 2 tablespoons peanut oil
- 2 red bell peppers, sliced in half, seeds removed, cut into ⅓-inch pieces
- 1 red onion, sliced into ⅓-inch strips
- Pinch salt
- 1½ cups (250 g) pineapple chunks (see Hot Take, page 95)

FOR THE CHICKEN:

- ½ recipe Pull-Apart Seitan Chick'n (page 115), lightly squeezed to remove excess broth, torn into bite-size pieces
- About ¼ cup (30 g) cornstarch
- 2 tablespoons peanut oil

FOR SERVING:

- Jasmine rice
- Thinly sliced scallions

NOW BEGIN THE STIR-FRY

1 Preheat the peanut oil in a wok over medium-high heat. Sauté the pepper and onion in the oil with a pinch of salt. Let the vegetables char a bit, but retain their snappines, about 5 minutes. Transfer the veggies to the sauce in the pot and add the pineapple as well.

TIME TO MAKE THE CHICK'N

1 While the veggies are cooking, put the chick'n in a mixing bowl and sprinkle it with cornstarch, tossing to coat. The chick'n should be slightly moist so that the cornstarch sticks. When you remove the veggies from the wok, immediately add the peanut oil and chick'n and sauté for about 7 minutes, spraying with cooking spray as needed, while the chick'n browns.

2 Now pour the sauce and veggies into the wok with the chick'n. Stir for about 3 minutes, until hot. Serve over rice, garnished with scallions.

BUTTERMYLK FRIED CHICK'N

Serves 6

This recipe needs no introduction. But my publisher insists that every recipe gets one! So listen up, this is FRIED CHICK'N. Pull out that Dutch oven or the tabletop fryer you received for Mother's Day and were like "What! I'm not even a mother!" And let's fry these babies UP. Chick'n is soaked in a seasoned buttermylk batter for a few hours, then coated and fried to crispy magnificence. It's pure indulgence and, I believe you are obligated to say this where fried chick'n is concerned, it's . . . finger-licking good [audience groans].

Serve with all the sides: Mashed Potatoes (page 110), Coleslaw (page 27), Onion Gravy (page 152),or just eat out of a bucket!

- 1 recipe Pull-Apart Seitan Chick'n (page 115)

FOR THE BUTTERMYLK BATTER:

- 2 cups (480 ml) unsweetened soy milk
- 3 tablespoons apple cider vinegar
- 1 teaspoon lemon pepper
- 1 teaspoon salt
- 1 teaspoon paprika
- 2 teaspoons poultry seasoning, prepared or homemade (page 89)

FOR THE SEASONED FLOUR:

- 2 cups (250 g) all-purpose flour
- 1 teaspoon salt
- ½ teaspoon paprika
- ½ teaspoon ground white pepper
- ⅛ teaspoon cayenne pepper
- 1 teaspoon garlic powder
- 1 teaspoon onion powder
- Peanut oil, for frying

1 Tear each bundle of chicken into 3 pieces, so that you have 12 pieces that are about 4 inches (10 cm) long, and organically shaped. Lightly squeeze each over the kitchen sink to remove excess broth.

2 Make the buttermylk batter: In a large bowl, stir together the soy milk, vinegar, lemon pepper, salt, paprika, and poultry seasoning. Add the chicken pieces and let marinate, refrigerated, for at least 2 hours, flipping occasionally.

3 Prepare the seasoned flour: In a baking pan, mix together the flour, salt, paprika, white pepper, cayenne, garlic powder, and onion powder. Have an empty baking sheet ready to place the coated chick'n on.

4 Place the bowl of marinated chick'n next to the flour mixture. Take a piece of marinated chick'n and dredge it in the flour, using your dry hand to coat it. Transfer to the empty baking sheet. Continue until all the chick'n pieces are coated.

5 Have paper bags lined up on a counter to absorb the oil after frying the chick'n. In a large Dutch oven, heat about 3 inches (7.5 cm) of peanut oil to 350°F (175°C). Add half the chicken and cook for about 8 minutes, until golden, using tongs to turn so all sides are fried. If you want to use a tabletop fryer instead, then prepare the oil according to the manufacturer's instructions.

6 Transfer to a paper bag to drain (see Hot Takes). Cook the remaining chick'n the same way.

HOT TAKES

Peanut oil is the way to go for fried chick'n. It tastes the best. It fries the best. But if you have an allergy or some other reason, then safflower oil is a close second.

I've always used brown paper grocery bags to absorb extra oil. But do people (besides me) even have paper bags anymore? If you don't, then paper towels will work, too. If people even have paper towels.

JERK CHICK'N WITH PINEAPPLE SALSA

Serves 4

- 4 cloves garlic, crushed
- 1½ cups (210 g) roughly chopped shallot
- 1 cup (240 ml) vegetable broth
- 2 habanero chiles, seeds removed
- 2 tablespoons chopped fresh ginger
- ¼ cup (60 ml) fresh lime juice
- 3 tablespoons tamari
- ¼ cup (60 ml) olive oil
- 3 tablespoons brown sugar
- 1 tablespoon smoked paprika
- 2 teaspoons dried thyme
- 1 teaspoon ground allspice
- ¼ teaspoon ground cloves
- ¼ teaspoon ground cinnamon
- ¼ teaspoon ground nutmeg
- ½ recipe Pull-Apart Seitan Chick'n (page 115)
- Pineapple Salsa (page 312)

There is no dish that compares to jerk chick'n. What a blessing it is (for me) that many of Brooklyn's Jamaican restaurants served a vegan version when I was growing up. It's fiery, tart, smoky, herby, and aromatic all at once, with a little bit of sweetness, too. I love that the flavors include thyme and ginger! What other cuisine can accomplish that kind of fusion? The pineapple salsa cools things down and also enhances and contrasts the smokiness. This is wonderful served over ginger mashed sweet potatoes. The key to jerk is the smokiness, which we achieve here with a cast-iron grill. I'm gonna go ahead and say there is NO substitute for grilling, so just invest in one already.

1 In a food processor fitted with a metal blade, chop the garlic up. Add the shallots and pulse to chop those. Add the broth, habaneros, ginger, lime juice, tamari, oil, brown sugar, paprika, thyme, allspice, cloves, cinnamon, and nutmeg. Puree for about 1 minute; it should be saucy with some texture remaining.

2 You should have 3 seitan chick'n bundles. Squeeze them over the sink to remove excess broth. Tear each into 3 pieces, so you have 9 pieces. Score small slivers all over the seitan chick'n, just deep enough to pierce the skin, about 10 times per piece, so the flavor soaks in. Place in an 11 by 13-inch (28 by 33 cm) baking dish and pour in the sauce to submerge the chick'n. Using gloved hands, rub the sauce all over the chick'n pieces to thoroughly coat. Let marinate for at least an hour, flipping occasionally.

3 Preheat a cast-iron grill over medium heat. Spray with cooking oil. Grill the jerk chick'n in two batches, using a thin metal spatula to flip the pieces and spraying with cooking oil as needed. It's ready when charred grill marks appear and things get smoky. About 8 minutes per side.

4 Transfer to a serving bowl and toss in the remaining marinade. Top with pineapple salsa and serve!

HOT TAKE

This version is a little less hot than I'm used to, mostly because I use habaneros instead of traditional scotch bonnet peppers, and I remove the seeds. I'd suggest trying it this way and adding a little cayenne if the spice level is too wimpy for you. On the other hand, if you already know you don't like spicy, try a seeded jalapeño.

CHICK'N CACCIATORE

Serves 4

Cacciatore means "hunter's stew," but instead of Bambi and Thumper, we are hunting the elusive wheat meat. An easy prey and an easy recipe that comes together all in one skillet. Crisped, seasoned cutlets are doused in a creamy wine-kissed tomato sauce packed with mushrooms, red pepper, capers, and herbs. It's finished with cashew cream. I prefer to serve cacciatore over mashed potatoes but some weirdos serve it with pasta.

- ½ recipe Pull-Apart Seitan Chick'n (page 115)
- ¼ cup (30 g) all-purpose flour
- 2 teaspoons poultry seasoning, prepared or homemade (page 89)
- ⅛ teaspoon salt
- 4 tablespoons (60 ml) olive oil, plus a little extra
- 1 cup (115 g) thinly sliced shallots
- 1 red bell pepper, seeded and thinly sliced
- 6 cloves garlic minced
- 8 ounces (225 g) cremini mushrooms, thinly sliced
- 1 teaspoon dried thyme
- 1 teaspoon dried oregano
- 1 teaspoon dried rosemary
- ½ teaspoon red pepper flakes, plus more for garnish
- Several dashes freshly ground black pepper
- ½ cup (120 ml) dry white wine
- ¼ cup (30 g) capers, drained
- 1 (15-ounce/430 g) can crushed tomatoes
- ½ cup (60 g) whole unroasted cashews
- 1 cup (240 ml) Chick'n Broth (page 299) or prepared vegetable broth
- Mashed Potatoes (page 110), for serving
- About 12 large basil leaves, rolled up and cut into thin ribbons, for garnish

1. You should have 2 chick'n bundles. Slice each on a diagonal into 4 cutlet shapes, about 3 inches by 2 inches (7.5 by 5 cm), so that you have 8 cutlets total.
2. Preheat a large skillet, preferably cast-iron, over medium-high heat. On a dinner plate, mix together the flour, poultry seasoning, and salt. Dredge the chick'n cutlets in the flour mixture to coat.
3. Add 3 tablespoons of the olive oil to the pan and cook the chick'n until lightly browned, about 3 minutes on each side. Transfer to a plate and set aside.
4. Do not rinse out the skillet because you're going to make the sauce in it. Add the remaining tablespoon olive oil to the pan. Sauté the shallots in the oil until translucent, about 3 minutes. Add the bell pepper and sauté for about 5 minutes. Scoot those veg aside and sauté the garlic in a tiny bit more olive oil, just until fragrant, then mix with the shallots and peppers.

CONTINUED →

5 Add the mushrooms, thyme, oregano, rosemary, red pepper flakes, and black pepper. Cook until the mushrooms are lightly browned and releasing moisture, about 5 minutes.

HOT TAKE

You have to be careful with the salt here, because the salty capers might overpower the other flavors. Simply salt to taste after the sauce has simmered for a bit.

6 Add the wine and deglaze the pan, scraping up any bits stuck to the bottom of the pan. Turn the heat up and let the wine reduce for about 3 minutes. Lower the heat a bit and add the capers and tomatoes. Let cook for 10 minutes or so as you make the cashew cream.

7 In a high-speed blender, blend the cashews and broth until completely smooth, 1 to 2 minutes, scraping down the sides with a rubber spatula to make sure you get everything.

8 Add the cashew cream to the sauce. Let the sauce simmer over low heat for about 15 minutes to allow the flavors to marry. Taste for salt and seasoning. Return the cutlets to the pan and toss to coat and warm them up.

9 Serve over mashed potatoes (or pasta if you must) and garnish with extra red pepper flakes and fresh basil.

CHICK'N OF THE WOODS AND WAFFLES

Serves 6

I'm a tireless advocate for sweet and savory. And, for that matter, breakfast for dinner! Naturally, I had to provide a recipe for a timeless classic like chicken and waffles. When it comes to meatless chick'n, you can't get more on-the-nose than juicy, flaky chicken of the woods mushrooms.

To achieve all the crunchy crevices you'd expect from fried chicken, double dip the mushrooms in a "buttermilk" slurry and seasoned flour. Here, although it's an unorthodox approach, I don't think you need to keep a wet hand and a dry hand. In fact, it's better if you let your fingers get battered and then put that clumpy batter right back into the flour dredge to achieve some beautiful crinkles. Once battered, there are two ways to fry: in the air fryer or shallow-fried in a cast-iron pan.

Serve with pure maple syrup and vegan butter for the complete experience!

1 Make the waffles: In a 2-cup (480 ml) measuring cup, use a fork to vigorously mix about half the milk with the flaxseed, until frothy. Add the remaining milk and the vinegar and set aside.

2 In the meantime, combine the flour, sugar, baking powder, baking soda, and salt in a large bowl. Make a well in the center.

3 Add the milk mixture to the flour along with ⅓ cup (75 ml) water, the oil, and vanilla. Mix until the batter is relatively smooth. A few lumps are a-OK.

4 Preheat a waffle iron and let the batter rest. Cook according to the waffle iron's directions, spraying the waffle iron liberally with oil or cooking spray between waffles.

HOT TAKE

If you can't find fresh chicken or hen of the woods mushrooms (also known as maitake), or just don't want to pay a million dollars per pound, you can use oyster mushrooms instead. If you still can't find oysters, then whole shiitakes work well, too! Just trim the tough stems and pick the ones with the largest caps you can find.

FOR THE WAFFLES:

- 2 cups (480 ml) unsweetened soy milk (or your preferred nondairy milk)
- 1 tablespoon ground flaxseeds
- 1 tablespoon apple cider vinegar
- 2 cups (250 g) all-purpose flour
- 3 tablespoons granulated sugar
- 2 teaspoons baking powder
- ½ teaspoon baking soda
- ½ teaspoon salt
- 2 tablespoons olive oil
- 1 teaspoon pure vanilla extract

CONTINUED →

FOR THE MUSHROOM FRIED CHICK'N:

- 1 pound (455 g) chicken of the woods mushrooms
- 3 tablespoons cornstarch
- 1 cup (240 g) cold unsweetened soy milk
- 1 tablespoon apple cider vinegar
- 1 tablespoon tamari
- 1½ cups (190 g) all-purpose flour
- 2 tablespoons nutritional yeast flakes
- 1 tablespoon plus 2 teaspoons poultry seasoning, prepared or homemade (page 89)
- 1 teaspoon sweet paprika
- ¾ teaspoon salt
- ⅛ teaspoon cayenne pepper
- Canola or other neutral oil or cooking spray, for frying

FOR SERVING:

- Pure maple syrup
- Vegan butter

5 Make the mushroom chick'n: Use your fingers to break the mushrooms apart into 3-inch pieces. Spoon the cornstarch into a medium bowl. Add the milk and vigorously mix with a fork until well combined. Mix in the apple cider and tamari and set the slurry aside.

6 In a large bowl, sift together the flour, nutritional yeast, poultry seasoning, paprika, salt, and cayenne.

7 Dip each mushroom into the seasoned flour, then into the slurry. Now back into the flour, making sure to coat it all over. Back into the slurry then finally back into the flour. You should have a pretty thick coating you can kinda pinch to create crevices. Make sure to utilize the clumps of flour that form from getting wet with slurry.

TIME TO FRY!

1 If shallow-frying: Preheat a large cast-iron pan over medium-high heat. Add about ¾ inch (2 cm) of canola or other neutral oil. Fry on both sides for about 5 minutes each. The mushrooms should be golden brown and crispy. Transfer to paper towels to drain.

2 If air-frying: Spray the mushrooms all over with cooking oil (canola or olive oil). Spray the air-fryer basket with oil as well. If you have an air-fryer with multiple shelves, position the chick'n on the middle shelf. Air-fry for 15 minutes at 400°F (205°C).

The best way to butcher hen of the woods mushrooms is with your hands! How vegan. If you use a knife you might risk cutting off precious "feathers." Simply pull off the nubby stem and then tear the mushrooms into desired pieces.

To get the timing perfect, make the waffles first and then either toast them to order or keep warm in the oven at 200°F (95°C).

CAULIFLOWER SCHNITZ'L

Serves 4

Time to pop on over to the vegan biergarten for a brew and some schnitzel by the fire! Or, if there's no vegan biergarten nearby, let's re-create the experience at home.

Schnitzel—pounded, breaded, fried meat—is a central European icon. There are millions of ways to prepare it, but my all-time favorite is with a creamy mustard sauce spiked with beer. Although I've never visited, it beckons me to mother Austria. I assume that when I do drop by, some diplomat will welcome me with a plate of this.

Here I'm replicating chick'n with cauliflower steaks! The secret to getting them perfectly fried and chicken-y is to lightly roast them first, bringing out the juiciness and toasty flavors. I won't lie, it takes a lot of dishes, so reserve this for when you have an army to help clean.

Schnitzel is typically served with any manner of potato dishes; mashed potatoes is a no-brainer, but potato salad would also be nice, and roasted or scalloped potatoes would receive no complaints. If you want to go another starchy route, try rice or pasta! Make the gravy while the cauliflower is roasting and cooling.

If you like, sneak some lemon slices onto the roasting tray for an additional pop of wow (see pic).

FOR THE CAULIFLOWER:

- 2 large heads cauliflower
- 3 tablespoons olive oil
- 1 tablespoon poultry seasoning, prepared or homemade (page 89)
- ½ teaspoon salt

FOR THE SLURRY:

- 1 cup (125 g) all-purpose flour
- 3 tablespoons cornstarch
- 2 cups (480 ml) cold unsweetened soy milk
- 1 tablespoon Dijon mustard

FOR THE BREADING:

- 2 cups (200 g) fine dry breadcrumbs
- 1 tablespoon poultry seasoning, store-bought or homemade (page 89)
- 1 teaspoon kosher salt (use less if poultry seasoning contains salt)

- Safflower oil, for frying

1 Line two baking sheets with parchment. Place four steaks on each sheet. Drizzle each with 1½ tablespoons of oil and sprinkle with poultry seasoning and salt. Toss to coat. Bake for 12 minutes, to lightly roast, rotating pans halfway. Remove from the oven and set aside to cool.

2 Now make the slurry and breading: In a wide-rimmed bowl, use a fork to mix together the flour and cornstarch. Add half the soy milk and stir well until it's a thick, smooth paste. Mix in the remaining milk and mustard.

3 On a large rimmed plate, mix together the breadcrumbs, poultry seasoning, and salt.

4 Now form an assembly line, from left to right: the roasted cauliflower, the slurry, the breadcrumb mixture, and finally a piece of parchment to place the prepared schnitz'ls on.

CONTINUED →

FOR SERVING:

- Starch of choice (see examples in headnote)
- 1 cup (30 g) lightly chopped fresh parsley stems and leaves
- Sliced lemon

5 Dip the cauliflower steaks one by one into the slurry, letting the excess drip off. Transfer to the breadcrumb bowl and use the other hand to sprinkle a handful of breadcrumbs over the cauliflower to coat it completely. Transfer to the parchment and repeat with the rest of the steaks. Make sure you use one hand for the wet batter and the other for the dry batter, or you'll end up with a breadcrumb glove.

6 Preheat a large cast-iron pan over medium heat.You'll need to fry in two or three batches. Preheat the oven to 250°F (120°C) to keep the schnitz'l warm after it's done cooking.

7 Pour a thin layer of oil into the pan, about ¼ inch deep. Fry the cauliflower steaks on each side until lightly browned, about 4 minutes. Transfer to a baking sheet and place in the oven while you make the next batches.

8 Serve over your preferred starch, spooning plenty of sauce over the top. Garnish with parsley and serve with fresh or roasted lemon slices.

HOT TAKES

I love russet potatoes for mashed potatoes, and I don't HATE the skin on, but I do prefer them peeled. You don't have to do a great job; a little peel left over is nice and rustic. If you use Yukon gold instead, peeling isn't necessary because they are so thin-skinned, and that sounds like a win. However, I still think that russets are fluffiest and best!

I know boiling potatoes sounds easy, but there's a right way to get the best flavor and texture. Submerge in cold, slightly salted water, and then bring the water up to a low boil and immediately down to a simmer. This ensures even cooking and prevents waterlogging the potato, which can make it too loose.

CREAMY BUTTERY MASHED POTATOES

Serves 4

Rich, creamy, BUTTERY mashed potatoes are a necessity in life, and these are the creamiest going. I love that they use simple ingredients that are probably in your pantry. But most importantly, they taste like they are loaded with butter and cream. And in typical "me" fashion, we achieve that with cashew cream and refined coconut oil. The method is simple: Mash, then whip with a hand blender. And, you know, even if you don't whip them, they'll still be pretty great. But whip for maximum fluff.

1 Place the potatoes in a 4-quart (3.8 liter) pot and submerge in cold water by about an inch (2.5 cm). Sprinkle in 2 teaspoons of salt. Cover and bring to a low boil.

2 Place the cashews in a high-speed blender with the vegetable broth and blend until completely smooth, scraping the sides of the blender with a spatula occasionally to get everything.

3 When the potatoes are boiling, lower the heat to a simmer, uncover, and cook for about 12 minutes, until fork tender. Drain the potatoes, and place them back in the pot.

- 2½ pounds russet potatoes, peeled and cut into 1½-inch (4 cm) chunks
- 2¾ teaspoons salt, plus more as needed
- ⅓ cup (30 g) whole unroasted cashews
- ½ cup (120 ml) vegetable broth, at room temperature
- ⅓ cup (75 ml) refined coconut oil, at room temperature
- Lots of fresh black pepper

4 Mash with a potato masher, to break the potatoes up a bit. Add half of the cashew mixture, the coconut oil, ¾ teaspoon salt, and pepper and mash with a potato masher until relatively smooth with no big chunks left.

5 Add the remaining cashew mixture, mix it in, and use a hand blender on high speed to whip the potatoes. They should become very smooth, fluffy, and creamy. Taste for salt and pepper along the way, transfer to a serving bowl, and serve!

MUSTARD CREAM SAUCE

Makes 3 cups (720 ml)

- 1 cup (115 g) thinly sliced shallots
- 2 tablespoons olive oil
- Pinch plus ½ teaspoon salt
- ¾ cup (90 g) whole unroasted cashews
- 1½ cups (360 ml) vegetable broth
- 1 cup (240 ml) pilsner beer
- Freshly ground black pepper
- 2 tablespoons whole grain Dijon mustard

Beer adds depth of flavor to this simple sauce. Don't be deceived by the short ingredient list; you get everything you want: richness, tanginess, and savory bursts of shallot.

1 Preheat a 4-quart (3.8 liter) saucepan over medium heat. Sauté the shallots in the olive oil with a pinch of salt for about 10 minutes, until lightly caramelized.

2 In the meantime, place the cashews and broth in a high-speed blender and blend until completely smooth, scraping down the sides with a rubber spatula to make sure you get everything. If you don't have a high-speed blender, see "Let's Get Nuts" on page 11.

3 Back to the shallots. Turn the heat up and pour the beer in along with the ½ teaspoon salt and several dashes of fresh black pepper. Let the beer bubble and reduce for about 3 minutes.

4 Reduce the heat to low. Add the cashew cream and stir until nicely thickened, about 5 minutes. Mix in the mustard. Taste for salt and seasoning.

BIG HUGS CHICK'N AND RICE SOUP

Serves 6

- 8 ounces (225 g) Pull-Apart Seitan Chick'n (page 115), pulled into 1- to 2-inch (2.5 to 5 cm) pieces (2 cups)
- 1 tablespoon olive oil
- ½ teaspoon salt plus a pinch
- 1 medium yellow onion, thinly sliced
- 2 tablespoons vegan butter, plus more if desired
- 2 large carrots, peeled and cut into ½-inch (12 mm) chunks
- 2 ribs celery, thinly sliced
- 2 cloves garlic, minced
- 1 teaspoon poultry seasoning, prepared or homemade (page 89)
- Freshly ground black pepper
- ½ cup (90 g) uncooked white jasmine rice, rinsed
- 2 quarts (2 liters) chick'n-style broth, store-bought or homemade (page 299)
- ¼ cup chopped fresh dill, plus more for garnish

Call me an iconoclast, but I prefer chick'n and rice soup to chick'n noodle! Especially with buttery jasmine rice. This soup has all the huggy ingredients: celery, dill, poultry seasoning with sage and thyme, and, of course, garlic and onion. As it cooks, your kitchen will fill up with the most nurturing aromas, like someone you love is cooking for you. And that someone, dear reader, is you. I use some vegan butter here, for body and richness. I recommend Miyoko's brand.

1 Preheat a 4-quart (3.8 liters) pot over medium heat. Sauté the chick'n in the olive oil with a pinch of salt until nicely browned. Remove from the pot and set aside.

2 In the same pot, sauté the onion in the butter with a pinch of salt for about 5 minutes, until translucent. Add the carrots and celery and cook for about 5 minutes. Add the garlic and sauté until fragrant, about 1 minute, using a little extra butter if you like. Add the poultry seasoning, 1 teaspoon salt, and pepper to taste and sauté another minute.

3 Add rice and pour in the broth. Cover and bring to a boil. Once boiling, bring down to a simmer and let cook for about 15 more minutes, until the rice is cooked and the carrot is tender.

4 Stir in the reserved chick'n and the dill and taste for salt and pepper. This definitely tastes better the longer you let it sit, but it can be enjoyed right away, too. Garnish with extra dill and serve!

HOT TAKE

If the pot you're cooking in is wide enough, like a Dutch oven is, you should be able to brown the chick'n in there before preparing the rest of the soup. Save yourself a dish, plus create little crispy bits that get swept up into the soup when you sauté everything else. If you're using a stainless steel pot that is more tall than wide, it's probably wiser to sauté the chick'n in a skillet and prepare the soup separately.

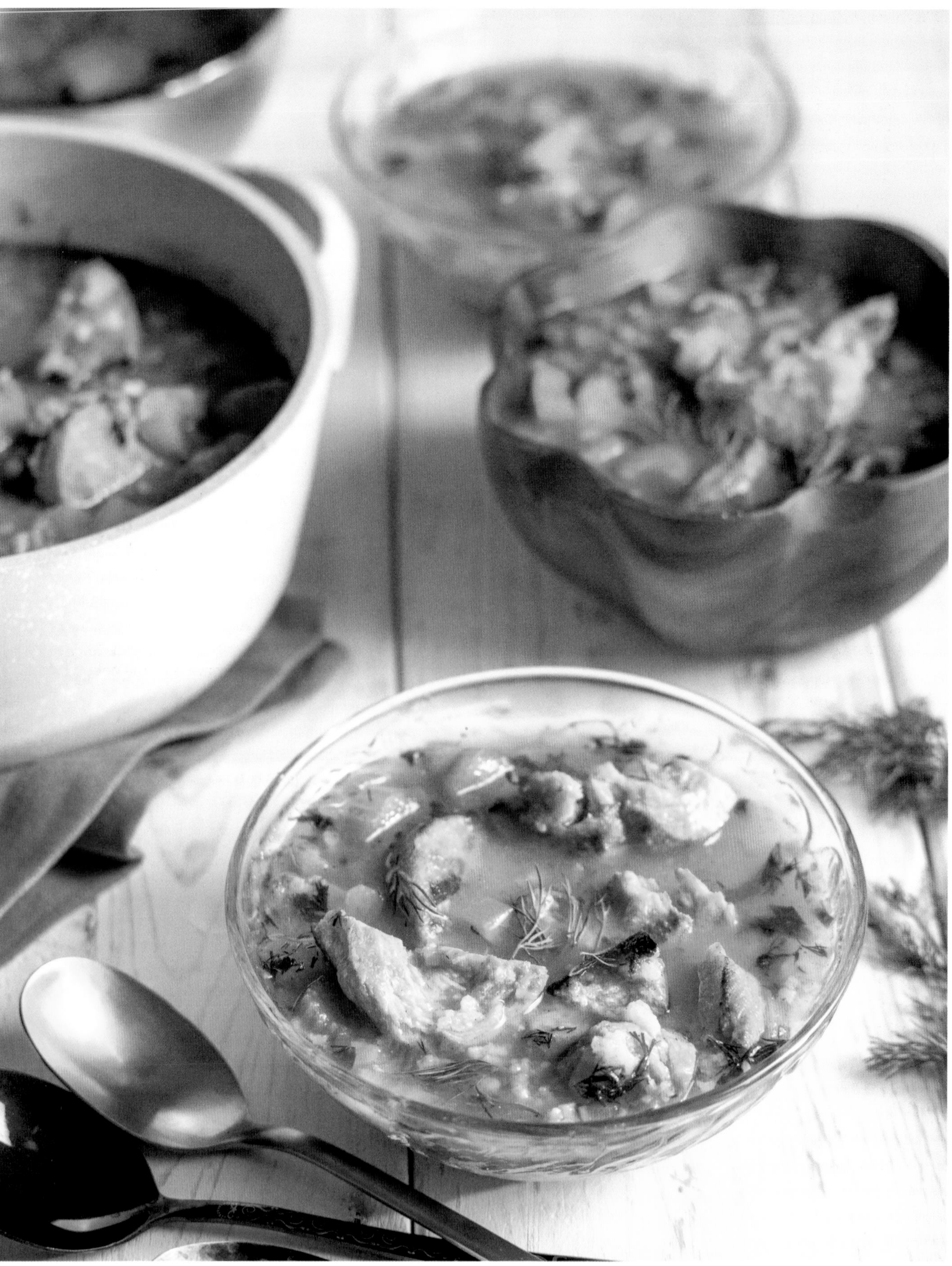

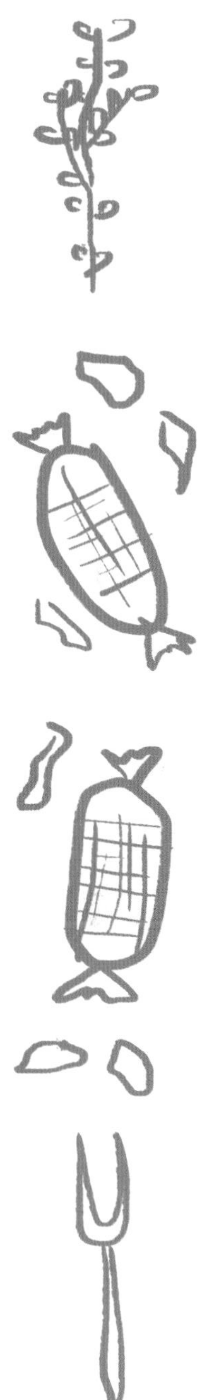

PULL-APART SEITAN CHICK'N

Makes 2¼ pounds (1 kg)

This is the layered, flaky textured vegan chicken of your dinnertime dreams! I wanted something comparable to store-bought vegan chick'n but, you know—better? It's just the thing to simmer away on a lazy Sunday afternoon then store and use throughout the week. The recipe is not difficult, but it does require a few specialized items, such as cheesecloth and twine, which will only make you feel more like a chef than you already do. The cheesecloth also gives the outer layer a nice pin-prick texture that's reminiscent of chicken skin and sears beautifully.

The gist of the recipe is that the raw seitan is processed into a soft dough that is both clumpy yet totally holds together. It's then gathered, pulled, twisted, bundled, and simmered, creating a pull-apart texture that could rival the finest fakest meat. But it tastes so much better when it comes from your kitchen! The flavoring is subtle and versatile enough to work in everything from South Asian stir-fries to Italian chicken Parmesan. There's just a touch of turmeric to lend luster and brighten up the color, while pea protein gives it a super meaty texture. Grilled, fried, or shredded for soups, it's so fantastically versatile and soaks up flavor like a champ.

CONTINUED →

OK, now that you have attended the Lady's School for Seitan, you should be well prepared to strike out on your own. Have fun and remember: You were made for this!

FOR THE SEITAN CHICK'N:

- **1 tablespoon olive oil**
- **2 teaspoons apple cider vinegar**
- **1½ teaspoons salt**
- **2 teaspoons onion powder**
- **1 teaspoon garlic powder**
- **½ teaspoon ground white pepper**
- **⅛ teaspoon ground turmeric**
- **¼ cup (15 g) nutritional yeast flakes**
- **½ cup (80 g) pea protein**
- **1½ cups (180 g) vital wheat gluten**

FOR THE BROTH:

- **10 cups (2.4 liters) chick'n-style broth, store-bought or homemade (page 299)**
- **8 bay leaves**

1 Have ready four 9-inch (23 cm) double-layered cheesecloth squares and twine.

2 In a food processor fit with a metal blade, whiz together 2 cups (480 ml) water, the olive oil, apple cider vinegar, salt, onion powder, garlic powder, white pepper and turmeric. Add nutritional yeast and pea protein and process until smooth, about 30 seconds.

3 Now add the vital wheat gluten and pulse in. Once it is all incorporated, process on low for about 5 minutes. It will be very stretchy, stringy, and pliable. Give the motor a break once in a while if your processor can't handle it.

4 Divide the dough into 4 even-ish pieces. From this point, be careful not to overhandle the seitan—you want it to retain its texture, which will allow it to separate nicely once cooked. Gently roll a glob of dough into an 8-inch (19 cm) roll. Fold in half, give a twist, and pull again so it's about 6 inches (15 cm) long. This creates the layers. Wrap in cheesecloth, snugly but not tightly; it will expand. Tie each end with twine. Proceed with the remaining pieces and let rest while you prepare the broth.

5 In a large (8-quart/7.5 liter) pot bring the broth and bay leaves to a boil. Lower the heat. Add the seitan bundles. Let stew, covered, very gently without boiling for about 15 minutes. When the skin is set, place the lid ajar for steam to escape and low boil for about 45 more minutes, using tongs to rotate every 15 minutes or so.

6 Cool completely in the broth. Squeeze out excess broth over the sink before using. Use according to recipe directions, but if you're just looking to use it "stand-alone," use your fingers to pull it apart into chunks. Or you can slice it up or shave it, depending on what you're making. It tastes best if browned in some olive oil first.

CREATING PERFECT SIMMERED SEITAN BUNDLES:

A ROMANCE NOVELLA

This recipe is not difficult. But often when people say something "isn't difficult," are they just talking you off the ledge? If it isn't difficult why would you have to even say that? Thus, in short, what I mean is that it's not difficult IF you pay attention and read the directions, because every step counts. So read this in bed, the night before you make it, and then dream of perfect little seitan bundles.

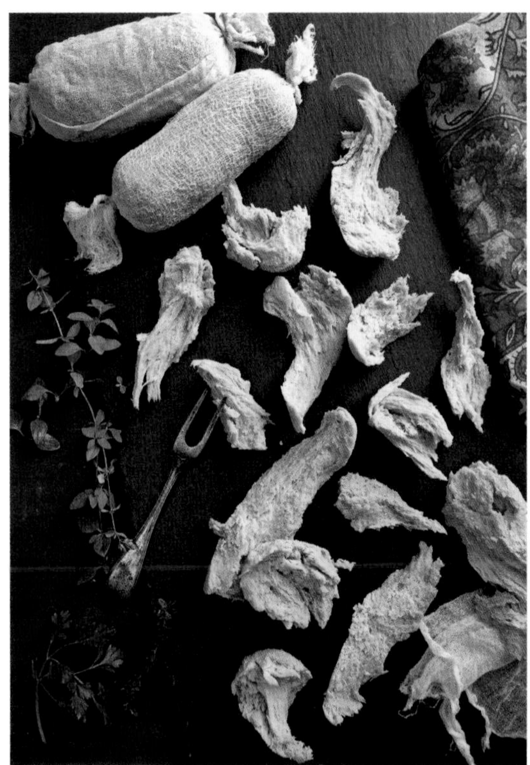

PART 1: CHEESECLOTH.
First of all, make sure you have cheesecloth and twine. Cut the cheesecloth into the proper sizes before beginning and set it aside. When wrapping, don't go too tight or it will make the chick'n denser than intended. It will still be good! But this isn't a bustier. Leave some slack, because the seitan soaks in moisture and plumps up, leading to the layery, light shreds we are going for. If that sounds vague, how's this: Make sure you can pull the cheesecloth about ½ inch (12 mm) away from the seitan once it's wrapped. So, snug and secure, with a little room to breathe.

PART 2: MIND YOUR BROTH TEMP.
If the broth is too hot you can waterlog the seitan, but this is very easy to prevent. Before adding the seitan, bring the broth up to a low boil, then lower the heat so that it's not boiling at all, just very hot. Then add the seitan bundles. When you add the seitan, the broth temperature will drop even more. Bring the heat up slightly. During this time, the seitan will be developing a "skin" which will protect it from becoming, as they say, "seitan brains." Once it is on this low heat for about 20 minutes, you can raise the heat to a low boil. Now it's really cooking! Cook this way for about 45 more minutes, with the lid ajar, using tongs to rotate the bundles every 15 minutes or so.

PART 3: COOL IT NOW.
The cooling-off stage is crucial, as if your seitan were heading from a hot spring to a spa at a ski resort. Turn the heat off and let the seitan cool in the broth. This can take an hour or so, but it's worth it for perfectly cooked fake chicken. If you have a cool place to put it, that's great. An open porch? A safe fire escape?

COMFORTING BEEF STEWS

Cozy winter nights. Breathtaking aromatics. Your favorite gigantic spoon. And a big hand-thrown ceramic bowl made by your grandma or roommate. Or maybe you bought it at a craft fair—in any case, that bowl is full of love. And love is the number one ingredient in beef stew, I realized, as this chapter ended up being way more romantic and nostalgic than I intended.

Could stew be the key to the heart? Every country and culture has a signature beef stew. And it flows through the veins into every part of the community, down to each specific person or family, right into our most cozy moment. Throw in something carby and life is complete.

Beef stews are an easy way to infuse a ton of flavor and texture, usually in a single pot. We use meaty ingredients with rich flavor like mushrooms, eggplant, and lentils. Onions caramelized with herbaceous flavors, which invoke nostalgic meaty memories. And tomato for a deepness that could even be described as bloody, in a Bloody Mary kind of way.

Of course there is also actually the fake meat role in these stews. Seitan and soy play a big part in this chapter, as they should. These recipes are fun and forgiving, heavy on the seasoning, light on the technique, and there for you when you need them.

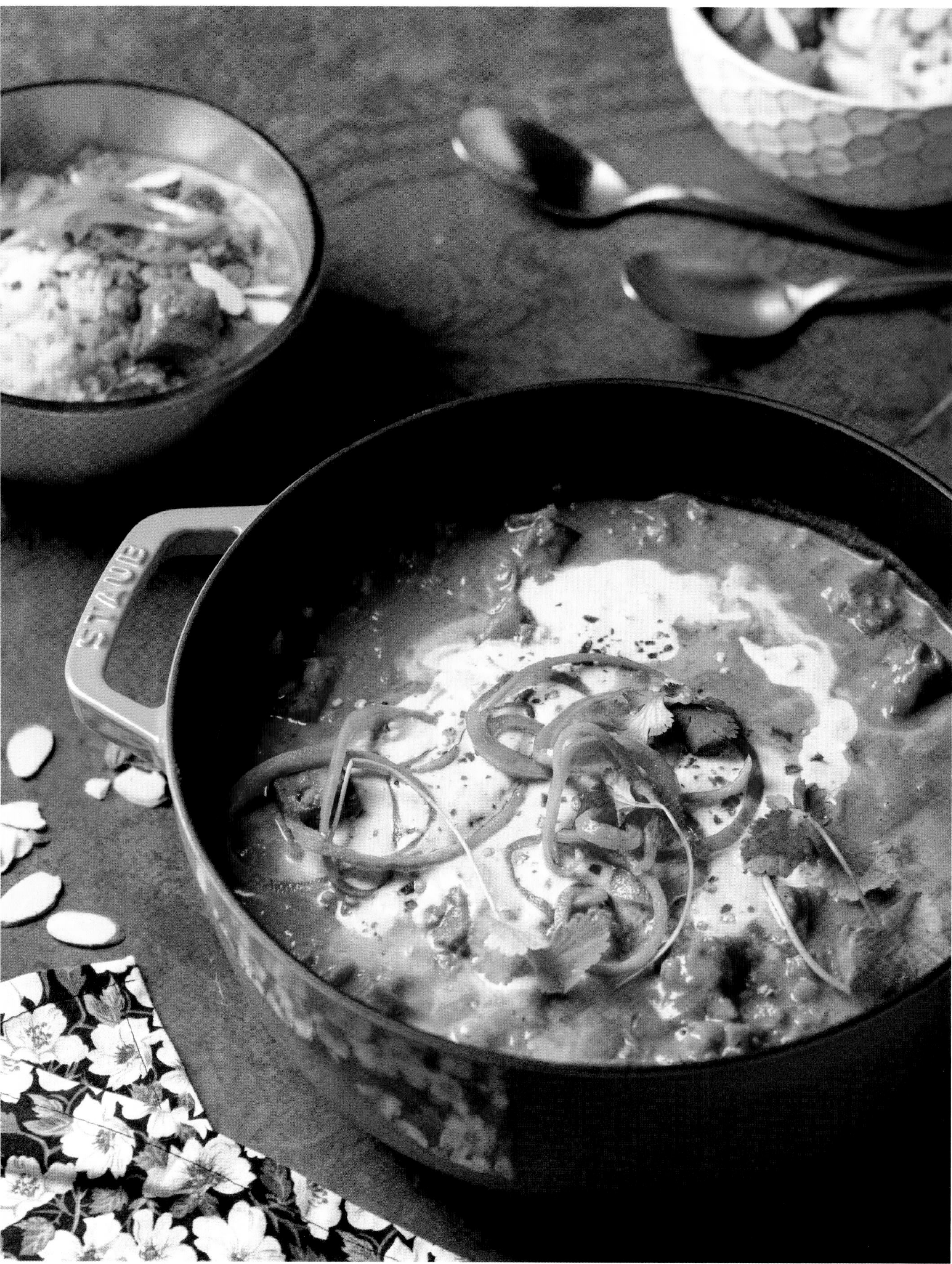
STAUB

ROGAN JOSH

Serves 6

The winter I turned eighteen I had a whirlwind romance. I lived in Brooklyn. He lived in Manhattan. He knew all the vegetarian places. One of our favorites was an Indian restaurant that was situated down a staircase. The winter air, my black scarf wrapped around my hair fragrant with vanilla perfume, and that kind of blood red lipstick you had to wear in the early '90s. And once inside those doors, the scent of ginger and cardamom, plus the only vegetarian Rogan Josh I have ever had. The aroma of that restaurant meeting with the winter air is something I will never forget.

Can I promise you such an intoxicating eating experience? With this dish, I can definitively say yes. Start with a peppery sauce laced with ginger, fennel, and cardamom, bolstered with coconut milk and a touch of lime instead of traditional yogurt. Top it off with plenty of cilantro and toasted almonds and serve with heaps of basmati rice for guaranteed success, every time.

I use red lentils to achieve the falling-off-the-bone effect of conventional beef. Personally, I really can't imagine using any other meat besides seitan here, but if you have a gluten allergy, rehydrated and sautéed soy curls would be just fine.

HOT TAKE

Rogan Josh is typically made with kasmiri chili powder, but after extensive research (thanks, Google) I found numerous suggestions to replace it with paprika. I chose a blend of sweet paprika and smoked paprika for well-rounded and balanced depth of flavor.

- 6 tablespoons (90 ml) refined coconut oil
- 1 quart (960 ml) Beefy Seitan (page 28), cut into 1-inch (2.5 cm) rustic chunks
- 1 large yellow onion, thinly sliced
- Pinch plus 1 teaspoon salt
- ¾ teaspoon fennel seed, crushed
- 3 bay leaves
- 6 cloves garlic, minced
- 1 heaping tablespoon minced fresh ginger
- 1 tablespoon mild curry powder
- 2 teaspoons garam masala
- 1½ teaspoons smoked paprika
- 1½ teaspoons sweet paprika
- ¼ teaspoon cayenne pepper, or more to taste
- 5 cups (1.2 liters) Beefy Broth (page 302) or prepared vegetable broth, plus more to thin
- 1 cup (200 g) red lentils
- 1 teaspoon agave syrup
- 2 tablespoons tomato paste
- 1 (15-ounce/430 g) can full-fat coconut milk
- 2 teaspoons fresh lime juice

CONTINUED →

FOR SERVING:

- Basmati rice
- ½ cup (50 g) sliced almonds, toasted (see Hot Take)
- 1 cup (30 g) loosely packed fresh cilantro sprigs
- Red pepper flakes (optional)
- Coconut Mint Raita (page 122; optional)
- Pickled Red Onions (page 311; optional)

HOT TAKE

Toast the almonds before beginning the recipe. You can use the cast-iron pan you are going to use for everything else. Preheat on low heat, then toast the almonds for about 5 minutes, until aromatic, tossing them once or twice. Transfer to a bowl to cool. No need to clean out the pan before making the rest of the recipe.

1. First sear the seitan. Preheat a large cast-iron pan over medium-high heat. Add 3 tablespoons of the coconut oil and the seitan in as much of a single layer as you can. Let cook for 3 to 4 minutes, until it gets a good sear. Use a thin metal spatula to flip. Continue cooking and flipping for about 10 more minutes until most sides are seared. Remove from heat and set aside.
2. Preheat a 4-quart (3.8 liter) pot over medium heat. Sauté the onions in the remaining 3 tablespoons coconut oil and a pinch of salt for 5 to 7 minutes, until lightly browned. Add the fennel and bay leaves and sauté a minute more. Add the garlic and ginger and cook for another 2 minutes.
3. Add the spices: curry powder, garam masala, both paprikas, and the cayenne. Toss them to coat the onions. Deglaze with a little of the vegetable broth, scraping up any bits from the bottom of the pan. Add the lentils, 1 teaspoon salt, the remaining vegetable broth, agave, and tomato paste. Cover and bring to a boil. Once boiling, lower to a simmer and cook until the lentils are tender, about 15 minutes.
4. Add the coconut milk and lime juice to the pan, along with the cooked seitan. Heat through. Turn off the heat and let the stew rest for 10 minutes for the flavors to marry. Remove the bay leaves and discard.
5. Taste for salt and seasoning, and thin with water if necessary. Serve in big bowls with basmati rice and top with the toasted almonds and cilantro and optional red pepper flakes, raita, and pickled red onions if desired.

COCONUT MINT RAITA

Makes 2 cups

- ½ a seedless english cucumber (or a 4-inch cucumber)
- ⅛ teaspoon salt
- 3 tablespoons fresh lime juice
- 1 tablespoon minced fresh ginger
- ½ teaspoon garam masala
- ¼ cup fine chopped fresh mint
- 1 (5 to 6-ounce/150 to 175 ml) can coconut cream

1. Grate the cucumber into a large bowl and mix in the salt, lime juice, ginger, garam masala, and fresh mint. Let sit for 5 minutes so the cucumber can release its juices. Use a rubber spatula to mix in the coconut cream. Taste for seasoning. Refrigerate for 30 minutes before using.

SURF AND TURF

Serves 6

This was a customer favorite at Modern Love Brooklyn. Seitan steaks soak up zesty, bright chimichurri and are then grilled to smoky, meaty heaven. They're placed atop a creamy chowder that tastes of the ocean, with mushrooms for clammy glammy texture, dulce flakes for fishy flavor, and of course you can't forget the chowder darlings carrots and onion. This is absolute meat-and-potato fare! You could stop there and have a fantastic meal . . . but don't. Roasted radishes add more "surf" to the mix, creating a shrimpy feel with minimal effort. Wilted mustard greens just seem to go with seafood and bring a nice spicy bite of freshness. When all is said and done, you've satisfied cravings across land and sea, and created a different beast altogether.

MAKE THE CHIMICHURRI

1 Pulse the garlic in a blender to chop it up a bit. Add the cilantro, parsley, vinegar, olive oil, broth, oregano, red pepper flakes, and salt. Blend until relatively smooth, with a little texture left.

MARINATE THE SEITAN

1 Slice the seitan into ½-inch-thick (12 mm) pieces the long way. You should get about 6 pieces per bundle of seitan. It's OK if they vary in size and shape a bit. You will have 12 pieces.

2 Pour the chimichurri into an 11 by 13-inch (28 by 33 cm) baking dish. Add the seitan steaks and smother in the sauce. Let them marinate for about an hour.

IN THE MEANTIME, START THE CHOWDER

1 Rinse out the high-speed blender. Blend the cashews with 2 cups (480 ml) water until completely smooth. This will take about 1 minute. Set aside.

2 Preheat a 4-quart (3.8 liter) pot over medium heat. Sauté the onions and carrots in the olive oil with a pinch of salt, for about 10 minutes, until the carrots are softened.

3 Add the shiitakes, oyster mushrooms, and celery. Cook briefly, for about 3 minutes, just until the mushrooms are softened. They should retain their texture.

4 Add the potatoes, ¾ teaspoon salt, pepper, dulce, tomato paste, and vegetable broth. Cover and bring to a boil. Once boiling, reduce the heat to a simmer. Cook for 10 to 15 minutes, or until the potatoes are tender. Keep a close eye so as not to overcook the potatoes.

HOT TAKE

To save some money, replace the oyster mushrooms with thinly sliced creminis. The shiitakes give enough texture to carry the fishiness, the oysters are just a nice touch.

FOR THE CHIMICHURRI STEAK:

- 6 cloves garlic
- 1½ cups (45 g) loosely packed fresh cilantro leaves and tender stems
- 1½ cups (45 g) loosely packed fresh parsley leaves
- ⅓ cup (75 ml) red wine vinegar
- ⅓ cup (75 ml) olive oil
- ⅓ cup (75 ml) vegetable broth
- 1½ teaspoons dried oregano
- ¾ teaspoon red pepper flakes
- ¾ teaspoon salt
- ½ recipe Beefy Seitan (about 2 bundles; page 28)

FOR THE CHOWDER:

- 1¼ cups (150 g) whole unroasted cashews
- 1 large yellow onion, cut into medium dice
- 2 medium carrots, peeled and sliced into ¼-inch-thick half-moons
- Pinch plus ¾ teaspoon salt, plus more to taste
- 2 tablespoons olive oil

- 6 ounces (170 g) shiitake mushrooms, thinly sliced
- 6 ounces (170 g) oyster mushrooms, sliced ¼ inch thick
- 3 stalks celery, sliced ¼ inch thick
- 2 medium-size Yukon gold potatoes, cut into ¾-inch (2 cm) chunks
- ½ teaspoon freshly ground black pepper
- 1 tablespoon dulce flakes
- 2 tablespoons tomato paste
- 3 cups (720 ml) Bay Broth (page 303) or prepared vegetable broth
- 2 tablespoons fresh lemon juice

FOR THE GARNISH:

- 2 cups (180 g) thinly sliced red cabbage
- Roasted Radishes (recipe follows)
- ¼ cup (13 g) finely chopped fresh parsley
- Lemon wedges

5 Stir in the cashew cream mixture and gently heat the chowder, uncovered, for about 7 minutes, until nicely thickened. Add the lemon juice and taste for salt and seasoning. Add a little extra water if it seems too thick. Keep warm until ready to serve while you cook the seitan steaks.

6 Preheat a cast-iron grill over medium-high heat. Spray with cooking oil. When the grill is hot, cook the seitan steaks in batches, six at a time. It should take 4 to 6 minutes on each side until charred grilled marks appear. Reserve the chimichurri sauce left in the dish for drizzling.

TO ASSEMBLE THE SURF AND TURF

1 Ladle about 2 cups (480 ml) chowder into each bowl. Place a handful of mustard greens on one side of the chowder. Top each serving with two steaks. Drizzle with the remaining chimichurri. Scatter radishes over the bowls. Sprinkle on the parsley and place the lemon wedges wherever looks cute. Serve!

ROASTED RADISHES

You'd be surprised what radishes are capable of! A little olive oil, salt, and a high-temp oven are all it takes to create this tasty snack. It's great for the Surf and Turf above, of course, but you also may want to scatter some on a salad or use it as a side dish anywhere you'd use potatoes.

MAKES 2 CUPS (130 G)

- 2 cups (130 g) round red radishes, sliced in half
- 2 tablespoons olive oil
- ¼ teaspoon salt

1 Preheat the oven to 425°F (220°C).

2 Line a baking sheet with parchment. Spread the radishes onto the sheet. Drizzle with olive oil and sprinkle with salt then toss to coat. Place facedown.

3 Bake for about 18 minutes, until golden brown.

JACQUES'S BOEUF BOURGUIGNON

Serves 6 to 8

- 2 (20-ounce/570 g) cans green jackfruit, packed in water
- 6 tablespoons (90 ml) olive oil
- Salt
- 2 cups (260 g) pearl onions
- 2 cups (230 g) sliced shallots
- ¼ cup (35 g) sliced garlic
- 2 cups (280 g) peeled and sliced carrots, in ¼-inch coins
- 3 tablespoons chopped fresh thyme
- 4 bay leaves
- 2 teaspoons smoked paprika
- 1½ cups (360 ml) dry red wine
- Freshly ground black pepper
- ½ cup (95 g) uncooked green or brown lentils
- 1 ounce (28 g) dried porcini mushrooms
- 5 cups (1.2 liters) vegetable broth or Beefy Broth (page 302)
- 2 tablespoons tomato paste
- ¼ cup (30 g) all-purpose flour
- 1 recipe Mashed Potatoes (page 110), for serving
- ¼ cup (13 g) chopped fresh parsley, for garnish

Is Julia Child smiling down on us for this one? Probably not. But damn, it's delicious. All the wine-kissed smoky satisfaction that you want in boeuf Bourguignon. Jackfruit is grilled and charred to rep the meat, along with its trusty sidekick, porcini mushrooms. Lentils add beefy body and smoked paprika brings that bacon kick that vegans love so much. Toasting slices of garlic for this stew creates big, garlicky bites that really make it, so don't you dare mince it instead. Pearl onions are an iconic component to Julia's recipe, so I use them here. They're cooked on the grill right after the jackfruit so that you aren't using too many dishes. But if you leave them out, no big deal. Julia is already disappointed in us so it can't get any worse. Serve over ridiculous amounts of mashed potatoes.

1 Drain and rinse the jackfruit. Pat dry. Remove and discard the core from the jackfruit pieces; it looks kind of like a seed. Toss the rest in a bowl with 3 tablespoons of the olive oil and a big pinch of salt.

2 Preheat a cast-iron grill over medium heat. When the pan is hot, place the jackfruit in as much of a single layer as possible. You will need to do this in two batches. Grill for about 5 minutes, until charred and smoky, then use a thin metal spatula to toss and grill again for 3 more minutes. Transfer to a bowl and set aside to add back later. Repeat with the second batch.

3 In the same bowl used for the jackfruit, toss the pearl onions in 1 tablespoon olive oil and a pinch of salt to coat. Place them on the hot grill. Let cook until softened and charred in some spots, flipping occasionally, about 15 minutes.

CONTINUED →

4 In the meantime, preheat a 4-quart (3.8 liter) pot over medium-high heat. Sauté the shallots and a pinch of salt in the remaining 2 tablespoons olive oil until translucent, 5 to 7 minutes. Add the garlic and carrots and sauté for about 5 more minutes. Add thyme, bay leaves, smoked paprika, and 1 teaspoon salt and toss around for a minute.

5 Pour in the wine to deglaze the pan, scraping the bottom with a wooden spatula, and bring to a boil. The liquid should reduce in about 3 minutes. While it's reducing, grind in ample amounts of fresh black pepper.

6 Add the lentils, porcinis, broth, and tomato paste, cover the pot, and bring to a full boil for 5 minutes or so. Lower the heat, leaving the lid ajar for steam to escape, and simmer until the lentils are tender, about 30 minutes.

7 In a measuring cup, mix the flour into ½ cup (120 ml) water with a fork until no lumps are left. Slowly add the water-flour slurry to the pot, mixing it in well. Let cook for about 10 minutes, stirring often. If it appears too thick, thin with a little water.

8 Mix in the reserved jackfruit and pearl onions and heat through. Shut off the heat and let the stew hang out for about 15 minutes, for the flavors to marry. Serve with mashed potatoes and garnish with parsley.

HOT TAKE

Double-check that the jackfruit is canned in water, not in syrup. You don't want any sweetness here; even if you wash it off, it would still be super weird.

MEATY PORCINI RAMEN WITH RUNNY CASHEW EGG

Serves 4

I love a creamy ramen. And yeah, I get little a jealous when I see a runny egg in a bowlful of noodles, getting everything all luscious. Like, what an easy way to add creaminess and flavor. But vegans do it better. This cashew sauce is eggy and creamy, so easy and impossible to mess up. It really does hit the spot. It's poured over a ramen made incredibly beefy with porcini mushrooms and a homemade broth. This recipe is semi-epic, but you can certainly use the runny cashew egg idea on a simpler ramen of your choosing.

So here's what's going on: You'll be making a rich, spicy broth from dried porcini mushrooms and miso. When the broth is strained, you grab all those rehydrated porcinis and cut them into meaty pieces. You'll be freezing tofu, toasting garlic, sautéeing veggies, and blanching scallions. Are you auditioning for *Top Chef* or something? Yes. That is exactly what you are doing.

FIRST, MAKE THE BROTH

1 Add 3 quarts (3 liters) water, garlic, kombu, ginger, porcini, and red pepper flakes to a large pot and bring to a boil. Lower the heat to a simmer and cook for about 30 minutes uncovered, until the liquid is reduced to about three-fourths of the original quantity. Remove from heat. Stir in the miso. Let the broth cool until it's easy to handle without burning yourself.

2 Once cool, use cheesecloth to strain the broth into a large bowl, squeezing as tightly as you can to get as much broth as possible. Open up the cheesecloth and pick out the mushrooms to reuse. Set the broth aside. Compost everything else. If you don't have cheesecloth, no prob. Use a mesh strainer and just push the broth out with your regular old hands.

HOT TAKE

Prepare the broth a night or two in advance so that when you get to the actual ramen making, it'll really only take 3 minutes. Or, like, 45. But still. Just make the broth on a night when you're making dinner anyway and have it cook away, hands free. The kombu gives the broth a sealike umami quality that makes it more of a traditional Japanese dashi, but the broth is yummy with or without it. (But yeah, better with it.)

FOR THE PORCINI BROTH:

- 6 cloves garlic, smashed
- 1 piece kombu (optional)
- 1-inch (2.5 cm) piece fresh ginger, cut into 3 or 4 pieces (don't peel)
- 1 ounce (28 g) dried porcini
- 2 teaspoons red pepper flakes
- 3 tablespoons red miso

FOR THE RUNNY CASHEW EGG:

- 1 cup (120 g) whole unroasted cashews
- 1 teaspoon kala namak
- ⅛ teaspoon ground turmeric

CONTINUED →

FOR THE RAMEN:

- 1 (16-ounce/455 g) package ramen noodles
- 3 to 4 tablespoons (45 to 60 ml) canola oil
- ¼ cup (35 g) thinly sliced garlic
- 1 (14-ounce/400 g) block extra-firm FTAP tofu (see page 89), cut into small cubes
- Dark green part of a scallion, thinly sliced (see Hot Take)
- 6 baby bok choy, white parts sliced off and reserved
- 2 tablespoons mirin
- 2 to 3 tablespoons tamari plus salt if needed

FOR THE GARNISH:

- Thinly sliced purple cabbage
- Spicy sesame oil
- Sriracha
- Light green and white parts of a scallion, curled (see Hot Take)

HOT TAKES

If you forget to freeze and thaw the tofu ahead of time, don't sweat it. Just give it a good press and you'll have a wonderful yet slightly less chewy tofu experience.

To make curly scallions, thinly slice the dark green parts of the scallions, which will go in the recipe to be sautéed. For the remaining light green and white parts, fill a bowl with ice water. Thinly slice the scallions lengthwise and submerge them in the ice. They will curl up and get cute!

WHILE THE BROTH IS COOKING, YOU CAN MAKE THE RUNNY CASHEW EGG

1 Simply blend the cashews, ¾ cup (180 ml) water, kala namak, and turmeric in a high-speed blender until completely smooth, scraping down the sides with a rubber spatula to make sure you get everything. It will take about 1 minute.

TIME TO MAKE THE RAMEN

1 Prepare the noodles in a separate pot according to package directions. Be careful not to overcook.

2 Preheat a wok or very wide pot over low heat and have a plate ready. Use 2 tablespoons of the oil to toast the garlic until nice and golden. Be very careful not to burn it; it should only take 2 minutes or so. Use a thin, slotted spatula to transfer the toasted garlic to the plate, leaving as much oil in the pan as you can.

3 Now turn the heat up, drizzle in a tablespoon or so more of the oil, and sauté the tofu cubes until golden brown, about 5 minutes.

4 Cut the reserved porcinis into bite-size pieces. Sauté them in the wok for 5 to 7 minutes, drizzling in an extra tablespoon or so of oil if needed. Add the scallion greens and the white parts of the bok choy. Sauté for 2 minutes. Add the mirin and stir for another minute.

5 Measure the broth and make sure it comes to 2 quarts (2 liters). Pour it into the wok and heat through. If you need to add a little water to thin it that's fine. Bring to a boil. Add the green parts of the bok choy to wilt. Add 2 to 3 tablespoons of tamari and taste for salt.

6 Build the bowls: Portion the noodles into big bowls. Ladle in the broth and soup stuff so that it covers the noodles. Spoon about ¼ cup (60 ml) eggy sauce into each bowl in one motion (in other words, don't drizzle it, just pour slowly over one section of the ramen). Garnish with toasted garlic, sliced cabbage, spicy sesame oil, sriracha, and the curled scallion.

新作
SRIRACHA HOT
CHILI SAUCE

TEMPEH IS FOR LOVERS CHILI CON CARNE

Serves 6

This is a 100 percent meat chili. No beans, just meat for miles. I wanted to mimic a Texas chili that brags about how it has no beans. Still, if you add beans, I won't be mad. And let's just ignore the fact that, technically, tempeh is made from soybeans. It makes the best ground meat, especially in stews. Even folks that don't like tempeh (I know, how could they not?) tend to enjoy it in this form: completely cooked to death, soaked in juicy flavors, with an absolutely carnivorous texture. Red miso gives that extra burst of deep, delicious flavor that will make mouths water every time you cook up a batch. Serve with cornbread if you know what's good for you! Some Shreddy Cheddy (page 291) and a nice dollop of So Very Sour Cream (page 200) with some extra hot sauce won't hurt, either.

- 2 (8-ounce/225 g) packages tempeh, crumbled into popcorn-size pieces or smaller
- 5 tablespoons (75 ml) olive oil
- Salt
- 1 large yellow onion, cut into small dice
- 4 jalapeños, seeded and chopped
- 6 cloves garlic, minced
- ¼ cup (10 g) chopped fresh cilantro leaves
- 3 tablespoons mild chili powder
- 2 teaspoons ground cumin
- 1 teaspoon dried oregano
- 2 tablespoons red miso
- 1 (15-ounce/430 g) can diced tomatoes
- 3 tablespoons tomato paste
- 2 cups (480 ml) Beefy Broth (page 302) or prepared vegetable broth
- 2 tablespoons of your fave Mexican-style hot sauce (more or less, to taste)
- 2 teaspoons pure maple syrup

FOR SERVING:

- Shreddy Cheddy (page 291)
- So Very Sour Cream (page 200)
- Hot sauce
- ½ cup (40 g) sliced scallions

1. Preheat a cast-iron pan over medium heat. Sauté the tempeh in 3 tablespoons of the olive oil with a dash of salt for about 20 minutes, until seared. Remove the tempeh to a plate and set aside.
2. In the meantime, preheat a 4-quart (3.8 liter) pot over medium heat. Sauté the onions and jalapeños in the remaining 2 tablespoons olive oil and a pinch of salt for 5 to 7 minutes, until lightly browned. Add the garlic and sauté a minute more, until fragrant.
3. Mix in the cilantro, chili powder, cumin, oregano, and 1 teaspoon salt. Toss to coat the onions. Stir in the miso to coat the onions. Add the tomatoes, tomato paste, broth, hot sauce, and maple syrup and give it a stir. Bring to a simmer and cook for about 20 minutes, stirring occasionally.
4. Add the cooked tempeh to the pot and cook for another 20 minutes, tasting as you go. Thin the chili with some more vegetable broth as needed.
5. Turn the heat off and let rest for about 10 minutes before digging in. Top bowls of the chili with cheddar, sour cream, hot sauce, and scallions.

CHICKPEA AND BEEF TAGINE

Serves 6 to 8

- ½ recipe Beefy Seitan (page 28)
- 5 tablespoons (75 ml) olive oil
- 1 yellow onion, cut into medium dice
- 2 cups (490 g) baby carrots, sliced in half diagonally
- 6 cloves garlic, minced
- 1 tablespoon minced fresh ginger
- 1 tablespoon whole coriander, crushed
- 1 teaspoon sweet paprika
- 8 pieces saffron
- 2 teaspoons Aleppo pepper
- 2 teaspoons ground cumin
- ¼ teaspoon ground cardamom
- 3 cinnamon sticks
- 1 (15-ounce/225 g) can crushed fire-roasted tomatoes
- 1½ cups (360 ml) Beefy Broth (page 302) or prepared vegetable broth
- 1 (15-ounce/430 g) can chickpeas, rinsed and drained (1½ cups)
- 1 teaspoon salt
- ½ cup (75 g) goldenberries or raisins
- 1 cup (120 g) coconut cream
- 2 tablespoons fresh lemon juice

FOR SERVING AND GARNISH:

- Couscous or jasmine rice
- Harissa
- 1 cup (130 g) shelled pistachios, finely chopped
- 1 cup (30 g) loosely packed fresh mint leaves

Cooking with seductively scented strands of sunset-hued spice—it doesn't get any sexier than saffron. This tagine is like an edible love letter, romantic and gorgeous. Cooking with dried fruits seems like advanced cheffery, but all you do is toss them in and the simmering stew does the rest, plumping them up to burst with sweetness in every bite, enriching savory seitan and tender chickpeas. Aleppo pepper, ginger, and cinnamon all come together in a rich, creamy, tomato base. Topped off with fresh mint and pistachio, it's a scandalous rendezvous of all the best Moroccan flavors! Sounds fancy, but it's all pretty simple. Serve with couscous or rice and a dab of harissa for extra heat. I used goldenberries because I couldn't find raisins one day! But you will probably have the opposite experience. Use golden raisins if you can find them, but regular old raisins work perfectly well, too.

1 First, sear the seitan. Preheat a large cast-iron pan over medium-high heat. Cut the seitan into strips, about 2 inches (5 cm) long and ¼ inch (12 mm) thick. You should have about 3 cups. Add 3 tablespoons oil and the seitan in as much of a single layer as you can. Let cook for 3 to 4 minutes, until it gets a good sear. Use a thin metal spatula to flip. Continue cooking and flipping for about 10 more minutes until nicely seared. Remove from heat and set aside.

2 Preheat a 4-quart (3.8 liter) pot over medium heat. Sauté the onions in the remaining 2 tablespoons oil and a pinch of salt, for 5 to 7 minutes, until lightly browned. Mix in the carrots and cook for about 5 minutes just to soften a bit. Add the garlic, ginger, and crushed coriander and cook for another 2 minutes.

3 Add the paprika, saffron, aleppo pepper, cumin, and cardamom. Toss to coat the onion. Deglaze with a little of the vegetable broth, scraping the bottom of the pot with a spatula. Mix in the cinnamon sticks, tomatoes, broth, chickpeas, 1 teaspoon salt, and the raisins. Cover and bring to a boil. Once boiling, lower the heat to a simmer and cook for 15 minutes uncovered.

4 When the carrots are tender, add the coconut cream and lime, along with the cooked seitan. Heat through. Turn the heat off and let the stew rest for 10 minutes, for the flavors to marry.

5 Taste for salt and seasoning, and thin if necessary. Remove the cinnamon sticks. Serve in wide bowls with couscous and harissa. Top with pistachios and mint.

BREW

IRISH BEEF STEW

Serves 8

If there were vegans in those taverns on *Game of Thrones*, they would have been eating this beef stew with a big chalice of mead and some wolf bread. The broth is silky but thick with stout, and absolutely brimming with all the good stewy things: onions, potatoes, carrots, and, of course, the beef! Homemade sausages made with beer are the star of the bowl, soaking up all the luscious flavors this stew has to offer. You don't have to slay any dragons or book a trip to Ireland to get it, so why not make some tonight?

- 4 banger sausages (page 150)
- 3 tablespoons olive oil
- 1 large yellow onion, cut into medium dice
- 1¼ teaspoons salt plus a pinch
- 4 cloves garlic, minced
- 2 teaspoons dried thyme
- 1 teaspoon dried rosemary
- 2 ribs celery, sliced
- 2 medium carrots, peeled and cut into ¾-inch (2 cm) chunks
- Freshly ground black pepper
- 1¼ cups (300 ml) stout beer
- 3 tablespoons tomato paste
- 8 ounces (225 g) Yukon gold potatoes, cut into ¾-inch (2 cm) chunks
- 6 cups (1.4 liter) Beefy Broth (page 302) or prepared vegetable broth
- ⅓ cup (40 g) all-purpose flour
- ¼ cup (9 g) chopped fresh parsley, for garnish

1 Slice the sausages in half, then cut them on a diagonal into ½-inch-thick (12 mm) semicircles. Preheat a 6-quart (5.7 liter) pot over medium heat. Sauté the sausages in half of the olive oil for about 5 minutes, until lightly browned. Transfer to a bowl and set aside.

2 In the same pot, sauté the onions in the remaining 1½ tablespoons oil with a pinch of salt for 5 to 7 minutes, until lightly browned. Add the garlic, thyme, and rosemary and sauté for about 1 minute, until fragrant.

3 Add the celery and carrots and sauté for 5 minutes. Grind in a healthy amount of fresh black pepper as the celery and carrots are cooking.

4 Add the stout and mix with a wooden spatula, scraping the bottom of the pan to deglaze. Raise the heat, let cook, then reduce the heat for about 5 minutes.

5 Mix in the tomato paste. Add the potatoes, 4 cups (960 ml) of the broth, and 1¼ teaspoons salt. Cover the pot and bring to a boil. Once boiling, lower the heat to a simmer and cook until the potatoes are tender, about 10 more minutes. Be careful not to overcook them.

6 In a measuring cup, mix the remaining 2 cups (480 ml) broth with the flour. Once the potatoes are tender, slowly add the water and flour mixture to the pot, stirring constantly as you go. Let the stew thicken for about 10 minutes or so. Add the sausages to the pot to warm through. Let sit for about 10 minutes before serving. Garnish with parsley to serve!

COCONUT ROASTED ROOT VEGETABLE BEEF STEW

Serves 6 to 8

Root veggies, coconut, and ginger make me feel like the Princess of Autumn. That combo is comforting enough, but add some beef to the mix and suddenly I'm promoted to Queen. Rutabaga, carrots, and golden beets are roasted first, bringing out hints of sweetness and ethereal fragrance. Then they're dunked into a bright, creamy coconut stew with seared beefy seitan and caramelized shallots. There is no better meal to eat while you gaze at the foliage from your castle. If you need to swap out one root veggie for another, say, heirloom turnips or some parsnips, that works just fine.

- 12 ounces (340 g) rutabaga, peeled and cut into ¾-inch (2 cm) chunks
- 12 ounces (340 g) carrots, peeled and cut into ¾-inch (2 cm) chunks
- 12 ounces (340 g) golden beets, peeled and cut into ¾-inch (2 cm) chunks
- 3 tablespoons olive oil
- 1 teaspoon salt, plus more for roasting and sautéing
- 3 cups cubed Beefy Seitan (page 28)
- 2 tablespoons refined coconut oil
- 1½ cups (170 g) thinly sliced shallots
- 4 cloves garlic, minced
- 2 tablespoons grated fresh ginger
- ½ teaspoon red pepper flakes
- ½ teaspoon ground turmeric
- 2 tablespoons tomato paste
- 4 cups (960 ml) vegetable broth
- 1 (15-ounce/430 g) can full-fat coconut milk
- 2 tablespoons fresh lime juice
- 1 tablespoon agave syrup

FOR SERVING:

- Jasmine or basmati rice
- Fresh cilantro sprigs
- Pickled Cherry Tomatoes (page 311; optional)

1. Preheat the oven to 425°F (220°C). Line two large baking sheets with parchment.
2. Divide the rutabaga, carrots, and beets between the prepared baking sheets. Drizzle with the olive oil and sprinkle with a little salt. Toss to coat. Roast the root veggies for 35 to 40 minutes, flipping them and rotating the pans once, until golden and tender.
3. In the meantime, preheat a 4-quart (3.8 liter) pot over medium-high heat. Sauté the seitan in half the coconut oil, until lightly browned on all sides, about 5 minutes. Transfer to a bowl and set aside.
4. In the same pan, sauté the shallots, garlic, and ginger in the remaining tablespoon of coconut oil with a pinch of salt, for 5 to 7 minutes, until the shallots are translucent. Add red pepper flakes and turmeric.
5. Mix in the tomato paste and 1 teaspoon salt until heated through. Add the broth, coconut milk, lime juice, and agave.
6. At this point, the root veggies should be ready. Add them to the pot, along with the beef. Turn the heat off. Let sit for 10 minutes, then serve over rice, garnished with cilantro and pickled cherry tomatoes.

LASAGNA BOLOGNESE STEW
WITH OLIVES AND KALE

Serves 6

Here we have another version of lentil meat made into a filling veggieful stew! This time, we toss the lentils in before they cook. This releases their natural juices into the broth, lending it even more meaty body. It comes together like a deconstructed lasagna with all the ingredients we love: noodles, olives, ricotta, tomato of course, and (maybe making its first appearance in this book) kale. This is definitely a weeknight meal, ideal for those times when you want lasagna, but not enough to actually make lasagna.

- 1 medium yellow onion, cut into small dice
- 2 ribs celery, thinly sliced
- 1 red bell pepper, seeded and diced
- 2 tablespoons olive oil
- 1 teaspoon salt, plus a big pinch
- 8 cloves garlic, minced
- 2 tablespoons nutritional yeast flakes
- 1 teaspoon dried thyme
- 1 teaspoon dried oregano
- ¼ teaspoon red pepper flakes
- Several grinds freshly ground black pepper
- 4 cups (960 ml) Beefy Broth (page 302) or prepared vegetable broth
- ¾ cup (145 g) dried brown or green lentils
- 1 (28-ounce/795 g) can fire-roasted diced tomatoes
- ½ cup (115 g) tomato paste
- ½ cup (75 g) pitted black olives, sliced in half
- 8 ounces (225 g) kale, chopped
- 8 ounces (225 g) lasagna noodles
- ½ cup (15 g) loosely packed fresh basil leaves (you'll be using more for garnish)

FOR THE TOPPINGS:

- 1 recipe Nutty Ricotta (page 290)
- 1 cup (155 g) sliced black olives
- Red pepper flakes
- ½ cup (15 g) loosely packed fresh basil leaves

1. Preheat a 6-quart (5.7 liter) pot over medium-high heat. Sauté the onion, celery, and bell pepper in the oil with a big pinch of salt for 8 to 10 minutes, until the onion is lightly browned.
2. Add the garlic and sauté until fragrant, about 30 seconds. Add the nutritional yeast, thyme, oregano, red pepper flakes, and 1 teaspoon salt and toss to coat the veggies, letting the nutritional yeast toast a bit, for 2 minutes or so. Grind in fresh black pepper.
3. Add the broth and scrape the bottom of the pan with a wooden spatula to deglaze. Stir in the lentils. Cover and bring to a boil. Once boiling, lower to a simmer, keep covered, and cook until lentils are tender, 20 to 30 minutes.
4. Add the diced tomatoes, tomato paste, olives, and kale. Bring to a boil, letting the kale wilt. Break the lasagna noodles up into about 3-inch (7.5 cm) pieces and stir them in. Cook until the pasta is tender, about 20 minutes. Stir occasionally and add a little water if things start to look too thick.
5. When the pasta noodles are cooked, dinner is ready! Stir in the fresh basil to wilt. Taste for salt and seasoning. Let sit for about 10 minutes so that the flavors can marry. Scoop into bowls, garnish with dollops of ricotta, the sliced olives, red pepper flakes, and more fresh basil.

PIGS ARE FRIENDS NOT FOOD

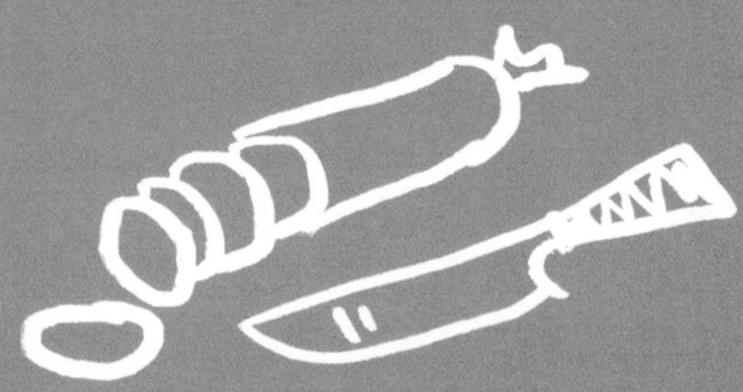

OK, we get it. "I can't live without bacon!" But the flavors we crave, the ones that are associated with all things bacon-y and sausage-y, are not necessarily from the lovable animal themselves. Rather, they are developed through smoking, curing, and seasoning. And that's what we are going for in this chapter: smoky, spicy, aromatic, and deeply umami flavors that just explode all over your taste buds.

Introducing smoke to your food doesn't have to be complicated. You can start with beginner methods, then graduate to dude-who-sits-around-discussing-wood-chips-on-Reddit.

But first, the easy ways: products that have already been smoked. Smoked paprika, smoked salt, chipotle, and—in moderation—liquid smoke. All of these are readily available in most supermarkets. But I also recommend finding more obscure smoked items online. Smoked sun-dried tomatoes are heaven sent, adding tang, texture, and, of course, smoke. Bonus: They are shelf stable. Smoked garlic is another bang for your smoky buck.

If you are ambitious and want to go the extra step, though, I am rooting you on. Smoking items at home gets the most scrumptious, eyes-rolled-back-in-your head results. See page 167 for stovetop smoker fun!

But it's not all smoke and mirrors. Spice blends that evoke porqi-ness include fennel, anise, sage, and all manner of peppers and chilis. To "cure" our fake meats, vinegars and miso provide acidity, tanginess, and that "I've been hanging out in a cellar for months" vibe.

Seitan plays a large role (and roll) here. But texture from mushrooms and tempeh, sun-dried tomatoes, and even grains to add "fat"—those are all in our fake meat arsenal and ready for your snout.

PEPPERONI PIZZA

Makes 2 pies

Here's an idea: Replace all awards with pepperoni pizza. Best actress? Here's a pepperoni pizza; hold that up and thank the academy. The Stanley Cup? Skate that pepperoni pizza around and pour some beer on it. Never mind an Olympic gold medal, just go ahead and hang a pepperoni pizza around your neck.

If you choose to make the whole thing from scratch and become a legend in your own home, just prepare any of the elements up to four days ahead of time. I wouldn't plan on making all the components on the day of and still being able to watch the evening news. But also, who watches the evening news? You can simplify the process by buying the crust, buying the cheese, and even buying the sauce. If there's just one thing you make, though, make the darn pepperoni!

- 1 recipe Pizzeria-at-Home Pizza Dough, at room temperature (recipe follows)
- 1 recipe Pizza Sauce (recipe follows)
- Olive oil, for greasing and various things
- 8 balls Fresh Mozz-Shew-Rella (page 286) or Minute Melty Mozzy Sauce (recipe follows)
- 2 logs Proper Pepperoni (recipe follows)
- ½ cup (15 g) loosely packed fresh basil leaves
- Crushed red pepper, for finishing

1 Preheat the oven to 500°F (260°C).

2 Lightly flour a clean, preferably cold counter. Roll one portion of the pizza dough into a ball and then flatten it with your hands into about an 8-inch (20 cm) circle. Use a rolling pin to roll it until it's about 13 inches (33 cm) across. It doesn't have to be a perfect circle.

3 Lightly grease a baking sheet. Transfer the dough to the sheet and reshape it a little if necessary.

4 Spread ¾ cup (180 ml) of the pizza sauce onto the dough, leaving a ¾-inch (2 cm) rim around the edge without sauce. In a coffee mug, mix together about 3 tablespoons olive oil with a tablespoon of pizza sauce. Brush the edges of the pizza crust with this mixture. You can use a spoon or your hands to brush it on, just giving it some added flavor and color.

5 Slice the cheese balls into ¼-inch-thick rounds and place them randomly on top of the pizza. Or, if using the melty mozz, drizzle or dollop it on the pizza. Slice the pepperoni into thin slices, somewhere between ⅛ inch and ¼ inch thick. Place them randomly on top of the pizza.

6 Bake in the preheated oven for 10 to 12 minutes. When done, the edges should be golden and the cheese melted.

7 Remove from the oven and scatter basil leaves across the top. Sprinkle with crushed red pepper and slice! Make the next pizza the same way.

HOT TAKES

If you don't feel like making mozzarella from scratch but don't want to buy it either, check out the quick-fix mozzarella sauce I've provided on page 147 as an option. It'll get the job done!

There's no shame in rolling out your dough instead of tossing it in the air like a pro. But remember to let dough sit at room temperature for at least an hour before attempting to stretch or roll it. Cold dough likes to snap back in place, so it's hard to work with.

CONTINUED →

PIZZERIA-AT-HOME PIZZA DOUGH

Makes two 14-inch (36 cm) crusts

This is the best recipe for home cooks who don't have a baking stone or pizza pan but still want a nice thin, crisp crust. The secret is cornmeal! It bakes just beautifully on a regular old baking sheet, no fancy equipment needed. If your baking sheet isn't quite large enough, go ahead and make your pizza into an oblong shape, rather than a traditional round. I guarantee that no one will complain.

- 1 cup (140 ml) lukewarm water
- 1 tablespoon granulated sugar
- 2¼ teaspoons (1 packet) active dry yeast
- 2 tablespoons olive oil, plus more for the bowl
- 2 cups (250 g) all-purpose flour (or a little less; see directions)
- 1 teaspoon salt
- ½ cup (80 g) medium-grind cornmeal

1. Add the water and sugar to the bowl of a standing mixer fitted with a dough hook. Sprinkle in the yeast and let sit for 5 minutes to bloom, which means it should fizz a bit.

2. Stir in the olive oil then add 1 cup (125 g) of the flour along with the salt. Mix on low speed until well incorporated, and then turn the speed up to medium and continue to mix for 3 minutes.

3. Add another ½ cup (65 g) of the flour, and the ½ cup (80 g) cornmeal and mix well, starting on low and then switching to medium speed. Knead on medium for about 5 minutes. You may occasionally have to get in there with your hands if the dough starts climbing up the hook. It should become smooth and elastic and slightly tacky. At this point, incorporate the remaining flour by the tablespoon, with the mixer running. When it starts to seem dry, stop adding flour. This could be anywhere between ¼ cup (30 g) and ½ cup (65 g). Knead again on medium speed until the dough is elastic and easy to stretch, about 8 more minutes.

4. Meanwhile, drizzle about 2 tablespoons olive oil into a large bowl. The dough will double in size, so make sure the bowl is spacious.

5. Remove the dough from the mixer, form into a ball, and place in the bowl, tossing it around to coat with the oil. Cover the top in plastic wrap and put in a warm place. Let the dough rise for about an hour, or until doubled in size.

6. Punch the dough down and knead lightly when you're ready to use. If using it later, divide dough into two balls, and place in a storage container with a lid for up to 3 days. The dough will rise again in the fridge, so make sure the containers are large enough. You can also store it in plastic bags.

MINUTE MELTY MOZZY SAUCE

Makes 2 cups (480 ml)

Pour this sauce over everything: pizza, casseroles, the neighbor's rosebushes for all I care. Blend, bake, and boom—you're set whenever a little melty mozzarella is needed. If it's going on a pizza, just drizzle about ¾ cup (180 ml) in a zigzag pattern or splatter dollops all over the top after applying the pizza sauce.

- **1 cup (125 g) whole unroasted cashews**
- **2 tablespoons nutritional yeast flakes**
- **1 tablespoon tapioca flour**
- **1 tablespoon mellow white miso**
- **½ teaspoon salt**

1. In a high-speed blender, place the cashews, nutritional yeast, tapioca flour, miso, ¾ cup (180 ml) water, and the salt, then blend away until completely smooth. Scrape down the sides with a rubber spatula to make sure you get everything.

CONTINUED →

PROPER PEPPERONI (AKA PROPPERONI)

Makes 4 logs

The key to great pepperoni is incorporating lots of texture, bright color, and bold flavor. We do that in a few ways here. The sun-dried tomatoes add flecks of red against the pink meat, which is tinted with beet powder, and white beans are coarsely chopped to look like little fatty bits. Finally, whole grain mustard is kneaded in to create that authentic pepperoni feel, like you're looking up at a galaxy of a million spicy stars.

- 3 cloves garlic
- ¼ cup (30 g) sun-dried tomatoes in oil
- 3 tablespoons refined coconut oil, melted
- 2 tablespoons beet powder
- 1 teaspoon salt
- 1 teaspoon granulated sugar
- 1 teaspoon anise seed
- ¾ cup (135 g) cooked white beans (one-half of a 15-ounce/430 g can), rinsed and drained
- 1¾ cups (210 g) vital wheat gluten
- ¼ cup (40 g) pea protein
- ¼ cup (15 g) nutritional yeast flakes
- 2 teaspoons smoked paprika
- 1 teaspoon onion powder
- 1 teaspoon garlic powder
- ½ teaspoon ground black pepper
- ½ teaspoon red pepper flakes
- 2 tablespoons whole grain mustard

1 Prepare four 10-inch (25 cm) squares of aluminum foil and parchment for wrapping and stack them, parchment on top of foil. Prepare your steamer.

2 Pulse the garlic in a blender. Add the sun-dried tomatoes, coconut oil, beet powder, salt, sugar, anise, and 1½ cups (360 ml) water. Blend until semi-smooth with some texture left. Pulse in the beans so that there are a few whole and half beans left. Set the mixture aside.

3 In a large bowl, whisk together the vital wheat gluten, pea protein, nutritional yeast, smoked paprika, onion powder, garlic powder, black pepper, and red pepper flakes.

4 Add the wet mixture to the dry along with the stone ground mustard and knead the dough for about 5 minutes, until springy.

5 Divide the dough into 4 even parts. An easy way to do this is to split the dough in half and then into quarters. Roll each piece of dough into a ball then mold and roll into about a 6-inch (15 cm) sausage shape. Wrap each log of dough in parchment-lined foil, twisting the ends like a Tootsie Roll. Don't worry too much about shaping it; it will snap into shape while it's steaming.

6 Steam the wrapped sausages in the steamer for 40 minutes, turning once. Let cool completely before using.

BANGERS AND MASH

Serves 4

Fun to say—more fun to eat. When I visited London, there were so many vegan-friendly spots serving bangers and mash and I ordered it every time. Does that make me the one person in the world who thinks British food is good? These sausages are luscious and rosy, made with beer and the usual sausage suspects (like onion and paprika). What really makes them stand out is the caraway seed! It's so hard to explain the flavor of caraway; imagine if licorice and coriander had a baby, and its godparents were a lemon tree and a dill plant. See? Hard to explain, but you'll understand when you taste it. The sausages are served in a rich gravy of caramelized onions, all over creamy mashed potatoes and beautiful bright, buttery peas with a little fresh mint for bursts of green. Anarchy in the UK, indeed.

FOR THE BANGERS:

- ½ cup (90 g) cooked navy beans
- ¾ cup (180 ml) brown ale
- 2 tablespoons olive oil
- 2 tablespoons red miso
- 2 tablespoons whole grain mustard
- 2 tablespoons tomato paste
- 1 tablespoon tamari
- ¼ cup (15 g) nutritional yeast flakes
- 2 tablespoons beet powder
- 1 teaspoon garlic powder
- 1 teaspoon onion powder
- 1 teaspoon crushed caraway seed
- 1 teaspoon smoked paprika
- ½ teaspoon dried thyme
- ½ teaspoon ground white pepper
- 1¼ cups (150 g) vital wheat gluten

FOR THE ACCOMPANIMENTS:

- Olive oil, for cooking
- Creamy Buttery Mashed Potatoes (page 110)
- Buttery Frozen Peas with Mint (recipe follows)
- Onion Gravy (recipe follows)

1 Make the bangers: Prepare four 10-inch (25 cm) squares of aluminum foil and parchment, parchment stacked on top of foil, for wrapping and steaming. Prepare your steamer.

2 In a bowl, mash the beans until no whole ones are left. Add the ale, olive oil, miso, mustard, tomato paste, and tamari and mix well.

3 Mix in the nutritional yeast, beet powder, garlic, onion, caraway, paprika, thyme, and white pepper. Add the vital wheat gluten and mix well. Knead for about 5 minutes.

4 Divide the dough into 4 equal parts. An easy way to do this is to split the dough in half and then into quarters. Roll each piece of dough into a ball then mold and roll each one into about a 6-inch (15 cm) sausage shape. Wrap the dough in parchment-lined foil, twisting the ends like a Tootsie Roll. Don't worry too much about shaping it, it will snap into shape while it's steaming.

5 Place the wrapped sausages in the steamer and steam for 40 minutes, turning once. Let cool completely before using.

6 Assemble the bangers and mash: Preheat a large cast-iron pan over medium heat. Cut the bangers in half the long way, on a diagonal. Sear in olive oil until nicely browned, about 4 minutes.

7 Scoop a big old scoop of mashed potatoes into the center of a large rimmed plate. Make a divot in the center. Place the peas in the divot. Place two cooked bangers halves on top. Pour gravy all over! Repeat to make four plates in all and serve.

CONTINUED →

ONION GRAVY

Makes 1 quart (960 ml)

- 3 medium yellow onions, halved and sliced into thin half-moons
- 3 tablespoons refined coconut oil
- 2 tablespoons all-purpose flour
- ¼ cup (60 ml) dry red wine
- 2 teaspoons red miso paste
- 2 cups (480 ml) Beefy Broth (page 302) or prepared beef-style broth
- Salt, if needed
- ½ teaspoon ground black pepper

You can achieve incredible depth of flavor just by cooking onions low and slow. Using coconut oil adds butteriness and traditional anchovy-based Worcestershire sauce is completely outshined by the umami of red miso. To make it extra fake meaty, use Beefy Broth (page 302). It's incredibly nuanced and savory, with natural sweetness from the caramelized onions. If you opt for store-bought broth, adjust the salt as necessary, since the amount of salt in packaged broth can vary.

1 Preheat a large, heavy-bottomed pan over medium-low heat. Sauté the onions in 2 tablespoons of the coconut oil for about 25 minutes, stirring often, until they start to caramelize. Cover the pan when you are not stirring.

2 Add the remaining tablespoon oil and let it melt. Sprinkle in the flour and cook for about 2 minutes, coating all the onions and getting them a bit toasted.

3 Pour in the wine to deglaze the pan, scraping the bottom with a wooden spatula. Let it cook for about 2 minutes.

4 Mix in the miso to dissolve. Stream in the broth, stirring constantly. Add salt, if needed, and the pepper. Simmer until thick, stirring occasionally, for 10 to 12 minutes. Taste for salt and seasoning.

BUTTERY FROZEN PEAS WITH MINT

Makes 2 cups (290 g)

- 1 (16-ounce/455 g) package frozen peas
- ¼ teaspoon salt
- 2 tablespoons refined coconut oil
- 3 tablespoons finely chopped fresh mint

No one is cottage-core enough to shell their own peas, but frozen peas are the best frozen vegetable so that's OK. They are frozen at the height of freshness, no doubt by hordes of cottage-core workers. This recipe is, well, not really a recipe. It's frozen peas, coconut oil, fresh mint, and salt. It doesn't need to be anything else.

1 Empty the frozen peas into a pot with about ¼ cup (60 ml) water, cover, and heat over low until warmed through. You can also microwave them according to package directions.

2 Drain the peas. Place them in a bowl and add the salt, coconut oil, and mint. Toss to melt the oil and coat the peas. Taste for salt and serve!

TEMPEH LARB

Serves 4-ish

My cravings for Thai food run deep, and larb satisfies every time. I've seen it made with both pork and chick'n, but I choose the pork-y route here, using tempeh instead. The sauce is tangy, spicy, and sweet, with a savory funkiness meant to mimic fermented fish sauce. It's all poured over ground tempeh along with lots of fresh herbs, then scooped into lettuce cups and topped with toasted rice powder. If you're in an incredible rush, you can skip the rice powder, I suppose, but it adds an unforgettable layer of toasty flavor; a defining characteristic of classic larb. Using a store-bought green curry paste is a smart shortcut to add those lemongrass and ginger notes in a hurry.

1 Preheat a wok or cast-iron pan over medium heat. Dry toast the rice for about 10 minutes, until aromatic and lightly browned. Transfer to a blender and let cool completely while you make everything else. You will use the pan again for the minced tempeh; no need to wash it.

2 Make the dressing: In a large mug, use a fork to mix together all the ingredients until the miso is well combined. Set aside.

HOT TIP

Pay attention to the directions! Some of the dressing is reserved to top the lettuce cups. Believe me, you don't want to miss a drop of this sauce.

- ¼ cup (45 g) uncooked glutinous (sticky) rice

FOR THE DRESSING:

- ¼ cup (60 ml) fresh lime juice
- 2 tablespoons rice vinegar
- 2 tablespoons red miso
- 3 tablespoons brown sugar
- 1 tablespoon sriracha
- ¼ teaspoon kelp powder

CONTINUED →

FOR THE TEMPEH:

- 2 (8-ounce/225 g) packages tempeh
- 3 tablespoons refined coconut oil
- 1 medium red onion, quartered and thinly sliced
- 3 cloves garlic, minced
- 2 tablespoons prepared green curry paste
- 1 teaspoon red pepper flakes, plus more for garnish
- ⅓ cup (15 g) roughly chopped fresh basil leaves
- ⅓ cup (17 g) roughly chopped fresh mint leaves
- ⅓ cup (15 g) roughly chopped fresh cilantro

FOR ASSEMBLING:

- 16 iceberg lettuce leaves
- Big handful fresh cilantro (tender stems and leaves)
- Lime wedges

3 Prepare the tempeh: Crumble the tempeh into small pieces, ranging from pea to popcorn size. Preheat the wok or cast-iron pan over medium-high heat.

4 Sauté the tempeh in 2 tablespoons of the coconut oil, flipping often with a thin spatula, until lightly brown, about 15 minutes. Remove tempeh from the pan and set aside.

5 In the same pan, sauté the onion in the remaining tablespoon oil for about 3 minutes. You want it to retain some crunch. Add the garlic, curry paste, red pepper flakes, and chopped basil, mint, and cilantro. Swish the contents around to toast the curry paste a little, about 2 minutes.

6 Add ½ cup (120 ml) of the dressing to the pan and mix it up so that the curry paste is well incorporated. Return the tempeh to the pan along with 2 tablespoons water. Cook for about 5 minutes to soak up the flavor. Taste for salt but remember you'll be topping the larb with the reserved dressing and that is somewhat salty.

7 The rice in the blender should be cool now. Pulse and blend into a powder. Let the powder settle before lifting the lid.

8 Layer the lettuce leaves in groups of two so that you have 8 lettuce cups. Spoon the larb into the cups. Drizzle with the remaining dressing. Sprinkle it with the rice powder and additional red pepper flakes (if you like it spicy), and top with fresh cilantro. Serve with lime wedges.

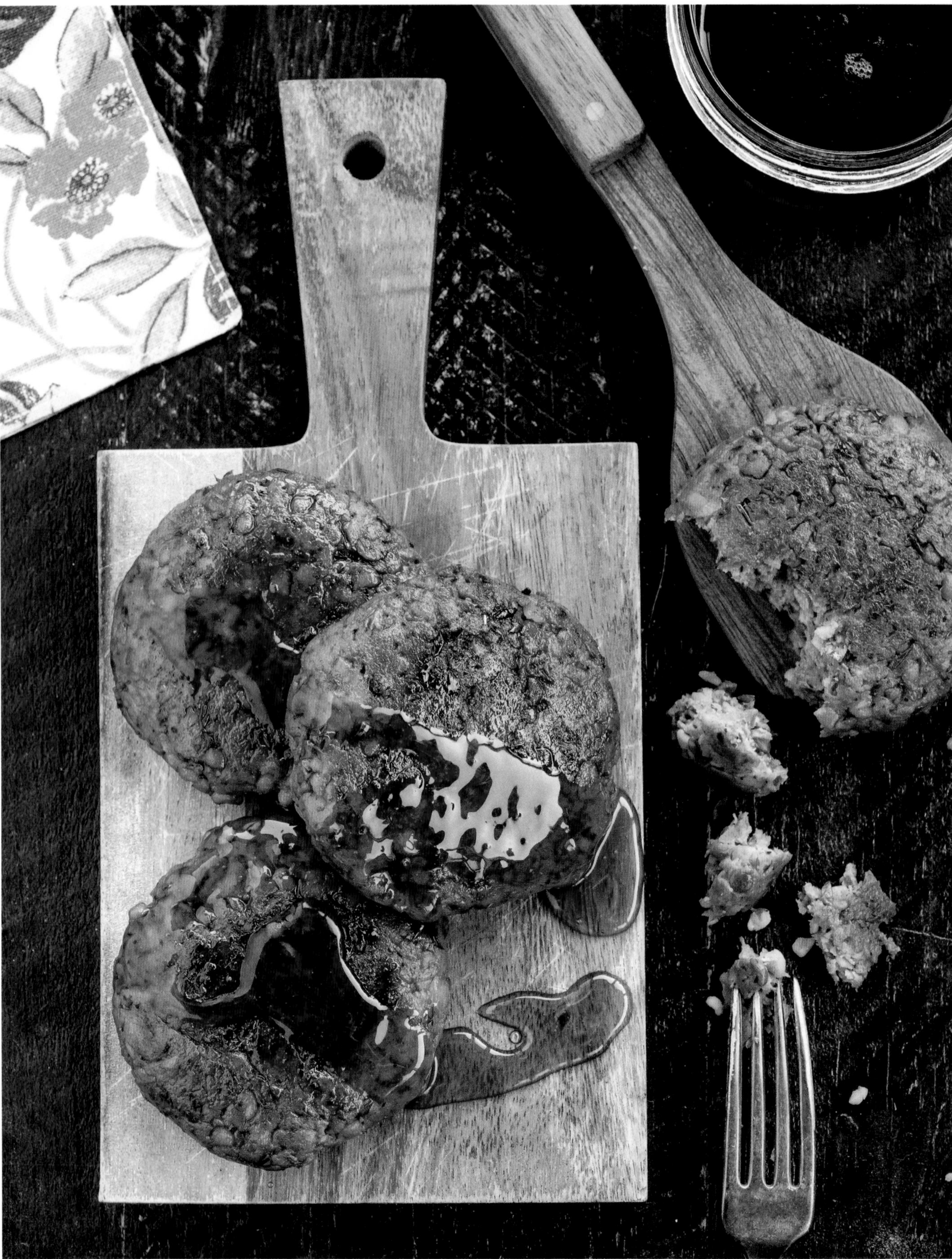

BREAKFAST SAUSAGE

Makes 8

Imagine sizzling discs of juicy meat sputtering away in the pan. The aroma drifts through the whole household, awakening all the sleepyheads in their beds. This is THAT breakfast sausage. But how, you ask? Tempeh is mashed for meaty substance, lentils provide flavor and texture, mayo adds for fatty richness, with a hint of liquid smoke for authenticity, and vital wheat gluten holds it all together. Then there are the spices: sage, thyme, anise, and nutmeg. Finish with a hit of maple syrup and you're ready to tackle Sunday. I like to drizzle extra maple syrup on after they've been cooked, too. Coconut oil gives the best, fattiest, sizzliest results, so try not to sub it if you don't have to.

- 1 (8-ounce/225 g) package tempeh
- ¼ cup tamari
- 1 tablespoon apple cider vinegar
- 1 cup (190 g) overcooked lentils (lentils from a can work great)
- 3 tablespoons vegan mayo, prepared or homemade (page 309)
- 2 tablespoons pure maple syrup
- ½ teaspoon liquid smoke
- 2 tablespoons nutritional yeast flakes
- 2 teaspoons dried sage
- 1 teaspoon garlic powder
- ½ teaspoon dried thyme
- ½ teaspoon ground black pepper
- ¼ teaspoon anise seed
- ¼ teaspoon ground nutmeg
- 1 cup (120 g) vital wheat gluten
- Refined coconut oil, for cooking

1 Have ready eight 10-inch (25 cm) pieces of aluminum foil lined with parchment paper. Also, set up and preheat your steamer.

2 Crumble the tempeh into bite-size pieces in a 4-quart (3.8 liter) pot. Submerge the tempeh in water by about 3 inches (7.5 cm). Add 2 tablespoons of the tamari and the apple cider vinegar.

3 Place the pot on the stove and bring to a full boil, uncovered. Boil for about 15 minutes. Drain the tempeh and let cool completely. Once cool, use your hands to mash it up pretty well.

4 In a large bowl, mash the lentils until no whole ones are left. Add the mashed tempeh, mayo, maple syrup, remaining 2 tablespoons tamari, liquid smoke, nutritional yeast, dried sage (rubbed between your fingers), garlic powder, thyme, black pepper, anise seed, and nutmeg. Mix really well.

5 Add the wheat gluten and mush everything together with your hands, getting it really well incorporated, about 2 minutes.

6 Break the mixture up into 8 equal pieces. Form each piece into a ball and then flatten into a disc about ½ inch (12 mm) thick. Use the palms of your hands to turn the disc, creating somewhat even sides that aren't flat. In other words, shape it more like a tire than a flying saucer.

7 Wrap each disc in parchment-lined foil. Take care to make them circular again once wrapped. Steam with a tight lid for about 40 minutes. Let cool completely before unwrapping and cooking.

8 To cook, preheat a large skillet over medium heat and cook the patties on each side in a thin layer of coconut oil, until lightly browned, about 4 minutes.

SAUSAGE OATMEAL PANCAKES

Makes 6 pancakes

- 1½ cups Breakfast Sausage (page 157)
- 1 tablespoon refined coconut oil, plus additional for cooking pancakes
- 1¼ cups (155 g) all-purpose flour
- ½ cup (45 g) quick-cooking rolled oats
- 2¼ teaspoons baking powder
- ¼ teaspoon salt
- 1½ cups (360 ml) unsweetened soy milk or your fave vegan milk
- ¼ cup (60 ml) unsweetened applesauce
- 1 tablespoon safflower oil or any mild vegetable oil
- 1 tablespoon granulated sugar
- ½ teaspoon pure vanilla extract

FOR SERVING:

- Vegan butter
- Flaky sea salt, such as Maldon
- Pure maple syrup

Some recipes make you question everything you thought you knew. Who am I? How did I get here? The answer, for me, is not complex. I love pancakes. I love oatmeal. I love vegan sausages. But combining a million good things doesn't always mean you will end up with another good thing. So I messed around and found out. And I am here to tell you: Combining all these things leads to an even better thing. Pancakes that are savory, with a fluffy yet hardy texture. The most filling delicious breakfast! A steady stream of maple syrup poured over the top doesn't hurt one bit. I also sprinkled on a little flaky sea salt to up that sweet and salty combo. Without further ado, Sausage Oatmeal Pancakes. Your new favorite breakfast.

1. Tear or cut the sausage into small pieces, ranging in size from a pea to popcorn. In a nonstick pan over medium heat, cook the sausage pieces in coconut oil to lightly brown them, about 3 minutes. Once cooked, transfer them to a plate and pop them in the freezer to cool completely while you make the pancake batter. No need to wash the pan; you will be using it for pancakes in a bit and the sausage oil will taste good!
2. Combine the flour, oats, baking powder, and salt in a mixing bowl. Make a well in the center and add the milk, applesauce, safflower oil, sugar, and vanilla.
3. Use a rubber spatula to stir the wet mixture a bit to combine, then incorporate it into the dry, mixing just until everything is moistened. Fold the cool, crumbled sausages into the batter. Let the batter rest for 10 minutes.
4. Preheat the pan over medium heat. Make the pancakes one at a time, melting some coconut oil for each one. Scoop a scant ½ cup (120 ml) batter into the pan and cook until bubbly, then cover with a lid for another minute or two so it cooks through. Flip and cook on the other side until lightly brown. Proceed with the rest of the pancakes. Serve hot with butter, flaky salt, and maple syrup.

I love cooking pancakes in refined coconut oil! So buttery and yum. But you can cook in canola oil or vegan butter if you prefer.

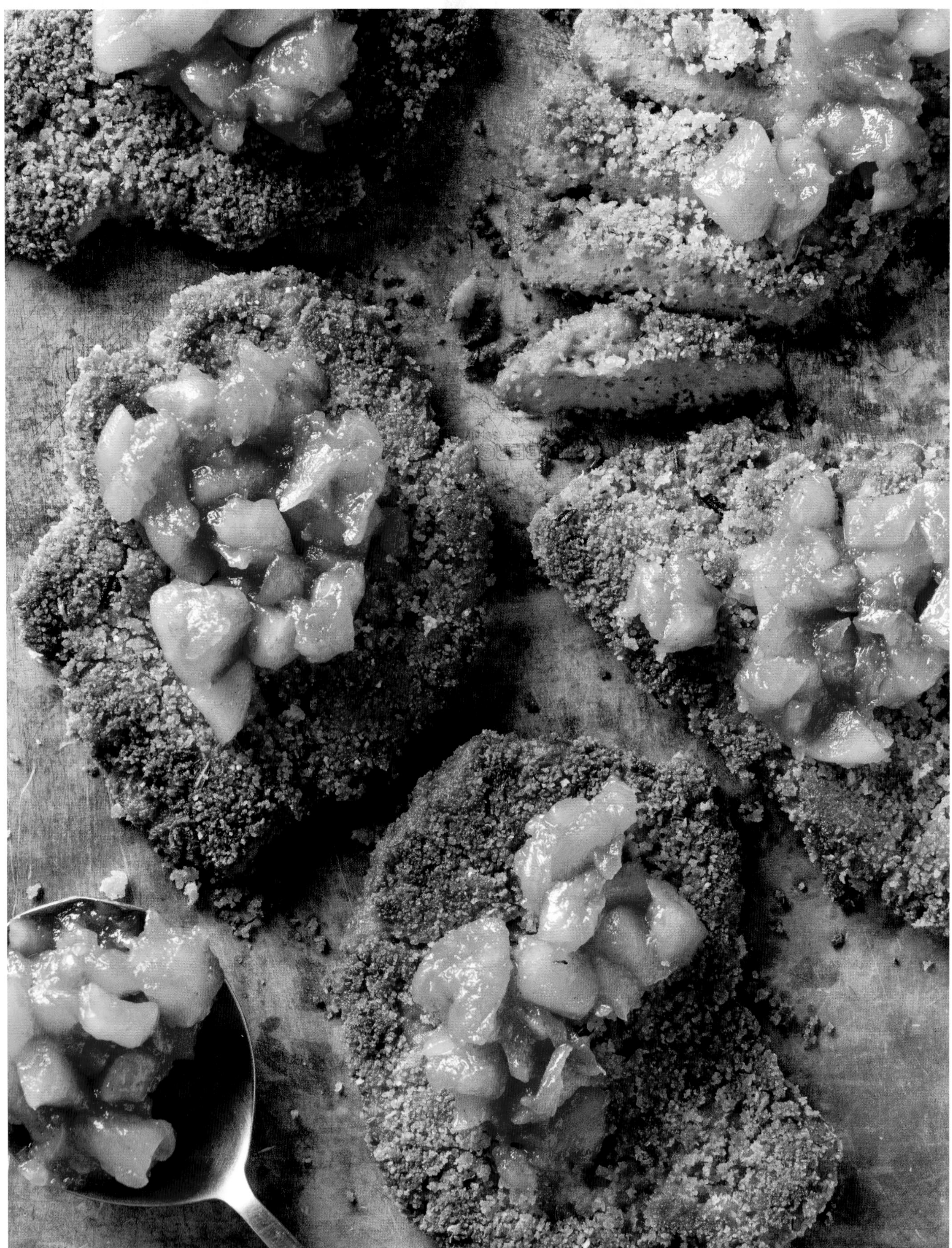

PORK CHOPS AND APPLESAUCE

Serves 4

You can't mention pork chops and applesauce without mentioning *The Brady Bunch*, so let's get that out of the way. "Porkchops and appleshaush." OK, great, now let's bring this classic into the twenty-first century! Tender seitan that feels fatty and porky is lightly breaded in rosemary and panko, then pan-fried until crisp and golden. It's best served with mashed sweet potatoes and, of course, applesauce. But the pork chops themselves can be used in any number of ways. They're smoke-kissed with a little smoked salt and some smoked paprika in the simmering broth. I cut the broth with water to keep it fairly light so that the broth doesn't impart an overpowering flavor. And the ingredient list is blissfully short! You can slice the porq and sauté, or grill it for a sandwich. It's a very versatile recipe for the beginner fake-meat maker. Veggie accompaniments I'd recommend are roasted brussels or grilled string beans.

FOR THE SEITAN PORK CHOPS:

- 1 cup (120 g) vital wheat gluten flour
- 3 tablespoons chickpea flour
- 1 teaspoon smoked salt
- ½ cup (120 ml) vegetable broth
- 2 tablespoons tamari
- 1 tablespoon apple cider vinegar
- 1 tablespoon olive oil

FOR THE BROTH:

- 4 cups (960 ml) vegetable broth
- ¼ cup (60 ml) soy sauce
- 6 bay leaves
- 1 tablespoon smoked paprika

MAKE THE SEITAN

1 In a large bowl, mix together the vital wheat gluten, chickpea flour, and smoked salt. Make a well in the center and add the vegetable broth, tamari, apple cider vinegar, and oil. Give it a mix with a big spoon, then use your hands to knead the dough into a very elastic dough, about 5 minutes.

LET THE DOUGH REST AS YOU PREPARE THE BROTH

1 In a 4-quart (3.8 liter) pot, combine the broth, 4 cups water, soy sauce, bay leaves, and smoked paprika. Cover and bring to a boil, then reduce the heat to a simmer.

2 To shape the pork chops, divide the dough into six equal parts with a knife or bench scraper. Shape each one into an oval, stretching them out a bit, to about 5 inches (12 cm) long. You can use a rolling pin for this, too.

3 Add each seitan piece to the simmering broth. Let them cook for about 15 minutes to develop a skin. Turn the heat up to medium to bring the broth to a low boil; cover again, leaving the lid a bit ajar, and let the seitan pork cook for about 15 more minutes. It should feel firm to the touch.

CONTINUED →

FOR BREADING AND FRYING:

- ¾ cup panko (60 g) breadcrumbs
- 3 tablespoons chopped fresh rosemary
- ¼ teaspoon salt
- ¼ teaspoon ground black pepper
- Olive oil, for cooking

FOR SERVING:

- 1 recipe Pretty in Pink Applesauce (right)

4 Let cool completely in the broth, placing the pot in the refrigerator once the broth stops steaming. You can transfer the seitan cutlets and broth to an airtight container and store in the refrigerator until ready to use.

5 Bread and fry the seitan chops: On a large dinner plate, mix together the panko, rosemary, salt, and pepper. Have ready a piece of parchment. Preheat a large cast-iron pan over medium heat.

6 Working one by one, remove each cooled cutlet from the broth, but don't shake the broth off. Press each side firmly into the breadcrumb mixture to coat. It won't be fully coated like fried chicken, but rather a light, imperfect breading. Place on the parchment until ready to fry.

7 You want a nice layer of olive oil in the pan, somewhere between ⅛ and ¼ inch. In two batches, pan-fry the chops for about 5 minutes on each side until golden, flipping occasionally.

8 The cutlets are ready to eat! Serve with a healthy amount of mashed sweet potatoes topped with plenty of applesauce, if you like..

PRETTY IN PINK APPLESAUCE

Makes 6 cups (1.4 liters)

Apples and a hint of cinnamon. You can't really go wrong. But know how to go really right? Make it pink! This applesauce is great with savory stuff, like the Pork Chops (above).

- 4 pounds (1.8 kg) Granny Smith apples, peeled, cored, and cut into ½-inch dice
- 3 tablespoons fresh lemon juice
- ½ cup (100 g) sugar
- ½ teaspoon ground cinnamon
- 1 teaspoon beet powder

1 In a 4-quart pot over medium-low heat, combine the apples, lemon juice, sugar, and cinnamon. Cover the pot and cook, stirring occasionally, until the sugar is melted and the apples are a bit cooked, about 15 minutes.

2 Uncover and cook until the mixture is bubbly, another 15 minutes or so. The apples should be very tender and saucy but still have some shape left in them.

3 Turn off the heat and stir in the beet powder.

4 Taste for sweetness. Let cool completely, then transfer to airtight containers and refrigerate until ready to serve.

KIELBASA AND CABBAGE SKILLET

Serves 4

Become your own Polish grandma. Fresh, homey flavors are brightened with mustard and dill. One major achievement of this stewy skillet is that the flavors are just as fitting in summer or winter. The kielbasa is flavored with marjoram and a hint of cloves, and when you slice one you see pearly little dots reminiscent of sausage fat. But it's adorable, because it is not in fact fat, it's grains! Pearled barley, to be exact. It's a fun time.

When all is said and done you're left with a new appreciation for cabbage. It's saucy and luscious, almost like a gravy, and of course full of big chunky meaty sausage bites. Have with a beer or a lemonade or both.

FOR THE KIELBASA:

- 3 cloves garlic, peeled
- ½ cup (30 g) smoked sun-dried tomatoes (see Hot Takes)
- 2 tablespoons olive oil
- 2 tablespoons tamari
- 1 teaspoon granulated sugar
- ½ teaspoon salt
- 1¼ cups (150 g) vital wheat gluten
- ¼ cup (15 g) nutritional yeast flakes
- 1 teaspoon onion powder
- 1 teaspoon garlic powder
- 1/16 teaspoon cloves (eyeball one-half of an ⅛ teaspoon measure)
- ½ teaspoon dried marjoram
- ½ teaspoon ground black pepper
- ½ teaspoon red pepper flakes
- ½ cup (80 g) cooked pearled barley (see Hot Takes)

MAKE THE KIELBASA

1 Prepare four 10-inch (25 cm) squares of alumimum foil lined with parchment for wrapping and steaming. Prepare your steamer.

2 In a blender, pulse the garlic to get it chopped up a bit. Add the sun-dried tomatoes, 1⅓ cups (315 ml) water, the olive oil, tamari, sugar, and salt. Blend until relatively smooth; some flecks of tomato are a-OK.

3 In a large bowl, mix together the vital wheat gluten, nutritional yeast, onion powder, garlic powder, cloves, marjoram, black pepper, and red pepper flakes. Make a well in the center. Add the mix in the blender into the center of the well. Add the cooked barley as well. Now combine the wet ingredients with the dry and knead for 5 minutes until it feels springy.

HOT TAKES

Smoked sun-dried tomatoes definitely up the game here, however, you can make some tweaks if you don't have that ingredient. Use regular sun-dried tomatoes, not the kind in oil. Make sure they are plump and not dried out. And add 2 teaspoons smoked paprika.

The barley needs to be cooked before making the recipe. You can cook ¼ cup (50 g) in ample water for about 20 minutes. Drain and it's ready! But a better idea is to make a whole pot of barley and have it for use another time!

CONTINUED →

FOR THE CABBAGE SKILLET:

- 3 tablespoons olive oil
- 4 kielbasa, each sliced on a bias into about 5 pieces
- 1 cup baby carrots, sliced in half on a bias
- 1 yellow onion, thinly sliced
- 6 cloves garlic, minced
- 6 cups sliced cabbage (about 1 pound/910 g)
- ½ teaspoon salt
- ½ teaspoon ground black pepper
- 2 cups (480 ml) vegetable broth
- 2 tablespoons tomato paste
- 2 tablespoons grainy Dijon mustard
- ¼ cup (13 g) chopped fresh dill, plus additional sprigs for serving

4 Divide the dough into 4 equal parts. An easy way to do this is to split the dough in half and then into quarters. Roll each piece of dough into a ball then mold and roll it into about a 6-inch (15 cm) sausage shape. Wrap each one in parchment-lined foil, twisting the ends like a Tootsie Roll. Don't worry too much about reshaping the dough, it will snap into shape while it's steaming.

5 Place the wrapped sausages in the steamer and steam for 40 minutes, turning once. Let cool completely before using.

MAKE THE CABBAGE SKILLET

1 Preheat a large wok or skillet over medium high. Sear the sliced kielbasa in 1 tablespoon of the olive oil, flipping often, until golden, about 5 minutes. Remove from the pan and set aside to add back later.

2 Add the remaining 2 tablespoons of oil to the skillet. Sear the carrots for about 10 minutes. Add the onions and cook for 15 minutes until golden. Add the garlic and sauté until fragrant, about 30 seconds.

3 Add the cabbage, salt, and pepper and cook until it wilts, about 15 more minutes. Add the broth along with the tomato paste, mustard, and dill. Turn the heat up to reduce the liquid, about 5 minutes. Toss the sausage back in to heat through. Serve with mashed potatoes or crusty bread. Sprinkle with fresh dill sprigs.

C4 | SUNDAY, OCTOBER 3, 2021
BRIEFLY
VOLLEYBALL
SPORTS
NEBRASKA
EVAN BLAND
World-Herald Staff Writer
Outfield work

TRUMPET MUSHROOM BACON

Makes about 1 quart (960 ml)

Let's get smoking! Investing in a stovetop smoker is worth it for this bacon alone. The ingredients are minimal because the trumpet mushrooms do the heavy lifting. They soak up smoky flavor, buckling just right. Crisp in some spots, chewy in others. What in the world did we do to deserve these miraculous fungi? Use in sandwiches—Join the Club Turki Sandwiches (page 19) are a great example. Toss into salads. Throw into a burrito. Top off a split pea soup. But who are we kidding, you know where to use bacon! Basically on everything.

- 1 pound (455 g) trumpet mushrooms
- 2 to 3 tablespoons olive oil
- ¾ teaspoons salt
- 3 tablespoons nutritional yeast flakes
- Stovetop smoker
- Applewood smoke chips, soaked in water for an hour

1 Slice the caps off the mushroom and reserve for another use. Very thinly slice the stems lengthwise, less than ⅛ inch thick if possible.

2 In a large bowl, toss the mushrooms in enough oil to coat and add the salt. Let rest for 30 minutes so that the mushrooms release moisture. If they seem dry about halfway through, mix in another tablespoon of oil.

3 Set up your smoker with the applewood chips and have it ready, smoking and on low heat. (See "Specialty Equipment and Accoutrements," page 14, for more info on stovetop smokers.)

4 Place the mushrooms in the smoker. It's OK if they are not in a single layer. Cover the smoker and let smoke for 5 minutes. Turn the heat off completely and continue to smoke for 10 minutes.

5 Meanwhile, preheat the oven to 350°F (175°C). Line two large baking sheets with parchment paper.

6 Remove the mushrooms from the smoker and place them in a single layer on the baking sheets. Bake for 15 minutes. Remove from the oven and flip the bacon. Rotate the pans and bake for 15 minutes more. The bacon should be somewhat crispy.

7 Remove from the oven and sprinkle both sides of the bacon with the nutritional yeast, then bake for 8 to 10 more minutes. The bacon slices should be crispy and chewy. Serve warm.

HOT TAKE

I KNOW! Trumpet mushrooms are so darn expensive. King oyster mushrooms are sometimes cheaper and easier to find. They work great here, too. Since you aren't using the caps in this recipe, save them (and any mushroom scraps) to grill or sauté for salads or pasta.

TEMPEH BACON

Makes 8 ounces (225 g)

- **2 tablespoons pure maple syrup**
- **2 tablespoons tamari**
- **2 tablespoons olive oil**
- **2 tablespoons smoked paprika**
- **8 ounces (225 g) tempeh, cut widthwise into ¼-inch slices**

The first time I ever tried tempeh, or vegan bacon, was back in the Rubik's Cube decade. You could find tempeh bacon at every healthfood store and every vegan brunch. We could not get enough of it, and honestly I still can't. Is the texture like bacon? No. But does it taste just like bacon? Still no. Tempeh bacon is not fooling anyone. But who cares? It is so smoky, toothsome, crispy, and satisfying that none of that even matters. Tempeh bacon is in its own lane, thriving. Do not hesitate to make a double batch, because you will absolutely use it in a million ways: Make a classic TLA (Tempeh Lettuce Avocado), serve it warm or cold in a salad, snack on it all day, top a pasta, serve with a scramble. Get ready to party like it's 1989!

1. In a wide shallow bowl, whisk together the maple syrup, tamari, olive oil, and smoked paprika. Add the tempeh slices and marinate for at least 20 minutes and up to an hour.
2. When the tempeh has marinated, preheat a large nonstick pan (cast-iron preferred) over medium heat. Spray the pan with a little cooking spray. Pan-fry the tempeh in a single layer for about 10 minutes, until slightly blackened in some spots, flipping occasionally with a thin metal spatula and adding splashes of marinade as you cook. Serve warm or chilled.

RIBBONY SEITAN BACON

Makes 20 bacon slices

Let me take you back to the decade when vegan bacon broke: the 2010s. Our hair was streaked, as was our bacon. Vegans everywhere began to ask, "If I don't photograph this food, is it even vegan?" and our bacon started looking like . . . bacon! I wish I could give credit where credit is due, but I have no idea what pioneer first thought to make two different colored seitans and combine them. I tip my hat to you, whoever you are. The fake meat version uses tapioca powder for stretchiness, smoked paprika for—you got it—smoke, and red miso and tomato paste for tang, saltiness, and color. It's steamed, sliced, seared, and ready for its close-up.

1 Prepare a steaming apparatus.

2 You'll make two separate doughs. Start with the pink dough: Add the vital wheat gluten, tapioca flour, nutritional yeast, onion powder, smoked paprika, and white pepper in a medium mixing bowl. Whisk to combine and form a well in the center.

3 Combine the liquids for the pink dough. In a small bowl, measure out ½ cup (120 ml) water, the tamari, olive oil, tomato paste, and miso. Whisk until cohesive, making sure to break up the miso and tomato paste. Add the wet mixture to the center of the dry ingredients. Work it in with your hands until it turns into a red dough, then knead for about 2 minutes to develop the gluten. Set aside.

4 Now make the white dough (for those light bacon fatty streaks): In a small bowl, combine the vital wheat gluten, tapioca flour, garlic powder, and salt. Whisk together and form a little well in the center.

5 Mix the liquids for the white streaks: In a measuring cup measure out 3 tablespoons water, the olive oil, rice vinegar, and sugar. Whisk to help the sugar dissolve then add to the center of the dry well. This dough will be wetter than the pink dough, so rather than having everything stuck to your hands, use a spoon to mix it all together.

FOR THE PINK SEITAN:

- 1 cup (120 g) vital wheat gluten
- ¼ cup (35 g) tapioca flour
- ¼ cup (15 g) nutritional yeast flakes
- 2 teaspoons onion powder
- 2 teaspoons smoked paprika
- ½ teaspoon ground white pepper
- 3 tablespoons tamari
- 2 tablespoons olive oil
- 2 tablespoons tomato paste
- 1 tablespoon red miso

FOR THE LIGHT STREAKS:

- ⅓ cup (40 g) vital wheat gluten
- 2 tablespoons tapioca flour
- 1 teaspoon garlic powder
- 1 teaspoon salt
- 1 tablespoon olive oil
- 1 tablespoon rice vinegar
- 1 teaspoon granulated sugar

ALSO:

- Olive oil or cooking spray, for cooking

CONTINUED →

TIME TO ASSEMBLE THE BACON LOAF!

1 Prepare an 18-inch (46 cm) piece of aluminum foil and cover that with a 12-inch (30 cm) square of parchment. Spray with cooking oil and set aside.

2 Divide the pink dough into 3 pieces. They don't need to be perfectly even, just eyeball it. Divide the white dough into 2 pieces. On a clean surface, spread one pink dough piece into a 6 by 8-inch (15 by 20 cm) rectangle. You can use a rolling pin but spreading it with your hands works just as well. If it's a little rough, that's fine! It'll look more natural and bacon-y that way.

3 Now take 1 piece of white dough and roughly spread it over the pink meat rectangle to cover. Make another pink dough rectangle and place it on top of the white layer. Spread the last white layer on top and then cover with the remaining pink meat dough for a third and final layer.

4 Shape and smoosh the loaf together a bit but keep it flat and rectangular. Place in the center of the prepared parchment and foil and wrap it up, but not too tightly. It will expand as it cooks.

5 Steam for 1 hour, then let rest in its wrapper for 20 minutes. Refrigerate to cool completely. When cool, unwrap the bacon loaf and slice it lengthwise into ⅛-inch-thick strips.

6 Preheat a large cast-iron pan over medium heat. Add a thin layer of olive oil or an ample amount of cooking spray. Sear the bacon strips in batches (whatever will fit without crowding the pan) for about 1 minute on each side until lightly browned.

HOT TAKE

Smoked paprika gets the job done, but this seitan is especially bangin' if you go all out and smoke it instead! If you'd like to give that a shot, replace the smoked paprika with sweet paprika. After slicing the seitan, layer the strips into the smoker and smoke on medium heat for 5 minutes. Turn the heat off and let smoke for 5 more minutes. Now go ahead and start your own seitan bacon business. (See "Specialty Equipment and Accoutrements," page 14, for more info on stovetop smokers.)

PANTRY MUSHROOM BACON

Makes 1 cup (65 g)

This recipe calls for a special talent: laziness. It begs you to take shortcuts. It insists you use as few ingredients as possible. It tells you to relax as it bakes in the oven. It even requires mushrooms that have already been sliced. And the results are incredibly and unfairly amazing. They taste like you smoked them for days in a vintage smoker that your grandpappy and his grandpappy before him used. Kinda. It's mushroom bacon. It's crispy, it's salty, it's smoky. Put it on everything, if you can muster the energy. Another bonus is that this bacon can be stored at room temperature. It dehydrates as it bakes, with results similar to a jerky.

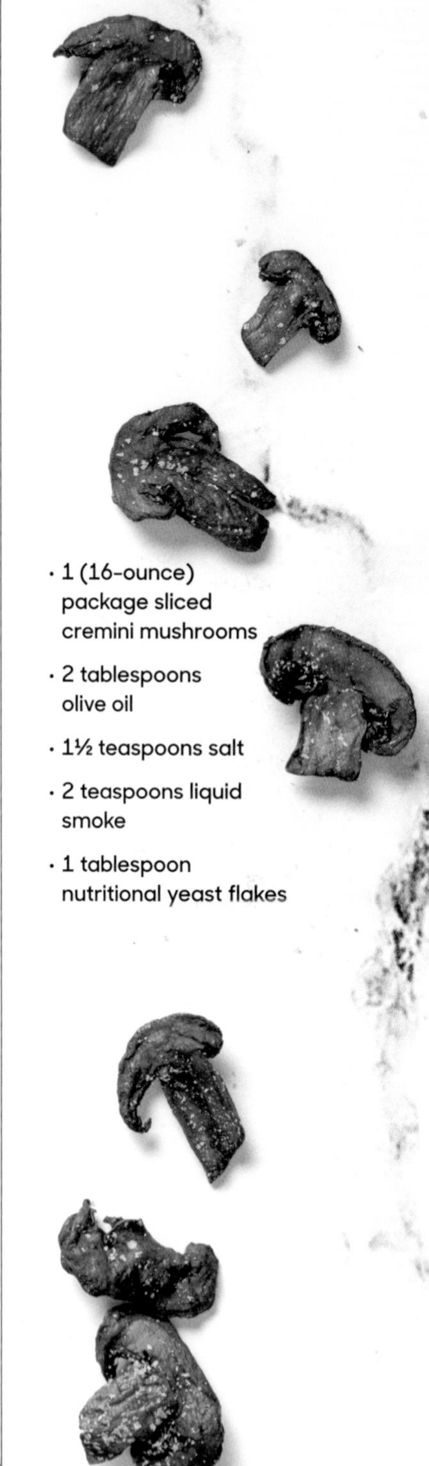

- 1 (16-ounce) package sliced cremini mushrooms
- 2 tablespoons olive oil
- 1½ teaspoons salt
- 2 teaspoons liquid smoke
- 1 tablespoon nutritional yeast flakes

1. Toss the mushrooms with the olive oil and salt in a medium bowl. Let sit for 1 hour until they release their juices.
2. Preheat the oven to 350°F (175°C) and line a baking sheet with parchment paper.
3. Drain the mushroom of excess liquid in a colander and return them to the mixing bowl. Sprinkle with liquid smoke and toss to coat.
4. Transfer the mushrooms to prepared baking sheet and spread out in a single layer. Bake for 30 minutes, stirring the mushrooms halfway through. Remove from the oven and lower the temperature to 325°F (165°C).
5. Sprinkle the mushrooms with nutritional yeast and use a thin spatula to toss to coat. Bake for another 15 minutes. The mushrooms should be crispy and firm.
6. Let cool on the baking sheet before using. They can be stored at room temperature in an airtight container for up to 3 days.

BEET'KIN BITS

Makes 2 cups

Did I just make beet-based bacon bits so that I could invent the word "Beet'kin"? Maybe. But these also happen to be exactly what you want to sprinkle on salads, of course, and on loaded baked potatoes with So Very Sour Cream (page 200), over split pea soup and any pasta that calls for a crunchy, salty flourish. These are bursts of smoky flavor that taste like an autumnal campsite (in a good way). Beets are grated and baked crisp, then smoked in cheesecloth. They make a wonderful little gift for the holidays! Get yourself a cute jar and write Beet'kin Bits on craft tape then watch your Secret Santa become putty in your hands. These bits store well at room temp for about a week if they've been dehydrated enough. However, if they feel especially moist, I recommend storing in the fridge for a week or so.

- **3 pounds (390 g) beets, peeled**
- **2 tablespoons olive oil**
- **1½ teaspoons salt**
- **Wood chips for smoking**

1. Preheat the oven to 325°F (165°C) and prepare a large rimmed baking sheet with parchment paper. Lightly spray with cooking oil.
2. Grate beets with a food processor or by hand and place on baking sheet. Toss with olive oil and salt. Spread out into a thin layer.
3. Bake beets for about an hour, stirring every 20 minutes.
4. While beets are baking, set up a smoker (page 14) and prepare about 16 inches (40 cm) of double-layered cheesecloth. Wet the cheesecloth and ring out excess water, then use it to line the perforated portion of your smoking apparatus.
5. Remove beet bits from oven and transfer to the smoker. Turn heat to high and smoke for 4 minutes (from the time they start smoking). Turn off heat and let sit, covered, for another 4 minutes.
6. Lift the cheesecloth out of the smoke table and shake the beet'kin bits back onto the baking sheet. Allow the beet'kin bits to cool fully before storing.

Beet Kin

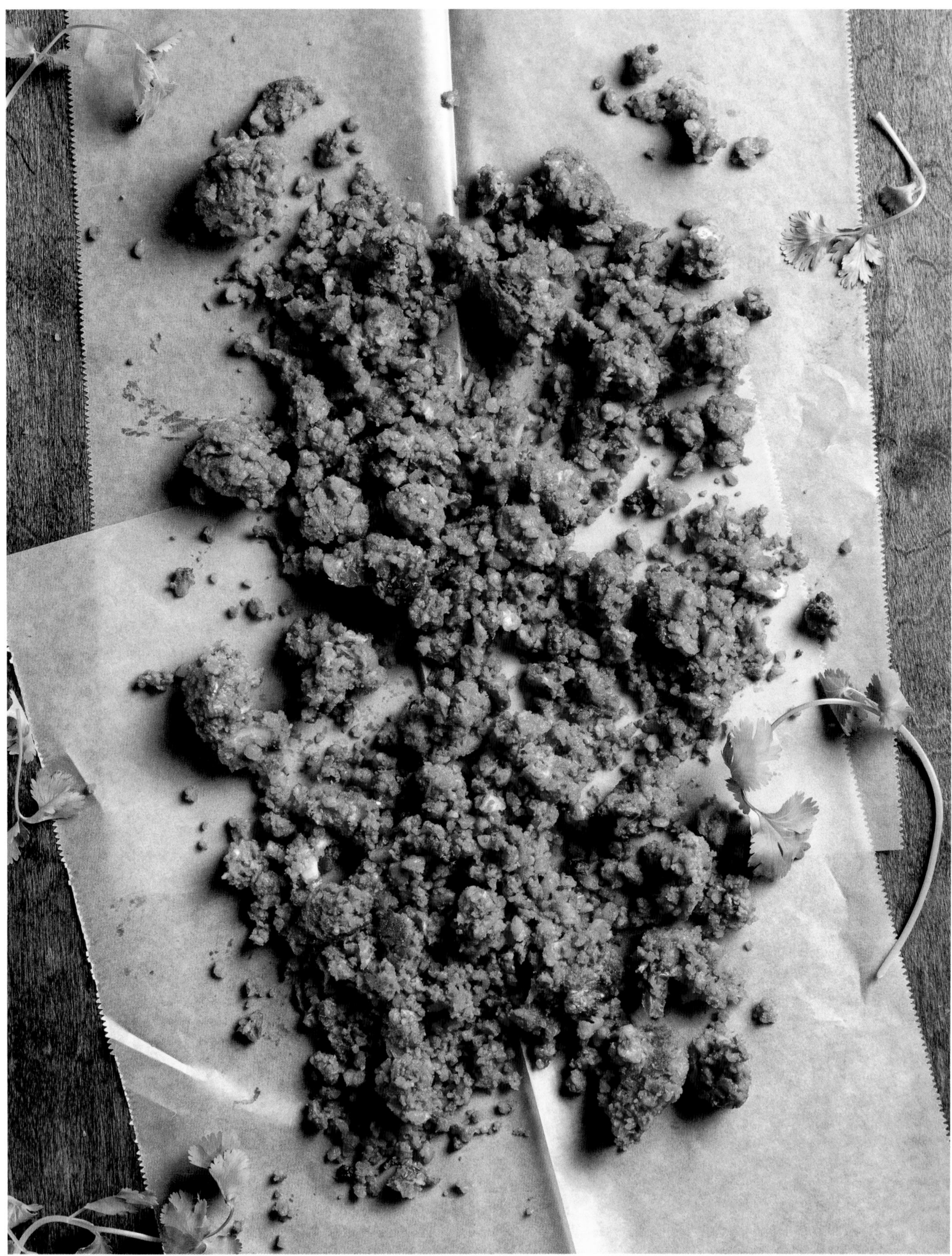

WALNUT SUN-DRIED TOMATO CHORIZO

Makes about 4 cups (475 g)

This chorizo is a wake-up call for any dish that needs a Spanish flair. Scramble, yes, but don't stop there. I think of it as the little black dress of vegan sausage; you can wear it anywhere. Use it to spice up pasta, over roasted potatoes, in taco salads, or over avocados with some spicy chili oil. Check out the Hot Take for more ideas! It's tangy and smoky and has a meaty bite that might even have you sneaking spoonfuls of it by itself in the middle of the night. Use warm or chilled. Fresh cilantro is a nice garnish but not totally necessary.

- 2 cloves garlic
- 3 cups (300 g) walnuts
- 1 small yellow onion, roughly chopped
- 6 sun-dried tomatoes in oil (about ⅓ cup/35 g tightly packed, including the oil)
- 1 tablespoon apple cider vinegar
- 2 teaspoons smoked paprika
- 1½ teaspoons ground cumin
- ⅛ teaspoon cayenne pepper
- ¾ teaspoon salt
- Fresh cilantro for garnish

1 Preheat the oven to 350°F (175°C). Line a large baking sheet with parchment paper and set aside.

2 In a food processor fitted with a metal blade, pulse the garlic until it's chopped. Add the walnuts and pulse to coarse crumbs. Add the onion and pulse again to chop.

3 Add the sun-dried tomatoes with their oil, along with the apple cider vinegar, paprika, cumin, cayenne, and salt. Pulse until all the ingredients are incorporated and resemble crumbled meat. You don't want to puree it, but don't leave large chunks of anything either. Pieces should be no larger than, let's say, a pea.

4 Spread the mixture out on the prepared baking sheet and bake for 10 minutes. Remove from the oven and it's ready to use!

HOT TAKE

MORE CHORIZO IDEAS:

- With a Fried Egg (page 56), hot sauce, and breakfast potatoes
- In a taco with all the fixins
- Or a taco salad!
- Over Spicy Clam Bar Linguine (page 185)
- Or pasta with regular old marinara
- With rice and beans
- On pizza
- As a filling for empanadas
- In queso
- In an omelet with spinach and cheese

PASTA AND NOODLES

I have a healthy addiction to noodles in every size, shape, and form. Sometimes I don't even know what I'll be making for dinner, but I put a pot of salted water on the stove and at some point, between slicing some onions and meditating on my space rack, inspiration hits.

These recipes are versatile and, for the most part, easy enough to throw together. For some, you'll need to have your fake meats ready. But by now you should always have a nice little collection of Chick'n or Pepperoni. Meanwhile, some come together right in the recipe, using ingredients like tempeh or lentils.

But often, it's all about the sauce. In this section, we will be creating depth of flavor, quickly and deliciously, whether it's with wines, miso, herbs, or some combination of all the above. The chapter is also very cream oriented, because that's often the most challenging part of cooking vegan. If you're craving creamy, we will get you there.

And let's also address the elephant in the room. There are thirteen recipes in this section, and three are for mac and cheese. But I couldn't help myself, and neither should you.

MEATBALL & SPAGHETTI NIGHT

Serves 4

One might say every night is meatball and spaghetti night and actually mean it. So perhaps we should call the other nights "non-meatball and spaghetti night." Now that we've established the importance of meatballs, every cook needs that one meatball recipe that they know by heart. It should be easy and require minimal dishes and ingredients, but, above all, it should be the best meatballs you've ever had. I hope that this is that meatball for you. It comes together in one bowl, using vital wheat gluten, tofu and Italian herbs, rolled between your palms into perfect little orbs and cooked to pan-fried perfection. Then you hit it with some broth and braise to cook all the way through. Of course these are perfect for spaghetti and meatballs, but play around with the recipe to "meat" all of your meatball-y needs.

FOR THE PASTA:

- 1 pound spaghetti
- 1 recipe Best Friend's Mom's Marinara (page 306) or 32 ounces prepared marinara

FOR THE BRAISED MEATBALLS:

- 1 (14-ounce/400 g) block extra-firm tofu, pressed for 1 hour
- 2 tablespoons vegan mayo, store-bought or homemade (page 309)
- 2 tablespoons tomato paste
- 2 tablespoons red miso
- 2 tablespoons nutritional yeast flakes
- 1 tablespoon tamari
- 1 teaspoon agave syrup
- 2 tablespoons dried onion flakes (or dried minced onion)
- 2 teaspoons garlic powder
- 1 teaspoon oregano
- 1 teaspoon dried thyme
- 1 teaspoon dried basil
- ½ teaspoon ground black pepper
- ½ teaspoon red pepper flakes
- 1 cup vital wheat gluten
- Olive oil for cooking
- 1 cup Beefy Broth (page 302) or prepared vegetable broth
- ¼ cup fresh chopped basil, for garnish

1. In a large mixing bowl mash the tofu as much as you can so that it resembles ricotta cheese but a little but smoother, with no large chunks. Use your hands to do the mashing. Mix in the mayo, tomato paste, miso, nutritional yeast, tamari, agave, onion flakes, garlic powder, oregano, thyme, basil, black pepper, and red pepper flakes.
2. Mush everything together with your hands, getting it really well incorporated, about 2 minutes. Add in the vital wheat gluten and knead for about 3 minutes.
3. Roll into ping-pong-size balls and place on a large dinner plate. Refrigerate for about 20 minutes.
4. Preheat a large skillet over medium-low heat. Pour a healthy layer of olive oil into the pan just to coat the bottom nicely.
5. Place the meatballs in the pan one by one, giving them a little spin to coat them in oil.
6. Cook for about 15 minutes, using a thin spatula to roll the balls around, cooking and browning them on all sides.
7. Turn the heat up for about 3 minutes. The pan needs to be hot for the braise. Have a lid for the pan at the ready.
8. Add the broth and immediately cover the pan. It should steam wildly. Let cook for about 2 minutes.
9. Lower the heat to medium, spin the balls, cover the pan again and cook for about 15 more minutes, turning often. Serve immediately, garnished with fresh basil.

SCALLOP DRUNKEN NOODLES

Serves 4

If I see vegan drunken noodles on a menu, I order them. Thick rice noodles, hanging from my fork like a delicious drape, dripping with a dark, spicy, slightly sweet, very savory, soy sauce. This version combines pork and seafood—two very forbidden foods from my Hebrew school days, which makes it even more appealing to me. Textured vegetable protein acts like ground pork, coating the noodles so the sauce clings to every scrumptious bite. Trumpet mushrooms are easily transformed into scallops—the chewiness just can't be beat. And although I hesitate to use vegetables in this cookbook (only slightly kidding), I couldn't resist adding some charred asparagus. This recipe isn't what I'd call difficult, but it's definitely impress-your-date material. Or impress your mom, or personal stylist, or whoever happens to be dropping by.

1 Blend all ingredients for the sauce together. You can also do this in a mixing bowl with a fork, but the blender is faster and smoother. A small blender, like a Magic Bullet, works really well.

2 In a small pot, submerge the textured vegetable protein in 3 cups (700 ml) water. Bring to a boil, simmer for 5 minutes, and drain. Set aside.

3 Bring a large pot of water to boil for the noodles. Cook al dente according to package directions and be careful not to overcook. Once cooked, place in a colander and rinse with very cold water. Place back in the pot and fill with ice and cold water, separating the noodles with your hands, to make sure they are cooled down. Drain in the colander again and set aside.

4 Preheat a large wok over medium high heat. Melt 1 tablespoon of coconut oil in the pan and sprinkle in a big pinch of salt. Cook asparagus for about 5 minutes, flipping often until seared but still crunchy. Remove from wok and set aside.

5 Now start the stirfry in the same pan. Lower heat to medium. Cook the garlic in the remaining oil to briefly toast, about 30 seconds. Add bell peppers, red onion, and red pepper flakes. Cook for about 5 minutes, to sear and soften.

6 Add the sauce and bring to a low simmer. Add the basil to wilt.

7 Add scallops and use tongs to toss to coat. Then add noodles and cook through. Fold in the asparagus.

8 Serve hot and immediately! Garnish with peanuts, radishes, basil, and lime.

- ½ cup textured vegetable protein
- 16 ounces wide rice noodles
- 12 ice cubes to make ice water

FOR THE SAUCE:

- 6 tablespoons red miso paste
- 2 teaspoons kelp powder
- ½ cup tamari
- ⅓ cup brown sugar
- ¾ cups Bay Broth (page 303) or prepared vegetable broth, plus more to thin

FOR THE STIR-FRY:

- 3 tablespoons refined coconut oil, divided
- ½ pound asparagus spears, cut into 2-inch (5 cm) pieces
- ¼ cup (45 g) sliced garlic
- ½ cup sliced bell peppers
- 1 large red onion, quartered and sliced
- 1 teaspoon red pepper flakes
- 1 cup loosely packed fresh basil leaves
- 8 ounces (225 g) Trumpet Mushroom Scallops (page 184), cooked

FOR GARNISH:

- 1 cup (150 g) roasted peanuts, finely chopped
- ½ cup matchstick-cut watermelon radishes
- Fresh basil leaves
- Lime wedges

HOT TAKES

The Drunken Noodles call for 8 ounces (225 g) mushrooms, but that means to weigh them once they have been trimmed. So you may need a full pound of the mushrooms to get suitable-size scallops. Do not fret. Simply use the scraps for another day. Gravy? Scramble?

Wide rice noodles are a must for this recipe! You can use rice sticks or rice fettuccine. If you absolutely must you can use the widest pad thai noodles you can find. It's very important to cook the noodles al dente and cool them immediately so that they don't turn to mush during the stir-fry process. Follow the directions in the recipe and it'll be fine!

You might also decide you want a different drunken noodles. Chick'n? Be'ef? No prob. Simple sauté half a pound (225 g) of the fake meat of your dreams before beginning the stir-fry and toss back in at the end.

TRUMPET MUSHROOM SCALLOPS:

A VEGAN ORIGIN STORY AND HOW-TO

Many moons ago, vegans figured out that if you slice trumpet mushroom stems into thick disks and then use a knife to create little crosshatch thingies, you have sea scallops. Much like the cavemen discovered fire, vegans discovered this. Early vegans gathered around trumpet mushrooms like the chimps at the beginning of *2001: A Space Odyssey*. Now trumpet mushrooms are fairly easy to find. I am going to make this its own little section because, really, you can use it in so many different ways. It's not quite a recipe, more of a handy method.

First, trim the mushrooms so that you remove the cap and any thin part of the stem. Reserve those for another use! Each scallop should range in circumference from about quarter-size to silver dollar-size and anywhere in between.

Slice the stems into about 1-inch-thick (2.5 cm) discs. Then score the tops of the discs in a crosshatch pattern, piercing the skin as little as possible, ideally less than one-eighth of an inch. This is a very satisfying process and even more gratifying when you see how beautifully the pattern crisps up, and how much flavor it will now absorb.

The most simple prep method: Preheat a cast-iron pan over medium-high. Cook the trumpet mushroom scallops in a thin layer of refined coconut oil and a sprinkle of salt for about 7 minutes on each side, until golden and gorgeous. Now serve them however you like! With a sauce, over a stir-fry or pasta, or as a fancy hors d'oeuvre.

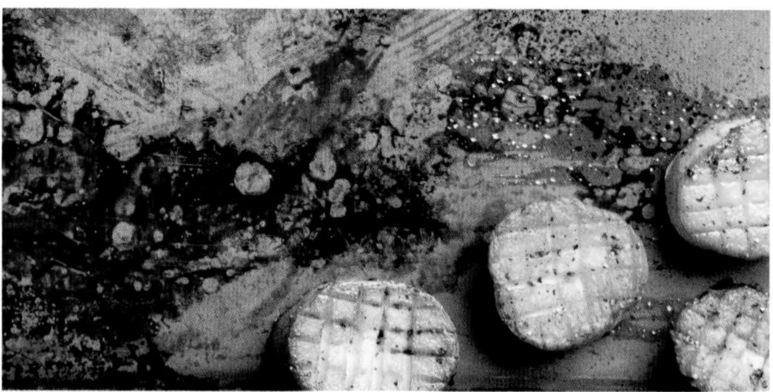

SPICY CLAM BAR LINGUINE

Serves 4

A spicy, garlicky, lemony pasta with chewy bits and whole clams scattered on top. That's how I remember this dish at clam bars in Sheepshead Bay. And sometimes I've missed it. But what if the clamshells on top were . . . edible? The part of my brain that processes vegan versions of things started to tingle. Potatoes. Sliced into ovals. Crispy like clamshells but you can eat them. And once again I get to put potatoes in pasta, which is my favorite pastime. To re-create the chewy parts, I used the classic trick of shiitake mushrooms equal any seafood. And the addition of lentils lends texture while soaking in flavor. Try to get potatoes that are between 2 and 3 inches (5 and 7.5 cm) long so they resemble clamshells. Any bigger and you will want to halve them before you thinly slice. When arranging them to serve, you can even put two together and have them sticking out like an open clamshell. Too cute!

FOR THE POTATO CLAM SHELLS:

- **12 ounces (340 g) Yukon gold potatoes, cut lengthwise into ¼-inch-thick slices**
- **3 tablespoons olive oil**
- **½ teaspoon salt**

1 For the clamshells, first roast the potatoes: Preheat the oven to 425°F (220°C). Line a baking sheet with parchment paper. Put the sliced potatoes in a bowl with enough cold water to submerge them. Let them soak for a minute or so to rinse off the starch. Drain completely and dry with paper towels as best you can.

2 Drizzle the baking sheet with the olive oil and salt. Add the potatoes and toss them around to get them coated in the oil, then arrange them into a single layer. Bake for 30 minutes, flipping once, until browned and crispy.

CONTINUED →

FOR THE REST:

- ½ teaspoon salt plus more as required
- 8 ounces (225 g) linguine
- 3 tablespoons olive oil
- 12 ounces (340 g) shiitake mushrooms, stems trimmed, caps sliced in half
- ¼ cup (45 g) sliced garlic plus 4 cloves minced garlic
- 1 onion, thinly sliced
- 2 tablespoons nutritional yeast flakes
- 1½ cups (220 g) cherry or grape tomatoes
- 2 bay leaves
- 2 tablespoons chopped fresh thyme
- ½ teaspoon red pepper flakes, plus more to finish
- ½ teaspoon kelp powder
- ¼ teaspoon dried oregano
- 1 cup (240 ml) dry white wine
- Generous amount freshly ground black pepper
- 1 cup (240 ml) vegetable broth
- ¾ cup (140 g) cooked brown lentils
- 2 tablespoons fresh lemon juice, plus more to finish
- ¼ cup (13 g) very finely chopped parsley, plus additional for garnish

3 In the meantime, prepare everything else: Bring 6 quarts (5.7 liters) salted water to a boil in a large pot. Boil the pasta until al dente according to package directions, then drain and set aside.

4 Preheat a large sauté pan over medium heat. Add 1 tablespoon of the oil and sear the mushrooms for about 5 minutes, sprinkling them with a little salt and tossing frequently. Remove from the heat and set aside.

5 Sauté the sliced garlic in the remaining 2 tablespoons oil and cook for about 1 minute until lightly browned. Add the onion and a pinch of salt and toss to coat. Cook until onion is translucent, about 5 minutes.

6 Add the minced garlic and sauté for about 3 seconds more. Then add the nutritional yeast and toss to coat, lightly toasting it for about 1 minute to bring out the flavor.

7 Add the tomatoes to the pan and toss around, letting them break down a bit for about 2 minutes. Add the bay leaves, fresh thyme, red pepper flakes, kelp powder, ½ teaspoon salt, and the oregano. Stream in the wine and toss everything around with a wooden spatula to deglaze the pan. Raise the heat and add a generous amount of freshly ground black pepper as the wine reduces and the tomatoes break down a bit, about 3 minutes.

8 Lower the heat back down to medium and add the veggie broth and lentils to heat through. Add the lemon juice and parsley and mix well. Return the mushrooms to the pan along with the linguine and let cook for about 3 minutes.

9 Place on a serving platter family-style and stick the potatoes strategically into the pasta swirls so that they resemble clam shells. Sprinkle with a little additional parsley and finish with plenty of lemon juice and more red pepper flakes.

CURRY UDON
WITH POTATO & CHICK'N

Serves 4

Q: What makes carbs even better? A: More carbs. I have a thing for noodles and potatoes together in every shape and form. This particular craving is based on one of my favorite Thai restaurants in Omaha. On the menu, it's called Southern Noodles. A creamy, spicy coconut curry with hints of star anise, smothered all over udon noodles, potatoes and tofu. Sautéed scallions are a must in this. Potatoes are roasted for maximum flavor, relaxing in the oven, while you prepare the sauce. Everything comes together like a carby dream! Sometimes I add broccoli to the mix, so sauté a little up separately if you're feeling green urges, then toss into the noodles when they're finished.

- 2 average-size russet potatoes, peeled and diced ½ inch
- 3 tablespoons olive oil, divided
- ½ teaspoon salt
- ½ teaspoon black pepper
- 10 ounces udon noodles
- 1 bunch scallions
- 3 cups Pull-Apart Seitan Chick'n (page 115), torn into bite-size pieces
- 2 tablespoons refined coconut oil
- 1 teaspoon minced fresh ginger
- 3 cloves garlic, minced
- 1 tablespoon curry powder
- 4 star anise pods
- 1 cup Chick'n Broth (page 299) or prepared vegetable broth
- 1 (15-ounce/445 ml) can coconut milk
- 1 tablespoon tamari
- 1 tablespoon sriracha

FOR GARNISH:

- ½ cup fresh cilantro sprigs
- Lime wedges to serve

1. First, roast the potatoes. Preheat the oven to 425°F (220°C). Place the potatoes in a large bowl and rinse them with cold water. Use paper towels to pat them completely dry. On a baking sheet lined with parchment, drizzle the potatoes with olive oil, sprinkle with salt and pepper, and toss to coat. You can finish it off with some spray oil to close the deal. Cook for about 20 minutes, tossing twice. Set aside once cooked. They will be tossed into the pan with everything else eventually.
2. Bring 4 quarts of water to a boil in a large pot. Boil noodles al dente according to package directions.
3. To prepare the scallions, thinly slice the white and light green parts. When you get to the dark green, slice them into large 1-inch pieces. Set the large pieces aside.
4. Preheat a large heavy-bottomed pan over medium heat. Sauté the chicken in 1 tablespoon coconut oil to brown, about 7 minutes. Use a little cooking spray if needed. Transfer to a plate and set aside.
5. Sauté ginger, garlic, and light slices of scallion in 1 tablespoon coconut oil, for about 2 minutes. Add the curry powder and star anise and toss to toast, about 1 minute. Add the vegetable broth to deglaze the pan. Then add coconut milk, tamari, sriracha, and the dark green scallion pieces.
6. Bring to a simmer for about 10 minutes. Add the potatoes and chick'n to the sauce and toss to coat, then add the noodles and toss again. Cook for 5 minutes or so, thinning with broth if needed. Discard the anise pods.
7. Transfer to wide bowls and garnish with cilantro and lime.

HOT TAKE

Rinsing potatoes before roasting seems like an extra step that might not be worth the effort, but listen: It is! The potatoes will get so golden and crispy you won't believe your taste buds. So take the extra step, be rewarded, and thank me later.

CACIO E PEPE E SALSICCIA

Serves 4

Cheese and pepper. And more cheese and pepper. And also, while we are at it, even MORE cheese and pepper, please! Cacio e Pepe is the hotness, and re-creating the flavors, vegan style, is child's play. Almonds for cheesy texture. Cashews for creamy richness. Nooch and miso—the usual tricks—for that cheesy bite. And then, wow, lucky us, black pepper is already vegan! Now let's up the ante with sausage. I crave tempeh sausage and that's what I used for most of my vegan life until other things were invented. This is a useful recipe because it's a weeknight-type meal that will certainly sneak its way into regular rotation when everyone is like I WANT CHEESE AND PEPPER, BUT I WANT SAUSAGE TOO BECAUSE I DESERVE THE VERY BEST. As a bonus, it doubles well. Serve with a simple little arugula salad, like I usually do. The Parmesan is a nice addition if you're up for it, but not totally necessary if it's, say, just a normal Tuesday.

- 8 ounces (225 g) linguine
- Salt, for cooking the pasta

FOR THE TEMPEH SAUSAGE:

- 16 ounces (455 g) tempeh
- 2 tablespoons olive oil, plus a little extra
- 4 cloves garlic, chopped
- 1 teaspoon chopped fennel seed
- ¼ teaspoon ground sage
- ½ teaspoon dried thyme
- ½ teaspoon onion powder
- 1 teaspoon smoked paprika
- ¼ teaspoon red pepper flakes
- 1 teaspoon apple cider vinegar
- 2 tablespoons tamari

FOR THE SAUCE:

- ½ cup (50 g) slivered almonds
- ½ cup (60 g) whole unroasted cashews
- 1 tablespoon mellow white miso
- 1 tablespoon olive oil
- 1 tablespoon fresh lemon juice
- ¼ cup (15 g) nutritional yeast flakes
- ½ teaspoon salt
- 1 teaspoon ground black pepper, plus extra for garnish
- Vegan Parmesan, prepared or homemade (page 285) (optional)

1 Cook the pasta in salted water according to package directions. Once cooked al dente, drain and set aside until ready to use.

2 Make the sausage: Preheat a cast-iron pan over medium heat. Crumble tempeh into bite-size pieces. Sauté the tempeh in 2 tablespoons oil until lightly brown, flipping often with a thin, metal spatula, about 15 minutes.

3 Push the tempeh to the side of the pan. Drizzle in a little more olive oil and cook the garlic in the oil for about 15 seconds, then combine it with the tempeh.

4 Add the fennel, sage, thyme, onion powder, smoked paprika, and red pepper flakes and mix. Add ¼ cup (60 ml) water, the apple cider vinegar, and tamari. Sauté for another 10 minutes or so. Add splashes of water if it's sticking to the bottom of the pan. Remove from the heat.

5 Make the sauce: In a high-speed blender, blend the almonds, cashews, 1¾ cups water, the miso, olive oil, lemon juice, nutritional yeast, and salt until relatively smooth. There will be a slightly grainy texture from the almonds.

6 Add the pasta to the tempeh sausage in the pan and toss. Add the sauce and black pepper and cook for about 3 minutes, stirring often, until thick. Serve with additional black pepper.

PASTA CARBONARA

Serves 4

If you think too much about it (and I do), carbonara is basically breakfast for dinner. A thick and silky eggy sauce that clings to the pasta, which is loaded with plenty of vegan bacon. I also incorporate diced tomatoes because they somehow up the classic hammy feel of the dish. In the end, it's a crowd-pleaser and exactly what everyone wants to twirl around their fork. The simple sauce comes together in minutes and can also be used for a vegan eggs Benedict or any dish that's calling out for a hollandaise. You may have some left over so don't be afraid to use it! The bacon choice is yours, although the Ribbony Seitan Bacon provides the most drama.

- 1½ teaspoons salt, plus more for pasta water
- 8 ounces (225 g) fettuccine
- 1 cup (120 g) whole unroasted cashews
- ¾ teaspoon ground turmeric
- 1 teaspoon garlic powder
- 1 teaspoon onion powder
- 1¼ cups (300 ml) vegetable broth
- 2 tablespoons mellow white miso
- 1 teaspoon kala namak
- ¼ cup (15 g) nutritional yeast flakes
- 2 cups (360 g) chopped fresh tomatoes
- 1 tablespoon olive oil

CHOOSE YOUR BACON:

- 1 recipe Trumpet Mushroom Bacon (page 167), lightly warmed
- 1 recipe Ribbony Seitan Bacon (page 171), cut into 1½-inch (4 cm) pieces and sautéed in a little oil for 2 minutes
- 1 recipe Pantry Mushroom Bacon (page 173), lightly warmed

1 Bring 6 quarts (5.7 liter) salted water to a boil in a large pot. Boil the pasta until al dente according to package directions.

2 In a high-speed blender, combine the cashews, turmeric, garlic powder, onion powder, vegetable broth, miso, kala namak, 1 teaspoon salt, and the nutritional yeast. Blend until smooth, about 1½ minutes, scraping down the sides with a rubber spatula once in a while to make sure you get everything.

3 Preheat a large pan over medium heat. Sauté the tomatoes in olive oil with the remaining ½ teaspoon salt, just until warmed through and juicy, about 5 minutes. Do not let them break down too much. Stir the cashew sauce into the tomatoes.

4 When the pasta is ready, drain and add it immediately to the pan. Toss to coat. Fold in half the bacon of your choice, and save the remainder to scatter over each serving.

PEPPERONI MAC & CHEEZE

Serves 6 to 8

Let's just cut to the cheeze. There are a lot of vegan mac recipes out there (and even three in this very book), but this cheeze sauce might just take the noodle. It's nut-free and that's cool in case you have allergies but also I am in love with it. The ease, the rich cheesiness, and the tangy flavor. What's more, the ingredients are so simple: coconut milk, sun-dried tomatoes, miso, nutritional yeast, and onion powder. And that is it. And it is good. Real good. The coconut flavor magically transforms into something completely creamy and savory when blended with these intensely umami flavors. Dice up some pepperoni on top and you are just where you need to be: at the gates of meaty, cheezy heaven. I topped mine with some calabrian chili paste because I like it spicy, but that is optional.

- 1 pound macaroni

FOR THE PEPPERONI:

- ½ cup chopped sun-dried tomatoes with some oil
- 3 Proper Pepperonis (page 149), quartered and diced

FOR THE SAUCE:

- 1 (15-ounce/445 ml) can coconut milk
- ¾ cup sun-dried tomatoes in oil (it was about ¼ cup of oil, if that helps)
- 2 tablespoons miso
- ½ cup (30 g) nutritional yeast flakes
- 2 teaspoons onion powder

TO FINISH:

- Calabrian chili paste (optional)
- 1 cup (40 g) finely chopped fresh basil

1. Preheat a large skillet over medium heat. Use a tablespoon of the sun-dried tomato oil to saute the pepperoni for about 5 minutes, until browned. Set aside until ready to use.
2. Add the chopped sun-dried tomatoes to heat through. Cover to keep warm.
3. Cook noodles al dente in salted water. Drain them and return to the pot.
4. Blend all sauce ingredients until totally smooth.
5. Add the sauce to the noodles. Mix to heat through. Taste for salt.
6. Serve topped with pepperoni, Calabrian chili, and basil.

TRUFFLED LOBSTER MAC & CHEEZE

If baked mac & cheese is your happy place, welcome home, sweetie! This is probably the most traditional of the macs, even with the addition of a little truffle oil. The taste and texture are designed after the kind of mac you can get at a little café in a sleepy coastal town on the Atlantic. It's chewy and gooey and, I don't know, almost fluffy. What's best is it's really very simple—kappa carrageenan gives the sauce that extra oomph, a super-cheezy texture that sets it apart. But it isn't all about the cheese! The lobster is a simple affair, too. Hearts of palm (aka lobster in a can) are breaded, fried, and shredded, then sprinkled with a little Old Bay for that fresh-from-the-sea flair. This will wake up the neighbors in that sleepy little town.

- 1 pound (910 g) macaroni

FOR THE SAUCE:

- 1¾ cup whole unroasted cashews
- 1¾ cups vegetable broth
- ⅓ cup sauerkraut juice
- 4 teaspoons truffle oil
- 4 teaspoons tapioca flour
- ⅓ cup nutritional yeast flakes
- 1 teaspoon onion powder
- 1¼ teaspoons salt
- 1 tablespoon kappa carrageenan

FOR THE HEARTS OF PALM LOBSTER:

- 2 (14-ounce/400 g) cans hearts of palm

1 Preheat the oven to 375°F (190°C). Lightly grease a 9 by 13-inch (23 by 33 cm), or 4-quart, casserole dish. Bring a large pot of salted water to boil for the noodles.

2 Cook the macaroni noodles al dente according to the package instructions. Drain, then add back to the pot they were cooked in.

3 Combine the cashews, vegetable broth, sauerkraut juice, truffle oil, tapioca, nutritional yeast, onion powder, and salt in a high-speed blender. Blend until completely smooth. Let cool for about 5 minutes. Add the carrageenan and blend for 10 seconds to combine it.

4 Reserve about a cup of the mac sauce and set aside. Put the remaining sauce into the pot with the noodles and stir to combine and coat completely. Transfer the saucy noodles to the casserole. Drizzle with the reserved mac sauce and use a rubber spatula to even it out a bit. Bake for 22 to 25 minutes, until lightly browned. Remove from the oven and set aside as you're preparing the lobster.

CONTINUED →

FOR THE SLURRY:

- 3 tablespoons cornstarch
- 1 cup (240 ml) cold unsweetened soy milk
- 1 tablespoon tamari

FOR THE BREADING:

- 2 cups (160 g) panko breadcrumbs
- 1 teaspoon kelp powder
- ½ teaspoon salt

- Safflower oil, for frying

TO SERVE:

- 3 tablespoons thinly sliced chives
- 3 teaspoons Old Bay Seasoning

5 Make the slurry and breading: Scoop the cornstarch into a large mixing bowl, add half the soy milk along with the tamari, and stir well until it's a thick, smooth paste. Mix in the remaining milk. On a large rimmed plate, mix together the panko, kelp powder, and salt.

6 Place the hearts of palm in the slurry bowl. Remove one by one, letting the excess drop off. Transfer to the panko bowl and use the other hand to sprinkle a handful of breadcrumbs over the hearts of palm to coat them completely. Bread all the other pieces in the same way. Make sure you use one hand for the wet batter and the other for the dry batter, or you'll end up with a breadcrumb glove.

7 Preheat a large cast-iron pan over medium-high heat. Pour in a layer of oil, about ¼ inch thick. Fry the hearts in the hot oil until golden, working in batches if necessary; it will take about 8 minutes total. Use a thin metal spatula to flip. Transfer to paper towels to drain the oil.

8 Use a fork and knife to gently cut the hearts in half, shredding a bit with the fork as you pull them apart. Place on top of the cooked mac (horizontally down the center looks nice) and sprinkle with Old Bay. Top with chives and serve!

BEEFY MUSHROOM STROGANOFF WITH A HIT OF BRANDY

Serves 4

A timeless classic! A laundry pile of buttery, meaty mushrooms and onions. Layers and layers of strogi flavors: rich, creamy, and earthy. Dried porcinis serve as the beef here, with their broth reserved for rich flavor that does much of the heavy lifting. However, the hit of brandy deserves its spot in the recipe title. It brings all the flavors together in a warm way. A scoop of sour cream melting all over is just the cream on top. Swirl it all together and have an amazing time. Fettuccine works well, no one will complain, but if you can find a vegan pappardelle online, go for it. There really is something special about those big old noodles that makes stroganoff even more stroganoff-y. On the label, the only ingredients should be semolina, water, and salt.

- 2 ounces (55 g) dried porcini mushrooms
- ¾ cup (90 g) whole unroasted cashews
- 8 ounces (225 g) fettuccine or pappardelle
- 1 medium yellow onion, thinly sliced
- 3 tablespoons olive oil
- Pinch plus ½ teaspoon salt, plus more as needed
- 4 cloves garlic, minced
- 8 ounces (225 g) cremini mushrooms, thinly sliced
- 1 teaspoon dried thyme
- 3 tablespoons brandy
- 2 tablespoons tomato paste
- 2 teaspoons whole grain Dijon mustard
- Vegan sour cream, store-bought or homemade (recipe follows)
- Several dashes freshly ground black pepper
- ½ cup (25 g) chopped fresh dill, for garnish

1. Bring 3 cups (720 ml) water to a boil in a saucepan. Add the porcini mushrooms. Boil for 10 minutes, then turn off the heat and let them cool.
2. Once the porcinis are cool, drain them into a colander with a bowl underneath to catch the broth. Reserve the broth and roughly chop the bigger mushrooms. In a high-speed blender, blend the cashews with the mushroom broth until totally smooth. Set aside.
3. Fill a large pot with salted water for the pasta. Start bringing it to a boil over medium-high heat, but wait to cook the pasta until the last moment so that you can serve it hot.

HOT TAKES

If you're making your own sour cream, do so a day in advance to make sure it sets up in time!

Beef it up! Sauté 2 cups thinly sliced Beefy Seitan (page 28) to fold in at the end.

CONTINUED →

4 Preheat a large, heavy-bottomed pan over medium heat. Sauté the onion in olive oil with a pinch of salt for about 10 minutes, until lightly browned. Add the minced garlic and sauté for 30 seconds or so.

5 Add the cremini mushrooms and thyme and cook until the mushrooms are lightly browned, about 5 more minutes. Pour in the brandy and cook for about 5 minutes to reduce.

6 Add the porcini mushrooms, tomato paste, mustard, salt, pepper, and the cashew-mushroom broth mixture to the pan. Stir until well combined and let the sauce cook and thicken for about 5 minutes. Taste for salt and seasoning.

7 Cook the pasta in the boiling salted water according to package directions. Once cooked tender, drain and place back in the pot, covered, until ready to use.

8 Serve the mushroom sauce over the pasta, with a scoop of sour cream on top. Garnish with the fresh dill.

SO VERY SOUR CREAM

Makes 4 cups

Smooth and tangy, and comes together like a breeze. And, also like a breeze, cools everything down. Modified from my *Superfun Times Vegan Holiday Cookbook*.

- **1 cup (120 g) unroasted cashews**
- **1 (15-ounce/430 g) can coconut milk**
- **½ cup (120 ml) fresh lemon juice**
- **¼ cup (240 ml) refined coconut oil, melted**
- **½ teaspoon onion powder**
- **Pinch salt (about 1/16 teaspoon)**

1 Puree the cashews in a high-speed blender with the coconut milk, lemon juice, melted coconut oil, onion powder, and salt. Blend until completely smooth, scraping the sides of the blender with a spatula occasionally to make sure you get everything, about 3 minutes.

2 Transfer to a container, cover, and chill for at least 3 hours to set.

TURKI TETRAZZINI

Serves 6

This sounds like it's gonna be so Italian, but then it so . . . is not. It's, essentially, a turkey pot pie in pasta form. And that is the most amazing invention ever! The Italian title refers to opera singer Luisa Tettrazini at the turn of the twentieth century. This was said to be her favorite dish, and it is indeed so good it just may make you sing *Rigoletto* at the top of your lungs, much to the chagrin of your neighbors. It's a casserole of bucatini and turki in creamy mushroom sauce with carrots and onions. Breadcrumbs and cheddar are crunchy and golden on top. Dig in and let your aria begin!

- 1½ cups (180 g) unroasted cashews
- 4 cups (960 ml) Chick'n Broth (page 299) or prepared vegetable broth
- ⅔ cup (80 g) all-purpose flour
- 3 tablespoons nutritional yeast flakes
- 8 ounces (225 g) bucatini
- ¼ cup (60 ml) olive oil, plus a few splashes
- 4 cups Roast Turki (page 20), torn into 1-inch chunks
- 1 medium onion, thinly sliced
- 2 cups carrots, sliced into thin coins
- 4 cups (340 g) sliced cremini mushrooms
- 1 teaspoon salt, plus a pinch
- 1 tablespoon onion powder
- 2 teaspoons poultry seasoning, prepared or homemade (page 89)
- ¼ teaspoon ground black pepper
- ½ cup (30 g) fresh parsley leaves, chopped
- ½ cup (50 g) breadcrumbs
- ½ cup (55 g) shredded hard vegan cheddar

1. Preheat the oven to 375°F (190°C). Lightly grease a 9 by 13-inch (23 by 33 cm), or 4 quart, casserole dish.
2. Combine the cashews, vegetable broth, flour, and nutritional yeast in a high-speed blender. Blend until completely smooth and set aside.
3. Meanwhile, cook the bucatini noodles al dente according to the package instructions. Drain and set aside.
4. Heat 2 tablespoons of the olive oil in a large sauté pan or cast-iron skillet over medium-high heat. Add the turki pieces and cook while turning the pieces often until lightly browned, about 6 minutes. Remove the turki from the pan and transfer to a plate.
5. In the same pan, heat the remaining 2 tablespoons of olive oil, then sauté the onion and carrot with a pinch of salt until the carrots are softened, about 7 minutes. Add the mushrooms and continue to sauté until they've released moisture and browned lightly.
6. Pour the blender mixture into the pan along with the onion powder, poultry seasoning, remaining 1 teaspoon salt, and black pepper. Cook, stirring often, until thickened, about 8 minutes.
7. Fold the turki, bucatini, and parsley into the pan. Reserve a little parsley for sprinkling to serve. If your pan isn't large enough to accommodate everything, transfer it all to a large mixing bowl and stir to combine.
8. Transfer the mixture into the casserole dish and top with breadcrumbs and shredded cheddar. Bake until golden and bubbly, 22 to 25 minutes. Let cool for a few minutes before serving.

MEATY SHELLS IN FRESH TOMATO SAUCE WITH FETA AND MINT

Serves 6

All of the four food groups are represented here: Meat. Cheese. Pasta. Tomatoes. Everyone loves marinara, absolutely, no question. But fresh tomato sauce is an entirely different animal. I mean vegetable. Or, fine, fruit, if you want to be a stickler about it. This recipe is designed for those summer tomatoes fresh off the vine—and to make it even fresher, mint, both in the sauce and topping the pasta off. It's the most beautiful, surprising, and simple way to change up your pasta and tomato sauce routine. Little shells are the perfect vehicle to capture the sauce and meat. I eat this with a spoon instead of a fork, even though doing so makes me feel like I'm in fourth grade. It's easier to get perfect bites that way, with just enough of everything—the sauce and some cheese and some meat and some mint. The flavors are so sophisticated it cancels that spoon right out.

FOR THE SAUCE:

- 8 cloves garlic, minced
- 3 tablespoons olive oil
- 3 pounds (1.4 kg) plum tomatoes, chopped (see Hot Take)
- 1 teaspoon salt
- 3 tablespoons chopped fresh mint
- Several dashes freshly ground black pepper

FOR THE PASTA:

- 1 pound (910 g) small shell pasta
- 2 cups (300 g) vegan feta, store-bought or homemade (page 290)
- 1 recipe MVP Meat (page 305)
- Fresh mint leaves, for serving

1 Make the sauce: Preheat a 6-quart pan over low heat. Cook the garlic in olive oil for about a minute, being careful not to burn or brown it. It should be very fragrant and lightly bubbling.

2 Add the tomatoes and salt and stir to deglaze. Turn the heat up to medium. Cover the pot and cook the tomatoes down until saucy, stirring occasionally, for about 30 minutes. Remove the lid, add the mint and pepper, and cook an additional 10 minutes, then remove from the heat. Taste for salt and seasoning.

3 Meanwhile, bring a large pot of salted water to a boil. Cook the shells according to the package directions. Drain and set aside.

4 Add the cooked shells to the tomato sauce and toss to coat. Transfer half the pasta to a serving bowl or platter. Scatter with half the meat. Add the remaining pasta. Scatter the remaining meat across the top and crumble on the cheese. Top with fresh mint leaves to serve.

HOT TAKE

The tomatoes can be pulsed in a food processor to get them nicely chopped without losing any of the juices.

SMALL THINGS

(INCLUDING WINGS)

Take this short quiz to see if this section is for you:

a. When at a restaurant, have you been known to order five appetizers, and zero entrées?
b. Do the servers at Bat Mitzvahs swerve their trays of hors d'oeuvres to try to avoid you?
c. Do you consider your stash of cocktail napkins your finest tableware?

If you answered YES to any of these, this section is for you, my friend.

As the title of this chapter implies, it's mostly a lot of wings, so let's start there. One thing is for sure: Vegans will turn anything into wings.

I love the motto on the Herbivore Clothing Company shirt everyone was wearing in 2010: "Wings are for flying, not frying." Wings are the ultimate symbol of freedom, and creating cruelty-free versions is an expression of that freedom. So let's do it!

But what is a vegan wing?

Off the bat, I should admit that I've never had a non-vegan wing. Skeptics might say, "Don't call it a wing!" Just call it a nugget or, if it's cauliflower, well, just call it cauliflower. But that doesn't sound like any fun.

If I had to define a wing I'd say: They're small and sloppy, about three bites big. They're slathered in sauce or rubbed in spice. May require further dipping (see: Rescue Ranch Dressing, page 281) but sometimes not. And you have to eat them with your hands, no utensils allowed. Have some upcycled cloth napkins nearby.

But let's not forget the other finger foods. Who can live without Sausage Pizza Roll Won Tons (page 232) or Pepperoni-Stuffed Mushrooms (page 231)? And that root vegetable marrow (page 227) will be the talk of the table for years to come. Also found here, the recipe we have all been waiting for: chick'n nuggets (page 221)! And these are the flakiest around.

Time to get the party started, *Fake Meat* style!

KATE'S BUFFALO TOFU WINGS

Makes 16 wings

Let's start with the OG of vegan wings. Once again, we take a trip to the golden era of veganism, the 1990s. We were lousy with veggie burgers and scrambled tofu. Packages of vegan cheese didn't even bother to advertise "IT MELTS," because we all knew it didn't. And no one, but no one, even considered that a wing could be vegan. Except Kate's Joint in Alphabet City. I could write a whole think piece on the place, but let's just focus on the buffalo wings. Fat rectangles of chewy tofu in an herbed breadcrumb coating, and dripping with buffalo sauce. On the side, a pinch dish of creamy tofu ranch. No table was without a few orders. On your first bite, everything just burst into your mouth in the most obscene way. Now you can create that feeling at home! So scruff up your tables, hire some crust punks to sit outside your window, and enjoy.

- 1 (14-ounce/400 g) block extra-firm tofu, sliced into 16 rectangles
- 1 teaspoon salt
- 3 tablespoons olive oil
- 1 tablespoon fresh lemon juice
- 3 tablespoons cornstarch
- 1 cup (240 ml) cold unsweetened soy milk
- 1 tablespoon tamari
- 2 cups (160 g) panko breadcrumbs
- 3 tablespoons chopped fresh rosemary
- Safflower oil, for frying

FOR THE SAUCE:

- ¼ cup (55 g) vegan butter, melted (I like Miyoko's)
- ¾ cup (180 ml) buffalo hot sauce (like Frank's Red Hot)

FOR SERVING:

- 2 cups (200 g) carrot sticks
- 2 cups (150 g) celery sticks
- Rescue Ranch Dressing (page 281)

1 Press each tofu rectangle with a paper towel to quickly dry it. Place in a single layer on a small baking sheet. Sprinkle with ½ teaspoon salt and drizzle with the olive oil and lemon juice. Toss to coat. Let rest while preparing everything else. You will be using this same tray for the breaded tofu.

2 Now make the slurry and breading: Scoop the cornstarch into a wide-rimmed bowl, add half the soy milk along with the tamari, and stir well until it's a thick smooth paste. Mix in the remaining milk. On a large rimmed plate, mix together the panko, rosemary, and remaining ½ teaspoon salt.

3 Dip a piece of tofu into the the slurry with one hand, letting the excess drip off. Transfer to the panko bowl and use the other hand to sprinkle a handful of breadcrumbs over the tofu to coat it completely. Return it to the tray and bread all the other pieces in the same way. Make sure you use one hand for the wet batter and the other for the dry batter, or you'll end up with crumb hand.

4 Preheat a large cast-iron pan over medium-high heat. Pour in a layer of oil, about ¼ inch thick. Fry the tofu in the hot oil until golden on the top and bottom, working in batches if necessary; it will take about 8 minutes total. The sides will get fried in the process, but add a little more oil if needed. Use a thin metal spatula to flip.

5 While the tofu is frying, make the sauce: Simply mix the melted butter with the buffalo sauce. You can melt the butter in a large ceramic bowl in the microwave then mix in the hot sauce to save on doing dishes.

6 Lift each wing from the oil and dunk it into the buffalo sauce to coat. Transfer to serving plates and serve immediately with the carrots, celery, and ranch.

HOT TAKES

I don't press the tofu for these. I don't know, Kate's might have, but I like the moisture when you bite into one, as well as the fact that it cuts down on a lot of prep time.

Kate's tofu wings were rect-angles, so I re-created the shape for mine. You can use any shape you like, but

(continued on page 211)

FIRECRACKER HONEE CAULIFLOWER WINGS

Makes 16 to 20 wings

Firecracker wings are sticky, sweet satisfaction. Here, we use a trailblazing combination of Frank's and sriracha. If you love these hot sauces separately (and everyone does), get ready for these babies to create a fireworks display. But remember: Fireworks scare animals and affect people with PTSD, so keep those explosions safely inside your mouth. Agave is a natural stand-in for honey, but if you want to go the extra mile, try the homemade Oh Honee Honee recipe for an even more authentic floral flavor. Cauliflower coated in panko is my go-to weeknight wing, no deep-frying required. They crisp up so nicely in the oven or air fryer.

1 First, make the sauce: In a small saucepan, use a fork to mix together the broth and cornstarch. When no big clumps are left, mix in the vinegar, tamari, both hot sauces, and agave.

HOT TAKES

News flash: You can mix and match literally any of the meat bases with any of the sauces. Firecracker Tempeh wings? Yass. Garlic-Parmesan Cauli Wings. Oh heck yes.

Any of the wings can be magically transformed into a full-on dinner! Maybe it's not magic. Maybe it's just like, add some rice, some sautéed veggies, and an avocado.

You can definitely air-fry the fried wings, if that's your thing! Air fryers vary so much I'm not going to give specific directions in the recipes; however, spray the breading with some oil before cooking, bake on the middle rack, and cook for about the same time the frying suggestions recommend. Generally, I don't flip when I air fry.

(continued from page 208)

don't expect any points for authenticity. Here are directions for butchering tofu to end up with the correct shape: sixteen stubby little rectangles. Don't press the tofu; a drain and a quick little squeeze with some kitchen towels to keep it dry are all you need. Now let's proceed.

Use a 14-ounce (400 g) rectangular block of tofu; this will work best. Place the tofu on one of its long sides and slice it in half down the middle into two planks, like you're making an open book. You should have two large rectangles. Now slice both of them in half the short way. You'll have four rectangles. Take each rectangle and cut it vertically into four pieces.

FOR THE FIRECRACKER SAUCE:

- ½ cup (120 ml) vegetable broth
- 1 tablespoon cornstarch
- ¼ cup (60 ml) rice vinegar
- 2 tablespoons tamari
- ¼ cup (60 ml) sriracha
- ¼ cup (60 ml) Frank's Red Hot sauce
- ¾ cup (180 ml) light agave syrup or Vegan for My Honee (page 306)
- 2 tablespoons refined coconut oil

CONTINUED →

FOR THE CAULIFLOWER WINGS:

- 6 cups (1.3 kg) large cauliflower florets (about 2 inches/5 cm), cut from 1 large head of cauliflower (or see suggestion in Hot Take)
- ½ cup (65 g) plus 2 tablespoons all-purpose flour
- 2 tablespoons cornstarch
- 1 cup (240 ml) cold water
- 1¾ cups (140 g) panko breadcrumbs
- 1 teaspoon ground white pepper
- 1 teaspoon salt
- 3 tablespoons olive oil

FOR SERVING:

- 1 large cucumber, sliced into long, thin strips
- 1 tablespoon black sesame seeds
- 1 cup (80 g) thinly sliced scallions

HOT TAKE

I don't often recommend purchasing precut vegetables, but in the case of cauliflower wings, I say you should do it! Just one caveat: Purchase two 12-ounce (340 g) packages. That way, if some of the florets are too small, you can use them for something else, like cauliflower rice or soup.

2 Place the pan over medium-low heat and let the sauce simmer for about 10 minutes, stirring often, until thickened, caramelized, and glossy. Add in the coconut oil and mix to melt. Turn the heat off and let the sauce cool until ready to use.

3 Now prepare the cauliflower: Preheat the oven to 450°F (220°C). Line a large rimmed baking sheet with parchment paper, spray with cooking spray, and set aside. Have cauliflower prepped and ready on the cutting board.

4 You'll need a large bowl for the batter and a big rimmed plate for the breading. Place the flour and cornstarch in the bowl. Add about half of the water and stir vigorously with a fork to incorporate. Add the rest of the water and stir until smooth. On the plate, mix together the panko, white pepper, and salt. Drizzle in the oil and use your fingertips to mix it up well.

5 From left to right, arrange the cauliflower, the batter mixture, the breading mixture, and lastly the prepared baking sheet. Dip each cauliflower floret into the batter mixture, letting the excess drip off. Transfer to the breading bowl and use your other (dry) hand to toss and coat, pressing the breadcrumbs into the crevices of the floret as you go. Coat completely. Transfer each coated piece of cauliflower to the baking sheet to form a single layer.

6 Bake for 10 minutes. Flip and bake for another 5 to 7 minutes. The florets should be varying shades of brown and crisp. Taste one to check for doneness; it should be tender with some bite.

7 Pour the firecracker sauce into a large bowl. Toss the fried cauliflower into the sauce in batches. Use tongs to gently flip them to coat all over.

8 Serve the wings over the cucumber strips and top with the sesame seeds and scallions.

MUSHROOM OYSTERS ON THE HALF SHELL

Makes 20

Indulge in all the glamour and romance of oysters! Small potatoes are roasted and filled with an aphrodisiac of flavor and texture: that slippery oyster (mushroom) infused with lemon and wine, with a hint of the sea and garlic galore. Coconut oil makes the filling rich and buttery. These are definitely a showstopper. Get out your most old-fashioned hors d'oeuvre trays and transport yourself to a 1960s NYC hotel lobby, where these are the fanciest things going. Serve with champagne on New Year's Eve or any eve!

1 Preheat the oven to 350°F (175°C). Line a large rimmed baking sheet with parchment.

2 Slice the potatoes in half lengthwise. Rinse in cold water and pat dry with paper towels. Place them on the prepared baking sheet. Toss with olive oil and salt, and then place them cut sides down on the sheet. Bake for 25 to 30 minutes, until the potatoes are completely tender on the inside and browned on the cut side.

HOT TAKES

The potatoes should be around 2 inches (5 cm) long. Choose Yukon Golds that are as equal in size as possible. Oblong red potatoes will work as well!

The oyster mushrooms should be cut into thin strips that are just about as long as the potatoes, for the most authentic-looking oysters. You can replace the oyster mushrooms with fresh shiitake caps, no big deal.

You may have some filling left over; better safe than sorry. I have no doubt you will figure out what to do with it!

FOR THE SHELLS:

- 10 baby Yukon Gold potatoes
- 1½ tablespoons olive oil
- ½ teaspoon salt

CONTINUED →

FOR THE FILLING:

- 6 cloves minced garlic
- 2 tablespoons refined coconut oil
- 2 cups thinly sliced oyster mushrooms (from about 8 ounces/225 g)
- ½ teaspoon smoked salt
- 2 tablespoons nutritional yeast flakes
- ½ teaspoon kelp powder (optional)
- Several dashes fresh black pepper
- ½ cup (120 ml) dry white wine
- 3 tablespoons finely chopped fresh parsley
- ¼ cup (60 ml) vegetable broth
- 1 tablespoon fresh lemon juice

FOR THE GARNISH:

- Finely chopped fresh parsley
- Fresh lemon slices

3 While the potatoes are baking, prepare the filling: Preheat a large pan over low heat. Cook the minced garlic in the coconut oil for about a minute, being careful not to burn it, just until the garlic is lightly cooked and very fragrant.

4 Add the mushrooms and sprinkle with smoked salt. Turn the heat up to medium high. Cook for about 15 minutes, until the juices are released and the mushrooms are lightly browned.

5 Mix in the nutritional yeast, kelp powder (if using), and black pepper. Toss to coat and cook for about 2 minutes. Add the wine and turn the heat up to high. Let the wine cook and bubble for about 5 minutes to cook off the alcohol.

6 Lower the heat. Add the parsley, broth, and lemon juice. Turn the heat off. Taste for salt and seasoning, adding more if needed. The potatoes should be done by now. Remove from the oven and let cool just until you can handle them, about 10 minutes.

7 Now make the potato shell cups. Use a paring knife to score the cut side of the potato about ⅛ inch from the edge. You're creating an oval that you will scoop out so that the potatoes have an edge. Use a small spoon to scrape out the insides of each potato, leaving about ¼ inch of potato intact at the bottom. Now you have potato cups! As for the scooped-out potatoes, just pop them into your mouth.

8 Warm the filling if it has cooled a bit. It should be saucy enough so that it's juicy when scooped into the shells. If it's not, add vegetable broth by the tablespoon to achieve sauciness.

9 Spoon the filling into the cups. Place on platters, sprinkle with parsley, and serve with lemon wedges.

PEANUT-LIME TEMPEH WINGS

Makes 16 wings

If I were a wing sommelier, I would have a lot to say about tempeh and peanuts. Something like "Tempeh's funky and nutty flavor is contrasted yet enhanced by this sweet, tangy, surprisingly savory peanut sauce." Tempeh wings are magical not just because they're so yummy, but also because breading isn't necessary! They crisp up nicely when shallow-fried all by themselves, then just need to be smothered in sauce. While the tempeh wings are cooking, the sauce comes together in the blender real fast.

- 2 (8-ounce/225 g) packages tempeh
- 1 teaspoon salt
- 3 tablespoons refined coconut oil, plus more as needed

FOR THE PEANUT SAUCE:

- 1 teaspoon minced fresh ginger
- 1 teaspoon toasted sesame oil
- 3 cloves garlic, minced
- ½ cup (120 ml) warm water, plus more to thin
- ½ cup (120 ml) natural creamy peanut butter
- ¼ cup (60 ml) fresh lime juice
- 2 tablespoons tamari
- 2 tablespoons sriracha
- 3 tablespoons agave syrup
- ½ teaspoon salt

FOR SERVING:

- 1 cup (115 g) thinly sliced radishes
- Extra sriracha, for drizzling (optional)
- ½ cup (75 g) roasted salted peanuts, chopped
- Fresh cilantro sprigs, for garnish
- Lime wedges

1. Cut each block of tempeh into 8 triangles. To do this, cut the block in half widthwise, then cut those halves in half widthwise. Now you'll have 4 stout rectangles. Cut each rectangle corner to corner to form the triangles.
2. Preheat a large cast-iron pan over medium-high heat. Sprinkle ¼ teaspoon salt into the pan, followed by 3 tablespoons coconut oil, or enough to form a thin layer.
3. Place the tempeh triangles in the oil, working in batches if necessary. Let them fry for about 5 minutes, until nicely crisped. Place a little coconut oil, about a teaspoon, on the top side of each tempeh wing. Sprinkle with the remaining ¾ teaspoon salt, flip, and cook for 5 more minutes.
4. Make the sauce: Blend together all the ingredients in a small blender until completely smooth. Transfer the peanut sauce to a large mixing bowl.
5. While the wings are still hot, place them in the sauce and use tongs to toss until fully coated.
6. Place the radishes artfully on a serving tray. Transfer the wings to the tray and drizzle on any remaining sauce from the bowl. Drizzle with sriracha, if you like, sprinkle on the peanuts, and top with cilantro sprigs. Serve with lime wedges for squeezing.

If I were to serve these in a restaurant, I would shallow-fry in cast iron. However, on a weeknight, if I have no one to impress, tempeh is a prime candidate for air frying. You should still coat the wings with a little coconut oil first to crisp the edges and sprinkle with a little salt to enhance the flavor. About 12 minutes at 400°F (200°C) should do it!

GRILLED CHIPOTLE BBQ WINGS

WITH AVOCADO RANCH

Makes 16 wings

Forget everything you thought you knew about wings. Grilled wings are a sea-changing moment. If you hadn't left Facebook so many years ago, you would definitely add "grilled wings" to your important life events, like births and job promotions. These barbecue babies are smoky and spicy, thanks to the chipotles in adobo. You start the sauce off gently, by seeding the peppers and draining the adobo juice. Then, as you cook it down, you can add some spiciness as you like with the reserved seeds and sauce. Seitan chick'n is pulled into organic slices then cut to create flat surfaces that are just begging for perfect grill marks. Those are slathered with the sauce, then broiled for extra caramelization. Everything is cooled down with a lux avocado ranch that keeps everyone coming back for more.

FOR THE CHIPOTLE BARBECUE SAUCE:

- 1 (8-ounce/225 g) can chipotles in adobo, adobo drained, seeds removed, and both reserved (see Hot Take)
- 2 tablespoons cornstarch
- 1¼ cups (300 ml) cold vegetable broth
- ½ cup (120 ml) light agave syrup
- ¼ cup (55 g) tomato paste
- 2 tablespoons tamari
- 1 teaspoon onion powder
- ½ teaspoon garlic powder
- 3 tablespoons fresh lime juice

1 Make the sauce: Place the seeded chipotle peppers in a blender along with the cornstarch, broth, agave, tomato paste, tamari, onion powder, garlic powder, and lime juice. Blend until smooth.

2 Transfer the sauce to a small pot. Heat on low-medium for about 20 minutes, stirring often, until reduced, bubbly, and slightly caramelized. Taste for spiciness and add some of the reserved adobo sauce and seeds if you'd like it hotter.

3 Let the sauce rest until cool enough to handle. You can place it in the fridge, stirring periodically, to expedite the process.

HOT TAKE

Do you have vinyl gloves on hand? Excuse the pun. But you absolutely cannot remove the seeds from the chiles bare-handed. Use a paring knife to slit open the chipotle peppers, and protect yourself by wearing kitchen gloves as you gently scrape out the seeds by hand. Reserve them, along with the excess adobo sauce, in a mixing bowl.

CONTINUED →

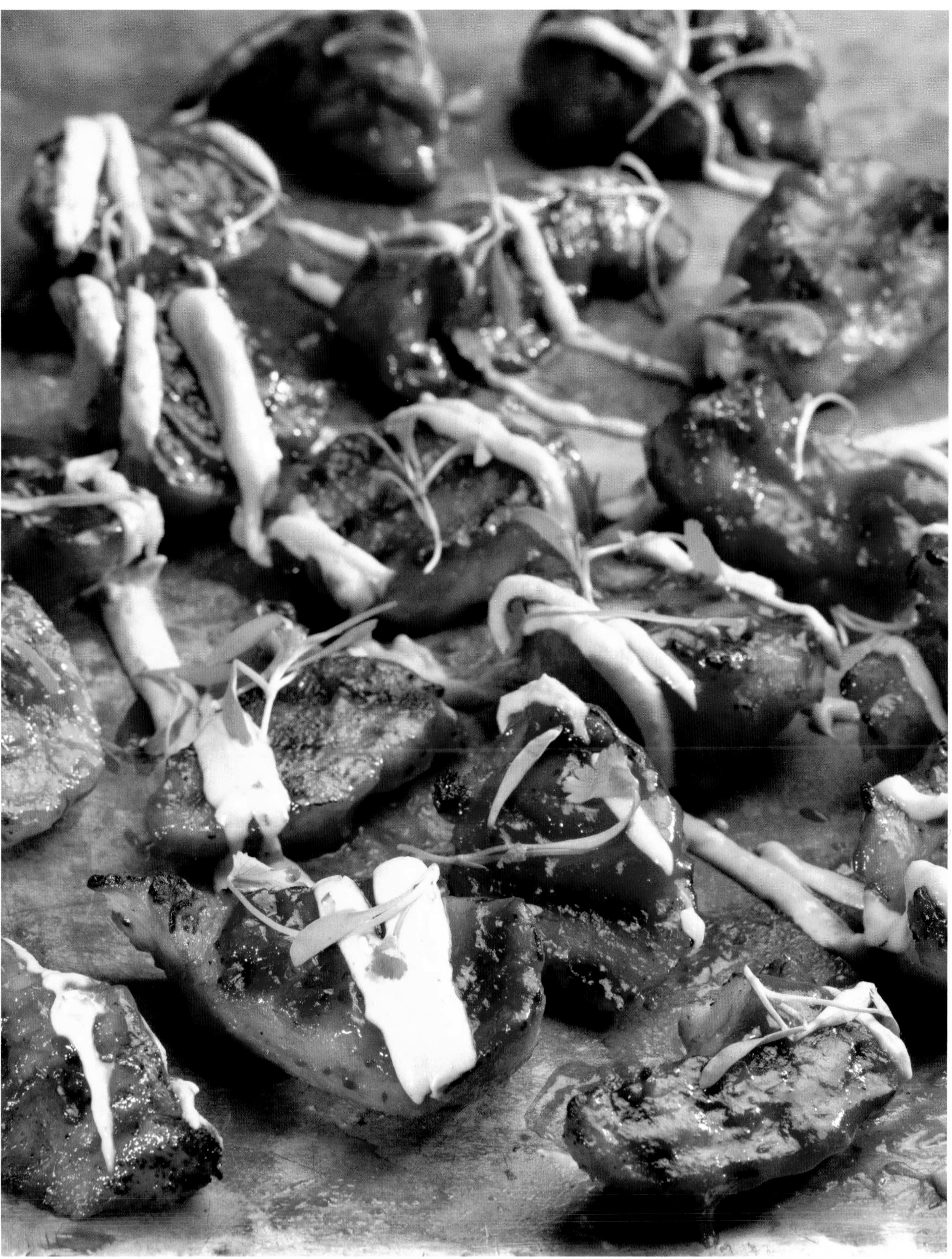

- ½ recipe Pull-Apart Seitan Chick'n (page 115)
- 2 tablespoons olive oil
- ¼ teaspoon salt

FOR SERVING:

- Avocado Ranch Dressing (page 281)
- ½ cup (20 g) fresh cilantro leaves or cilantro micro-greens

HOT TAKES

These wings are grilled, slathered, and then broiled to caramelize a bit. Since broilers vary, I gave basic instructions for how to finish them off, but keep a close eye so that they don't burn. If you're having the opposite problem and they aren't caramelizing, adjust the rack or heat as necessary. This is a good time to get to know your broiler if you aren't already acquainted.

On the other hand, if you have a kitchen torch, now is the time to use it! Instead of broiling the wings as the last step, you can torch them. Just make sure to read the safety instructions first and do not blame me if you set anything but a wing on fire.

4 Prepare the wings: To cut the chicken into wing-size pieces, pull each bundle apart into 4 pieces and then slice those pieces in half, giving you 16 wings. Place the wings in a large mixing bowl and sprinkle with the olive oil and salt. Toss to coat.

5 Coat the grill pan with cooking spray and set over medium-high heat. When the pan is hot, add the wings in batches, placing the flat sides down first. Grill for about 5 minutes, until dark grill marks appear. Use a thin metal spatula to flip and then grill the other side for 3 to 5 minutes.

6 Set the oven to broil on high heat and have ready a large rimmed baking sheet coated with cooking spray. Place the broiler rack about 4 inches (10 cm) below the heating element.

7 Place the sauce in a mixing bowl and toss in the grilled wings. Slather the wings with sauce and arrange in a single layer on the baking sheet. Broil for 2 to 5 minutes, depending on your broiler (see Hot Takes). The wings should be lightly caramelized.

8 Use a spatula to transfer the wings to serving plates. Serve with avocado ranch and garnish with the cilantro.

CHICK'N NUGGIES
WITH DIPPY SAUCE

Makes about 3 dozen nuggets

The biggest lie humanity has ever told itself is that chick'n nuggets are for kids. Sure, you can share them with kids, but let's not fool ourselves. A plate of chick'n nuggets can make for a perfectly respectable adult dinner. These nuggets are especially nuggety, with flaky and tender chicken that pulls apart when you sink your teeth in. A combination of TVP, navy beans, and wheat gluten makes this magic possible. It's as easy as nuggets. My method is pretty simple: We steam a few chick'n logs, than slice them up into discs and coat them in breadcrumbs!

FOR THE NUGGETS:

- 1 cup (70 g) textured vegetable protein (TVP)
- ¾ cup (135 g) cooked navy beans
- 3 cups (720 ml) cold water
- ¼ cup (60 ml) vegan mayo (storebought or homemade, page 309)
- 1 teaspoon onion powder
- ½ teaspoon garlic powder
- 2 tablespoons tamari
- 2 tablespoons nooch (aka nutritional yeast flakes)
- 1 teaspoon salt
- ½ cup (25 g) pea protein
- 1¼ cups (150 g) vital wheat gluten
- 2 tablespoons cornstarch
- ¼ cup (30 g) all-purpose flour
- 3 cups (300 g) dry bread-crumbs
- ¼ teaspoon ground black pepper

1 Make the nuggets: Bring 2 cups (480 ml) water to a boil in a small pot. Turn off the heat, mix in the TVP, cover, and let it sit for 20 minutes, until completely softened. Drain in a fine-mesh strainer and let cool. Once cool enough to handle, squeeze out any liquid with the back of a rubber spatula. Place in the fridge to cool further before processing.

2 Mash the beans into a puree. Mix in 1 cup (240 ml) of the cold water, the mayo, onion powder, garlic powder, tamari, nooch, and ½ teaspoon salt. Stir in the cooked TVP. Mix in the pea protein and vital wheat gluten, and use gloved hands to knead for about 3 minutes into a springy dough.

3 Prepare six 10-inch (25 cm) squares of aluminum foil and parchment for wrapping and steaming the nuggets. Prepare your steamer.

4 Divide the dough into 6 even pieces. Roll each piece of dough into a ball then mold and roll into about a 6-inch (15 cm) sausage shape. Wrap each piece of dough in parchment-lined foil, twisting the ends like a Tootsie Roll. Don't worry too much about shaping it, it will snap into shape while it's steaming.

CONTINUED →

- Safflower or canola oil, for frying

FOR THE SAUCE:

- ½ cup (120 ml) vegan mayo, prepared or homemade (page 309)
- 2 tablespoons mustard
- ¼ cup (60 ml) ketchup
- 2 tablespoons pickle juice
- 1 teaspoon smoked paprika

Dippy Sauce, as its name implies, is perfect for dipping. But some other sauces in this book are just as yum. Try any of the barbecue sauces (Chipotle, page 218; Five-Spice, page 46; or Backyard, page 244). Rescue Ranch Dressing (page 281) is an obvious winner, too.

5 Place the wrapped chick'n in the steamer and steam for 40 minutes, turning once. Let cool completely before proceeding. Once cool, unwrap each chicken log. Slice into ½-inch (12 mm) pieces, discarding the uneven ends. (Discarding actually means a snack for the chef to eat.)

6 Now, we will bread the nuggets. In a large, wide bowl, mix the remaining 2 cups (480 ml) cold water, the cornstarch, and the flour to create a slurry. On a large plate, mix the breadcrumbs, the remaining ½ teaspoon salt, and the pepper and place it right beside the slurry, with an empty tray next to that for the breaded nuggets. Place a handful of naked nuggets into the slurry. Use your left (nondominant) hand to retrieve a nugget, then dip it in breadcrumbs. Use your right (dominant) hand to cover it in breadcrumbs and toss to coat. Bread all nuggets.

7 Have ready paper towels or a paper bag for draining the oil. Preheat a large cast-iron pan over medium heat. Pour in about ½ inch (12 mm) safflower oil. The oil is ready when a tiny bit of breadcrumbs quickly bubbles when tossed in the pan. In batches, fry the nuggets on one side for about 3 minutes, flipping once and cooking for another 2 minutes, or until beautifully golden brown. Use a spatula to transfer nuggets to the paper towels to drain and add more oil as needed between batches.

8 Mix together all of the sauce ingredients and serve it alongside the nuggets!

D'ORITO-SPICED CHICK'N WINGS

Makes 16 to 20 wings

This is an all-consuming experience for your mouth. It's a familiar feeling, I'm sure; you bite into a chip and the tangy, cheezy powder melts on your tongue. You pucker. You go back for another, and another. There's orange powder everywhere but you could care less because you're in sour, savory heaven. Now you can experience that feeling in a wing! Cauliflower is coated in crispy rice flour and doused in a cheesy spice blend. They're pictured here with queso and pico but you could also serve these wings with ranch, and TBH, they're rightfully finger-licking on their own.

FOR THE D'ORITO DUST:

- 1½ cups (90 g) nutritional yeast flakes
- 2 tablespoons onion powder
- 1 tablespoon garlic powder
- ¼ cup (24 g) sweet paprika
- 1 teaspoon cayenne
- 1 teaspoon ground cumin
- ½ teaspoon ground black pepper
- 1½ teaspoons salt
- 1½ teaspoons citric acid

FOR THE CAULIFLOWER WINGS:

- 6 cups (1.3 kg) large cauliflower florets (about 2 inches/5 cm, from 1 large head of cauliflower (or see Hot Takes, page 211)
- 3 cups (480 g) rice flour
- 2 tablespoons cornstarch
- Safflower oil, for frying

FOR SERVING (OPTIONAL):

- Queso, prepared or homemade (page 291)
- Pico de gallo, prepared or homemade (page 313)

1. Make the D'orito dust first. Place all the ingredients in a blender and blend for 20 seconds. Let the dust settle before opening the lid; set aside.
2. Prepare the wings: Wash the cauliflower florets so they're clean and all wet. You'll want to keep them damp throughout the dredging so that the coating sticks.
3. Place the rice flour and cornstarch in a large mixing bowl. Take a few wet cauliflower pieces and roll them around in the flour to coat. Continue until all are coated.
4. Preheat a large cast-iron pan over medium-high heat. Add about ¼ inch oil. When the oil is hot, fry the cauliflower in batches until golden, flipping with tongs to brown all sides. It will take about 10 minutes total.
5. Place the D'orito dust in a large bowl. Lift the cauliflower from the oil and toss it in the D'orito dust to coat. Serve immediately!

HOT TAKE

Citric acid is the crucial ingredient here for that pucker-up D'orito moment. If you don't have any, you can achieve something kinda OK with 1½ teaspoons lemon pepper (without salt) and a squeeze of lemon to serve.

ROOT MARROW

Makes 12 to 14

Literally no one asked for it, but I could not resist creating a vegan bone marrow. And the world will thank me someday! This is one of my favorite recipes in the book. It's playful and visually stunning and something I literally dreamed about when I first imagined this cookbook. A rich, earthy, and savory filling that melts in your mouth in perfectly roasted earthy, sweet parsnip "bones." I know you came here for chick'n nuggets, but you will pop these into your mouth just as easily. They're a conversation starter, for sure, if you can talk with your mouth full.

- 4 pounds (1.8 kg) parsnips (about 6 large parsnips)
- 3 tablespoons olive oil
- 1 teaspoon salt
- Fresh ground black pepper
- ½ recipe What Am I, Vegetarian Chopped Liver? (page 72)
- Fresh thyme sprigs, for garnish

1 Preheat the oven to 375°F (190°C). Line a large rimmed baking sheet with parchment.

2 Trim the parsnips. Chop off the parts that aren't wide enough to stuff (see Hot Take). Hold on to the parts that are anywhere from 1¼ to 2 inches (3 to 5 cm) wide. Slice them crosswise into pieces that are about 2 inches (5 cm) tall.

3 On the prepared baking sheet, toss the parsnips with 2 tablespoons olive oil and the salt. Place the parsnips on their sides and roast them for about 40 minutes, turning once. They should be tender enough to easily poke through with a paring knife.

4 Lower the oven temperature to 350°F (175°C). Place the pan of parsnips on the stovetop to cool a bit. Once cool enough to handle (about 10 minutes), use a paring knife to cut a whole through the center of each that leaves ¼ inch of space on the sides. Don't cut all the way through to the bottom. Dig out each parsnip's "meat" with a teaspoon or, better yet, a grapefruit spoon, and pop it into your mouth.

5 Now fill each hole with the vegetarian chopped liver, packing it in tightly and smoothing it out on top. Place each parsnip back on the baking sheet, liver side up. Drizzle the liver with the remaining tablespoon of oil. Return to the oven and bake for 15 minutes, until the ,iver is warmed through and the parsnips are golden. Serve garnished with chopped thyme sprigs.

HOT TAKE

You won't be able to use the whole animal here. The parsnips need to be wide enough to stuff, so choose wisely. And even the widest parsnip will have spindly ends, so save those. You can roast the extra while preparing the parsnips for the recipe, and then snack on them while you cook everything else. Or save them for a soup!

ROSEMARY MINI DRUMSTICKS

Makes 16 drumsticks

If you like your hors d'oeuvres herby, chewy, savory, and, most importantly, absolutely adorable, this is the recipe for you. Marinated yuba does double duty: It forms a caramelized skin that is glazy and gorgeous, and inside it is the shredded meat of the drumstick. It's all bundled up on a skewer of rosemary that is fancy and functional. Use the whole twig of rosemary, not little sprigs; they need some bulk in order to stick them into the drumstick. Wrapping the drumstick is a two-person job, so call someone with dexterous fingers that you can trust.

- 4 dried yuba sheets (16 by 10 inches/25 by 40 cm)

FOR THE MARINADE:

- ⅓ cup tamari
- 1 cup water
- 2 tablespoons fresh lemon juice
- 1 tablespoon olive oil
- ¼ teaspoon liquid smoke
- 2 tablespoons nutritional yeast flakes
- 2 tablespoons cornstarch
- 2 tablespoons chopped fresh rosemary
- 1 tablespoon poultry seasoning, prepared or homemade (page 89)
- 1 teaspoon onion powder
- 2 teaspoons dark brown sugar
- 1 teaspoon kosher salt

FOR ASSEMBLY:

- 12 rosemary twigs

1 Soak the yuba sheets in warm water to rehydrate. Use a large frying pan for this, because it's wide enough to fit the sheets. Let them soak for about 30 minutes to an hour, flipping them around every now and again until soft and pliable.

2 In the meantime, whisk the marinade ingredients together in a mixing bowl, then divide half of the mixture into a separate bowl.

3 Once the yuba is soft, slice 2 sheets into 6 pieces each, so that you have 12 squares that are roughly 5 by 5 inches (12 by 12 cm). Place the squares in one of the marinade bowls.

4 Slice the remaining yuba into shredded ribbons. They don't have to be even; it's all going to get bunched up anyway. But aim for pieces that are about ½ inch (1.5 cm) wide. You can just ball the whole sheet up and go to town slicing. Place the ribbons into the other marinade bowl. Marinate for 1 hour.

5 Preheat the oven to 350°F (175°C). Have ready a baking sheet lined with parchment. Place a yuba square on a flat surface. Fill with a handful of shredded yuba (a scant ¼ cup will work). Now bunch the edges together and twist it at the base so that it has a "tail." This is where you need another set of hands: Have someone else tie the twine where the "tail" begins while you hold it in place, so that it resembles a drumstick.

6 Place the drumsticks on the baking sheet and coat with additional marinade. Bake for 20 minutes. Flip, brush with more marinade, and bake 10 more minutes.

7 Once baked, poke the rosemary through the bottom. You can use kitchen gloves so you don't burn your fingers, or just wait until the drumsticks are still warm but cool enough to handle. Serve!

PEPPERONI-STUFFED MUSHROOMS

Makes around 16 mushrooms

Here's a secret. Pepperoni flavors and seasonings can fool anyone into thinking they're eating pepperoni—even if there's no pepperoni in sight. These mushrooms are a testimony to that fact. They cut to the chase; you do not need to make a separate pepperoni for this recipe. Oh happy day! Instead, sun-dried tomatoes, mushrooms, and walnuts are spiked with fennel seed and pepper and other pepperoni inspo, to create the ILLUSION of pepperoni. This recipe is perfectly at home on date night with some wine, or date night alone with some wine, or family dinner with lots of wine.

FOR THE MUSHROOMS:

- 1 pound (455 g) stuffing mushrooms
- 2 tablespoons olive oil, plus more as needed
- 1 small red onion, very finely diced
- 1 teaspoon salt, plus more for seasoning
- 2 cloves garlic, minced
- 1 teaspoon fennel seed, crushed
- ½ teaspoon dried thyme
- ½ teaspoon red pepper flakes
- ¼ teaspoon ground black pepper
- ½ cup (50 g) dry breadcrumbs
- ½ cup (60 g) chopped walnuts (about pea size)
- ¼ cup (30 g) sun-dried tomatoes in oil, drained and finely chopped
- 2 tablespoons red wine vinegar

FOR THE GARNISH:

- 2 tablespoons chopped fresh parsley
- Food-safe rose petals to scatter around

1 Remove the stems from the mushrooms and set the caps aside. Roughly chop the stems and set them aside to be used in the stuffing later on.

2 Preheat a large, heavy-bottomed pan, preferably cast-iron, over medium-high heat. Add 1 tablespoon of the oil and sauté the onions with a pinch of salt until softened, 5 to 7 minutes. Add the remaining 1 teaspoon salt, the garlic, fennel, thyme, red pepper flakes, and ground black pepper; cook until fragrant, about 30 seconds.

3 Add the mushroom stems and cook until the mushrooms release moisture, about 5 minutes. Sprinkle the breadcrumbs into the pan and drizzle in the remaining 1 tablespoon oil. Toss to coat and lightly toast the breadcrumbs, about 3 minutes. Fold in the walnuts and sun-dried tomatoes.

4 Drizzle in ¼ cup (60 ml) water and the vinegar. Mix until the mixture holds together. If the filling seems dry, add a little additional water by the tablespoon. Turn off the heat and set aside just until cool enough to handle.

5 Preheat the oven to 350°F (175°C). Lightly grease a large rimmed baking sheet with olive oil and sprinkle with a little additional salt. The salt goes a long way to making sure the mushrooms aren't bland.

6 Spoon some filling into the mushroom caps and press it in. Then put additional filling on top of that so that it rises above the rim by about ¾ inch (2 cm). Transfer the mushrooms to the prepared baking sheet and drizzle each with a little olive oil. Bake for 20 to 25 minutes, until the mushrooms are tender and browned. Serve warm, sprinkled with parsley and decorated with rose petals.

SAUSAGE PIZZA ROLL WONTONS

Makes 20

- Cooking spray oil
- ½ cup (120 ml) marinara sauce
- ¼ cup (55 g) tomato paste
- 20 vegan wonton wrappers
- ½ cup (75 g) vegan feta cheese, store-bought or homemade (page 290)
- 4 Breakfast Sausages (page 157) or store-bought vegan sausage, cooked according to directions and crumbled

You know the opening scene in *Saturday Night Fever* when John Travolta is strutting down 86th Street eating two slices of pizza, one on top of the other? This is nothing like that! You can, however, get your hair perfectly in place and pop two of these bad boys into your mouth at once; it will be just as cool. I don't need to sell anyone on this recipe: It's meat, cheese, and dough! And it's easy. I chose feta here because it holds together nicely and melts just right—sturdy but creamy, just what the pizza roll ordered. The marinara is mixed with tomato paste to prevent it from spreading too much and becoming a mess. You are left with perfect pizza parcels ready for poppin'.

1 Preheat the oven to 425°F (220°C). Line a large pan with parchment. Spray with cooking oil.

2 In a small bowl, mix together the marinara sauce and tomato paste.

3 On a clean, dry work surface, place a wonton wrapper in front of you.

HOT TAKE

Check that your wonton wrappers are vegan! I used Nasoya, and they seem to be readily available in many supermarkets here in the old USA, so you should be able to find some.

CONTINUED →

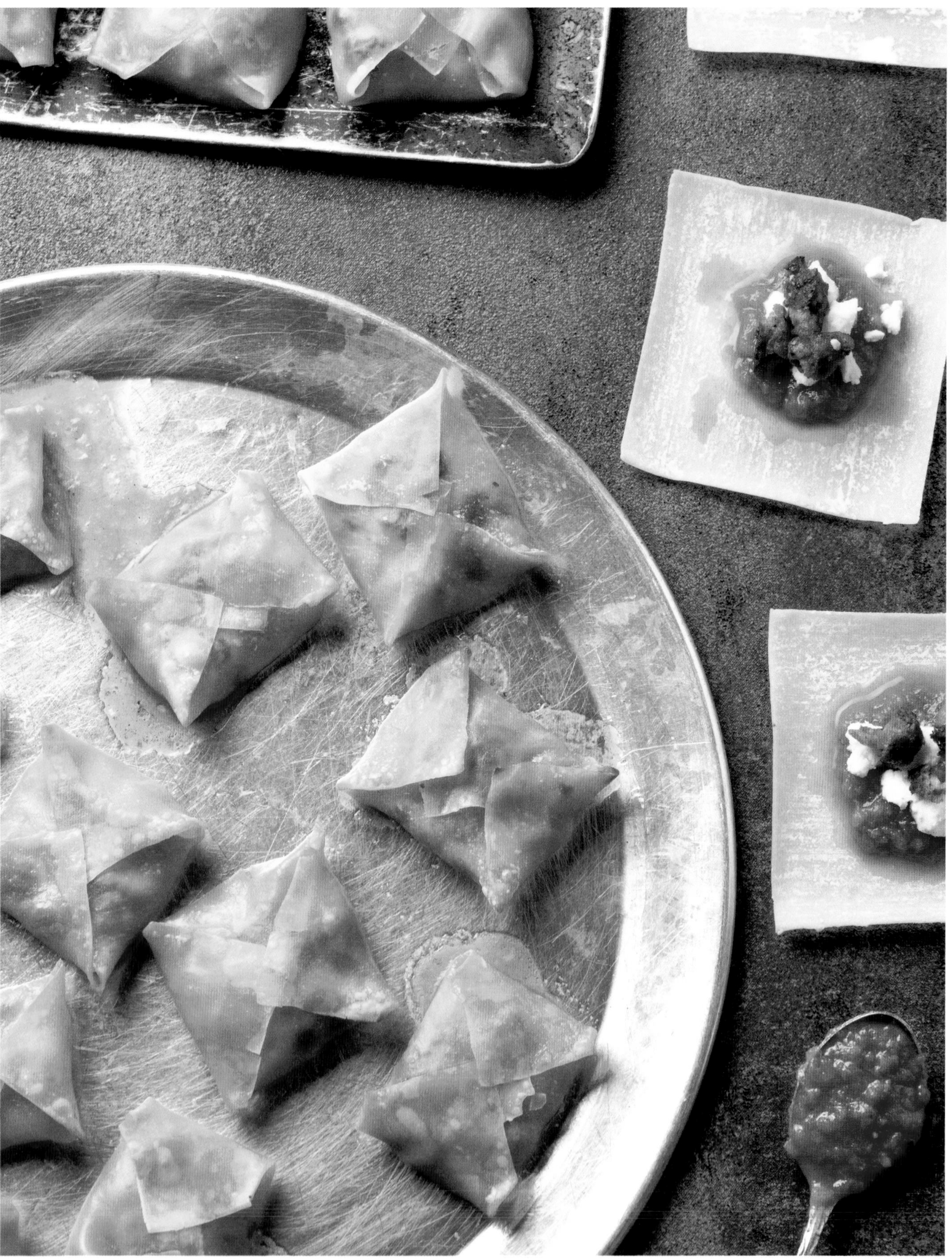

4 Add 1 teaspoon of the tomato sauce mixture right in the middle. On top of that, add about ¾ teaspoon cheese. Then a small amount of crumbled sausage on top (about 1 teaspoon).

5 With wet fingers, dab the edges of the wonton. Fold opposite corners over the filling, overlapping them like a hug. Use wet fingertips again to seal the edges. Fold the top and bottom corners to the center, creating a rectangle. With wet fingertips, seal the edges. Place on the prepared baking sheet and repeat with the remaining wonton wrappers.

6 Spray the wontons lightly with cooking spray. Bake for 12 to 15 minutes, until lightly browned and bubbly. Remove from the oven and place on a cooling rack for 3 minutes, then use a spatula to transfer to a serving tray.

PIGS BELONG IN A BLANKET

Makes 14

- 4 Hot Dogs (page 49), but make them smaller so you get 12 hot dogs instead of 8
- ½ recipe Life Is Rough Puff (page 250), or store-bought vegan puff pastry (see Hot Take)
- ¼ cup (60 ml) vegan mayo, prepared or homemade (page 309)
- 2 tablespoons unsweetened soy milk
- 1 tablespoon finely chopped fresh parsley, for garnish
- Dijon mustard, for serving

You don't want to be caught hosting a cocktail party without a batch of these! While the pigs are off somewhere cuddling in their beds, wrapped in the softest blankets, you are wrapping wheat-meat dogs in homemade puff pastry. No one has ever confused pigs-in-a-blanket with something fancy, but why shouldn't they? Golden buttery dough wrapped around smoky meaty bites that have all the appeal of a meat-stuffed croissant. And don't forget the mustard! If you need to make your life easier, you can use store-bought puff pastry; there are vegan brands out there, but if you really want to impress your forty-three TikTok followers, try your hand at Life Is Rough Puff (page 250).

1 Preheat the oven to 375°F (190°C). Line a large rimmed baking sheet with parchment. Cut each hot dog into three pieces that are about 2 inches (5 cm) long.

2 On a clean, dry surface, roll the puff pastry into an 8 ½ by 11-inch (21.5 by 28 cm) rectangle, with a short end facing you. To get the right long triangular shape for the blankets, the puff pastry will be first sliced the long way into strips and then those strips will be sliced diagonally.

HOT TAKE

I like my pastry simple, with no seeds to get in the way. But seeds do make for a striking (and tasty) appearance. If you'd like to gussy up your piggies, try sprinkling on ½ teaspoon of any of these after the glaze is brushed on: toasted sesame seeds, black sesame seeds, poppy seeds, za'atar, everything blend. Then bake as directed! You can even do a mix of these for added pizzazz.

CONTINUED →

HOT TAKES

If using homemade puff pastry, simply divide the dough in half before rolling out. That will get you the correct amount. If using store-bought, it often comes frozen in a 17-ounce package. Just use one sheet. Make sure it is thawed completely before using: Leave it in the fridge a day or two before you plan on using it.

The homemade hot dogs from this book can vary from 6 to 7 inches (15 to 17 cm). All you really want is for the ends of the dogs to stick out a bit from the pastry, which means you will need pieces that are just about 2 inches. I love the look of the ends poking out, with their funny shapes, so don't trim them. Also, don't sweat it if the size isn't a perfect 2 inches; just pop the extras into your mouth—that solves all your problems.

3 Slice the puff pastry vertically into six 1¼-inch (3 cm) strips, then slice each of those strips diagonally, from the top left corner to the bottom right corner.

4 Separate a strip and place its wider side in front of you. Place the hot dog piece on the wide side of the triangle, then roll up the pastry around the middle of the dog, ending with the point. Try to make sure that some hot dog is sticking out each end. Continue rolling up all the dogs. Now they're pigs in a blanket!

5 In a small bowl, mix together the glaze ingredients, mayo and soy milk. Use your fingers or a pastry brush to coat each pastry with the glaze.

6 Place the pigs in their blankets on the prepared baking sheet and bake for 18 to 20 minutes, until golden and puffy. Remove from oven and sprinkle with the parsley. Serve with mustard.

CENTERPIECES AND SHOWSTOPPERS

Fake meat is a celebration! And that's what this chapter is all about. Fun projects. Dazzling presentations. The fakest of fake meats. The talk of the town.

There's just something about the spectacle of a whole roast, or a slab of something, sitting in the center of the table, shimmering away. It brings everyone to the table, transforming another meal among many into irreplaceable memories carved forever into our brains and saved on our phones. That pot pie is going to feel like a Kardashian before the night is over.

Don't limit these recipes to only special occasions. Yeah, a Stuffed Faux Turki Roast is just what the Thanksgiving table ordered, but you can still dig into these recipes any old weekend when you have some time to spare and a deep desire for a glorious hunk of wheat steak.

This is where all those fake meat skills we practiced throughout the rest of the book will be put to the test. Don't worry, no one's grading your efforts, but these are more advanced techniques rather than entry-level stuff. TVP will be rehydrated and squeezed dry. Wheat meat will be kneaded. Beet powder will be flying through the air. Tofu will be pureed. At the end of it all, roasts will be stuffed, guests will be stuffed, and the question "Why fake meat?" will be answered. Period. Exclamation point. Mic drop.

STUFFED FAUX TURKI ROAST

Feeds 6 to 8

Always a classic. Always in style. For Vegansgiving, but really also for any holiday, this studded bundle of fun is the centerpiece of your dreams. It's a meaty blend of chickpeas and seitan, with a basic-but-in-a-good-way stuffing inside. The flavoring is delicious but subtle, so that you can pair it with stronger flavors, like all sorts of gravy. And if you want to have some fun with the filling, you can totally add in some chopped sausage, bacon, or nuts.

FOR THE STUFFING:

- 4 cloves garlic, minced
- 4 tablespoons (60 ml) olive oil
- 1 tablespoon chopped fresh rosemary
- ½ teaspoon dried thyme
- 6 cups ½-inch (12 mm) stale white bread cubes (see Hot Takes)
- 1 cup (240 ml) Chick'n Broth (page 299) or prepared vegetable broth
- ½ teaspoon ground black pepper
- ½ teaspoon salt, plus more if needed

1 Prepare the stuffing: Preheat a large skillet over low heat. Sauté the garlic in 2 tablespoons of the olive oil, just to warm through. Add the rosemary and thyme. Scatter the bread cubes in the pan and drizzle them with the remaining 2 tablespoons olive oil, flipping to coat. Add the broth, pepper, and salt and toss again so the bread is moist but still crunchy. Taste for salt. Let cook for about 10 minutes, then set aside to cool.

HOT TAKES

If you are using fresh bread cubes, bake the cubes for about 5 minutes in a 350°F (175°C) oven so that they are dry and slightly toasted.

This is a great roast for preplanning. It's perfect to make ahead, 1 to 3 days in advance. You can prepare and cook everything up to step 9, then follow from step 10 on the day you plan the big event.

CONTINUED →

FOR THE ROAST:

- **¾ cup (120 g) canned chickpeas, drained, plus ½ cup (120 ml) reserved chickpea liquid (aka aquafaba)**
- **1¼ cups (300 ml) Chick'n Broth (page 299) or prepared vegetable broth**
- **1¼ teaspoons salt**
- **4 tablespoons (60 ml) olive oil**
- **2 teaspoons liquid smoke**
- **1 teaspoon apple cider vinegar**
- **½ teaspoon agave syrup**
- **2 cups (240 g) vital wheat gluten**
- **¼ cup (15 g) nutritional yeast flakes**
- **1 teaspoon ground sage**
- **2 teaspoons onion powder**
- **1 teaspoon garlic powder**
- **½ teaspoon ground white pepper**

2 Prepare the roast: Preheat the oven to 350°F (175°C).

3 In a blender, puree the chickpeas, the aquafaba, 1 cup (240 ml) of the broth, the salt, 2 tablespoons of the olive oil, the liquid smoke, vinegar, and agave. Get it as smooth as possible, scraping down the sides with a rubber spatula as needed.

4 In a large bowl, mix together the wheat gluten, nutritional yeast, sage, onion powder, garlic powder, and ground white pepper. Make a well in the center and add the blended chickpea mixture. Use gloved hands to knead for about 3 minutes to make the seitan. It should be cohesive and easy to work with, like a sturdy dough.

5 Form the roasts. Prepare a piece of aluminum foil that is about 22 inches (55 cm) long (or big enough to wrap the turkey). Spray with cooking oil.

6 On a clean surface, use your hands or a rolling pin to flatten the seitan into a roughly 10 by 12-inch (25 by 30.5 cm) rectangle, with a long side facing you.

7 Place the filling in the lower third of the seitan rectangle, leaving about 2 inches (5 cm) of space on the left and right sides. Make sure the filling is compact; use your hands to form it into a nice, tight bundle.

8 Now roll! Roll the bottom part of the seitan up and over the filling. Keep rolling until it forms a log shape. Pinch together the seam and the sides to seal. It doesn't have to be perfect; things will snap into shape during baking.

9 Place the roll in the center of the prepared foil and wrap it up securely, twisting the ends of the foil. Transfer to a baking sheet and bake for 1 hour 20 minutes. Rotate the roll every 20 to 30 minutes for even cooking.

10 Let cool a bit then unwrap and remove the foil. Lightly grease with the remaining 2 tablespoons olive oil. Return the turki to the baking sheet and spoon the remaining ¼ cup (60 ml) vegetable broth over the top. Bake for another 15 minutes or so, to brown a little bit, basting with vegetable broth and turning about halfway through to prevent the roast from drying out. If heating from refrigerated, it will be closer to 20 minutes, rotating the turki often.

11 Let cool a bit, slice, and serve!

JACK'S BBQ SEITAN RIBS

Serves 4

There's something communal about ribs. Maybe everyone is just fighting to get an end piece, but in any case, they bring everyone together. These are chewy and toothsome and meaty and smoky and caramelized and messy and everything you want a rib to be. A mixture of jackfruit and seitan makes for a gristly texture that you need to chew and rip with your canines, just like a wild animal that doesn't eat animals. You only eat the beastly fruit named Jack. The method here is to make the seitan first, then slop it up with barbecue sauce and get it caramelized. Serve like a real BBQ event, with some grilled corn.

- 1 (14-ounce/400 g) can young jackfruit in water, rinsed
- 1¾ cups (210 g) vital wheat gluten
- 3 tablespoons nutritional yeast flakes
- 1 teaspoon garlic powder
- 1 tablespoon onion powder
- 2 teaspoons smoked paprika
- 2 tablespoons tamari or soy sauce
- 1 tablespoon olive oil
- 1 tablespoon tomato paste
- 1 tablespoon red wine vinegar
- 1 tablespoon pure maple syrup
- 3 cups (720 ml) prepared barbecue sauce or Stovetop Backyard BBQ Sauce (recipe follows)

1 Preheat the oven to 350°F (175°C). Have ready a large piece of aluminum foil lined with parchment paper, about 24 inches (60 cm) long.

2 Drain the jackfruit. Discard any large seeds and pull the pieces apart with your fingers until they resemble shredded meat (see photo, page 128).

3 In a large bowl, mix together the vital wheat gluten, nutritional yeast, garlic powder, onion powder, and paprika. Make a well in the center and pour in ¾ cup (180 ml) water, the tamari, olive oil, tomato paste, vinegar, and maple syrup. Add the jackfruit to the well and stir with a wooden spoon to combine. Use your hands to knead the mixture together for a few minutes until it's very springy and you can see gluten strands.

4 Roll the dough into a 10 by 6-inch (25 by 15 cm) rectangle. Score the ribs widthwise with a knife, pressing down hard but not cutting all the way through, so that you have 8 ribs, a little over 1 inch wide (2.5 cm) each.

5 Transfer the rectangle of ribs to the parchment paper–lined aluminum foil and fold into a neat package. Wrap loosely to cover. Place on a baking sheet and bake for 1 hour, flipping halfway through.

6 Remove the package from the oven and transfer it to a cooling rack. Carefully unwrap the rib loaf; it will be hot. Do not turn off the oven.

7 Spray the baking sheet with cooking spray, then pour 1½ cups (360 ml) of the barbecue sauce onto the baking sheet (first lining the pan with parchment if you don't want to be scrubbing your baking sheet forever, like we did for the photo). Spread the sauce out a bit so that when you return the ribs to the pan, they will fully cover the sauce.

CONTINUED →

8 Place the slab of ribs on the sauce and smother the tops with the remaining 1½ cups (360 ml) barbecue sauce (this works well if you use your gloved hands, but tongs will do the trick, too). Return the ribs to the oven and bake them for about 20 minutes, until they are lightly caramelized. Remove from oven.

9 Turn your broiler on and be ready to keep a close eye on the ribs. Place the ribs under the broiler for 3 to 5 minutes, checking for caramelization every minute or so. Be careful not to burn them!

10 When the ribs are nice and caramelized in spots, remove them from the oven. Cool until they are easy enough to handle but still warm enough to eat, about 10 minutes. Use a pizza wheel to cut along the scored lines, creating 8 ribs. Alternatively, you can use a sharp knife, pressing down hard with a downward motion to separate the ribs. Serve them on a platter, with additional barbecue sauce alongside, if you like.

STOVETOP BACKYARD BBQ SAUCE

Makes about 5 cups

This sauce simmers away on the stovetop, becoming thick, smoky, and caramelized while you do better things with your time.

- 3 tablespoons cornstarch
- 2 cups (480 ml) cold vegetable broth
- 2 cups (480 ml) prepared ketchup
- ⅔ cup (145 g) packed brown sugar
- ⅔ cup (165 ml) tamari
- ⅔ cup (165 ml) apple cider vinegar
- 2 teaspoons liquid smoke
- 2 tablespoons garlic powder
- 2 tablespoon onion powder
- ½ teaspoon cayenne pepper

1 In a 4-quart (3.8 L) saucepot, use a fork to vigorously whisk the cornstarch into the vegetable broth until it's mostly dissolved. Add the remaining ingredients and mix well.

2 Place the pot over medium heat, stirring occasionally, until the sauce comes to a boil. Once boiling, lower the heat to a simmer and let the sauce thicken for about 30 minutes. Stir occasionally. Remove from the heat and let cool for at least 30 minutes before using.

CAST-IRON STEAK AND ONIONS

Makes 2 big steaks to serve 4

If you're from Brooklyn—and you're probably not even though you say you are—then you celebrate with steak. Everyone knows this from every movie. Cavernous steakhouses that date back to the last, last century lurking all over the city, tucked under bridges or beside a forgotten waterway, with their historical plaques, creaky wood floors, and signed Frank Sinatra portraits on the wall. So let's celebrate, Brooklyn style. Whether it's a night of somber reflection or one of dancing and drinking (in your own home with only the members of your household and/or just your cat), this recipe works.

The method is a sear-braise combo for maximum juiciness. The steaks are cooked and removed from the pan, then you create a rich au jus by adding onions, garlic, miso, and red wine to the juices in the pan. Then the seared steaks are returned to the pan to cook through. The end result is some of the best seitan I have ever had! Seared and smoky, firm but tender. Plus it comes with its own sauce that's perfect for slathering. Serve with mashed potatoes or crinkle-cut fries.

FOR THE STEAKS:

- 1½ cups (180 g) vital wheat gluten
- 2 tablespoons nutritional yeast flakes
- 2 tablespoons beet powder
- 2 teaspoons salt-free lemon pepper
- 1 teaspoon onion powder
- ½ teaspoon mild mustard powder
- ⅔ cup (165 ml) water, at room temperature
- 3 tablespoons Bragg's liquid aminos
- 2 tablespoons tomato paste
- 2 tablespoons olive oil
- 2 teaspoons red wine vinegar

1 In a large bowl, combine the wheat gluten, beet powder, nutritional yeast, lemon pepper, onion powder, and mustard powder. Make a well in the center.

2 In a small bowl, mix together the room-temperature water, the aminos, tomato paste, olive oil, and vinegar until the tomato paste is incorporated.

3 Pour the wet ingredients into the well in the dry ingredients and mix until a lumpy ball forms. It will appear a bit dry. Now, use your hands (with gloves if you have them) to knead the mixture until all the ingredients are incorporated and there are no dry spots. If it's very cold in the kitchen, you may have a harder time kneading. Moisten your hands with warm water and keep going until you have a very stretchy dough; it should take about 3 minutes.

4 Shape the dough into a loose ball and divide the ball in half with a knife. Again, if it's cold, this process will take a bit longer as the seitan might spring back more as you cut. On a large cutting board, flatten each piece of dough into a kidney shape that is roughly ¾ inch (2 cm) thick and 8 inches (20 cm) in length. Using a rolling pin, roll and flatten them to form the steaks. Let the first one rest while you do the second one.

CONTINUED →

EVERYTHING ELSE:

- Olive oil, for cooking
- 1 medium onion, sliced
- Pinch salt
- 4 cloves garlic, minced
- ½ cup (120 ml) dry red wine
- 2 tablespoons red miso
- 3 bay leaves
- Freshly ground black pepper
- ¼ teaspoon dried thyme
- 4 cups (960 ml) Beefy Broth (page 302) or prepared vegetable broth
- Chopped fresh parsley, for garnish

HOT TAKES

The broth you use will affect the outcome. Make sure it isn't too salty because the sauce reduces a lot. If you're using a concentrated bullion mixed with water, like Better Than Bullion, that is fine, but go light with it and taste as you go to make sure it needs more. If you're making homemade, try Beefy Broth (page 302).

I really can't see one person eating a full steak like this, but feel free to prove me wrong. Aesthetically I wanted them to be this big, but realistically, the recipe for two steaks serves four hungry people.

5 Let both pieces of dough rest for about 10 minutes to allow the gluten to relax a bit, then repeat the rolling process. Again, the dough is more resistant if your kitchen is very cold so you might need to let it rest one more time. As the steaks rest the surfaces will get a little smoother, which is what you want for the sear and appearance.

6 Preheat a 12-inch cast-iron pan over medium-high heat. It should be very hot, and a drop of water should evaporate immediately. This is important because you want the steaks to hiss immediately, so they sear and do not stick.

7 Pour in a thin layer of olive oil to coat the bottom of the pan. Add the steaks and sear until both sides are dark brown, but not burnt, about 1½ minutes per side. Use a thin metal spatula to flip the steaks. Once they are seared, lower the heat to medium and let them cook until somewhat firm, about 10 more minutes, flipping 3 to 4 times and pressing down on them with the spatula.

8 When done, set aside the steaks on a plate; you will cook the sauce in the same cast-iron pan.

9 Turn the heat up to medium high. Drizzle about 2 tablespoons olive oil into the pan. Add the onion with a small pinch of salt and sear for about 3 minutes. Add the garlic and a little more oil if needed and cook the onions for about 2 more minutes, stirring often.

10 Pour in the wine and stir to deglaze, scraping up any brown bits on the bottom of the pan with a spatula, and reduce, about 3 minutes. Mix in the miso to dissolve. Add the bay leaves, a healthy dose of fresh black pepper (½ teaspoon or so), the thyme, and vegetable broth. Let the broth warm, reduce the heat to medium.

11 Once warm, return the steaks to the brothy pan and submerge them, spooning broth and onions over the top. Cover the pan and let cook for about 30 minutes. The broth should be simmering this whole time, but not boiling too rapidly so check occasionally. If the liquid is reducing too rapidly, you can add a little bit more broth.

12 OK, we're almost done! Remove the cover and flip the steaks. Turn the heat up and let the sauce reduce for about 15 minutes, uncovered. The broth will get really boily and active. Spoon sauce over the steaks while they cook. The steaks are done when they are no longer submerged and the sauce has thickened a bit and is really flavorful. Taste for salt and adjust if needed. Let them sit for 10 minutes or so before removing the bay leaves. Remove the steak from the pan, slice, garnish with parsley, and serve.

MADAME BEEFINGTON

Serves 6 to 8

- 1 recipe Life Is Rough Puff (see below), plus all-purpose flour for shaping the dough
- What Am I, Vegetarian Chopped Liver? (page 72)
- 1 recipe Roast Be'ef (recipe follows)
- ⅓ cup (75 ml) vegan mayo, prepared or homemade (page 309)
- 3 tablespoons unsweetened soy milk
- 2 tablespoons finely chopped fresh parsley

Beef Wellington puts everyone under its spell. Although it's been popularized as British fare, the exact origins are unknown. Some historians cite Napoleon as the inspiration, some claim maybe Julia Child just made it up. There's one thing we can say for sure: It's fancy as fork. And just as tasty. Tender meat wrapped in flaky pastry with a layer of buttery mushroom pâté in between. It's so festive you will be making up fake holidays on which to serve it! And if you feel like it, create your own origin story. Madame Beefington never tells.

To make this project manageable, make the be'ef recipe a day or three in advance. Let it cool in the broth and be ready for the world. You can also make the rough puff (see Hot Take) a day ahead!

1 To assemble the Madame Beefington, lightly flour a clean, preferably cold work surface. Roll out the pastry into a horizontal rectangle about ¼ inch thick. It should be about 10 inches (25 cm) wide and 14 to 16 inches (35 to 40 cm) long. Trim it to be 12 inches (30 cm) long and reserve the trimmings in the refrigerator to use for decoration if desired.

2 Spread a thick layer of the pâté in the center of the dough, across the waist. Place the roast beef on top of that, so it's facing you vertically. Then cover the rest of the roast beef in pâté. Fold up the sides of the pastry, top and bottom ends first, to completely encase the beef. Crimp the edges together and trim off any excess dough. Line a plate large enough to fit the roast with parchment and place the roast on the plate, seam side down. Refrigerate for 20 minutes.

3 Preheat the oven to 400°F (205°C). In a coffee mug, use a fork to mix together the mayo and soy milk to create a glaze.

4 While the oven is preheating, you can take this time to use the dough scraps to create any shapes you want to decorate the Beefington. We used a paring knife to create leaves and stuff, but you can do simple shapes, like hearts or diamonds, using a cookie cutter if you like. Or you can do nothing at all! It will still be cute. These decorations are baked separately so you don't feel rushed; keep them cold in the fridge and you can come back to them later.

HOT TAKE

Rough puff is a simpler version of puff pastry, but it still isn't that simple: The process still requires lots of rolling and refrigerating. However, it's a great way to feel like you're on *The Great British Baking Show* for an entire afternoon. You can absolutely use store-bought vegan puff pastry, though, if life is too rough even for rough puff.

CONTINUED →

5 When the oven is preheated, line a baking sheet with parchment. Transfer the Beefington, seam side down, to the pan. Score the dough in a chevron pattern (see pic, opposite), up the length of the pastry. Brush all over with the glaze. Bake until golden, about 30 minutes. If using cut-out shapes, please see step 6.

6 Have all the cut-out shapes chilled and at the ready. About 20 minutes into baking, remove the Beefington from the oven. Lightly brush the bottom of the pastry shapes with the glaze and place them on the Beefington as desired. Once placed, brush with glaze a final time. Return to the oven to bake until the decorative shapes are golden, too, about 10 more minutes.

7 Once baked, immediately remove the Beefington from oven and transfer it with the parchment to a cool surface; let cool for about 30 minutes before slicing and serving. Sprinkle with parsley and serve on your fanciest serving tray.

LIFE IS ROUGH PUFF

- ½ cup (120 ml) ice water
- 1 tablespoon apple cider vinegar
- 2 cups (250 g) all-purpose flour, chilled, plus more for rolling
- ½ teaspoon salt
- ¾ cups (1½ sticks/170 g) vegan butter, cut into ½-inch (12 mm) chunks and chilled in the freezer for an hour

1 Combine the ice water and vinegar and keep it cold in the freezer while you do everything else.

2 Place the flour and salt in a food processor fit with a metal blade. Pulse a few times to combine.

3 Place half of the butter in the food processor and pulse 10 times. Add the remaining 6 tablespoons (85 g) of the butter and pulse another 10 times, until the mixture forms small clumps ranging from pebbles to peas.

4 Stream the chilled water-vinegar mixture into the food processor while pulsing, about 10 to 12 times, until it comes together. Don't blend the dough; it should still be crumbly but hold together.

5 Lightly flour a clean, cold surface (a marble-type surface or stainless steel is great). Place the dough on surface and lightly form into a ball then press it into a rough rectangle, with a long side facing you. Using a rolling pin, roll out until about ½ inch (12 mm) thick. The rectangle will be about 16 inches (40 cm) wide and 6 inches (15 cm) long. The dough will be rustic and streaky but should hold together.

6 Time to fold! You will be folding it approximately into thirds. Fold one side of the dough over towards the other side, just a bit past the middle. And fold the other side over that one in the same way, so that you have three layers.

7 Wrap the dough in plastic wrap and place it in the freezer for 15 minutes. In the meantime, clean and dry the work surface and lightly flour it again.

CONTINUED →

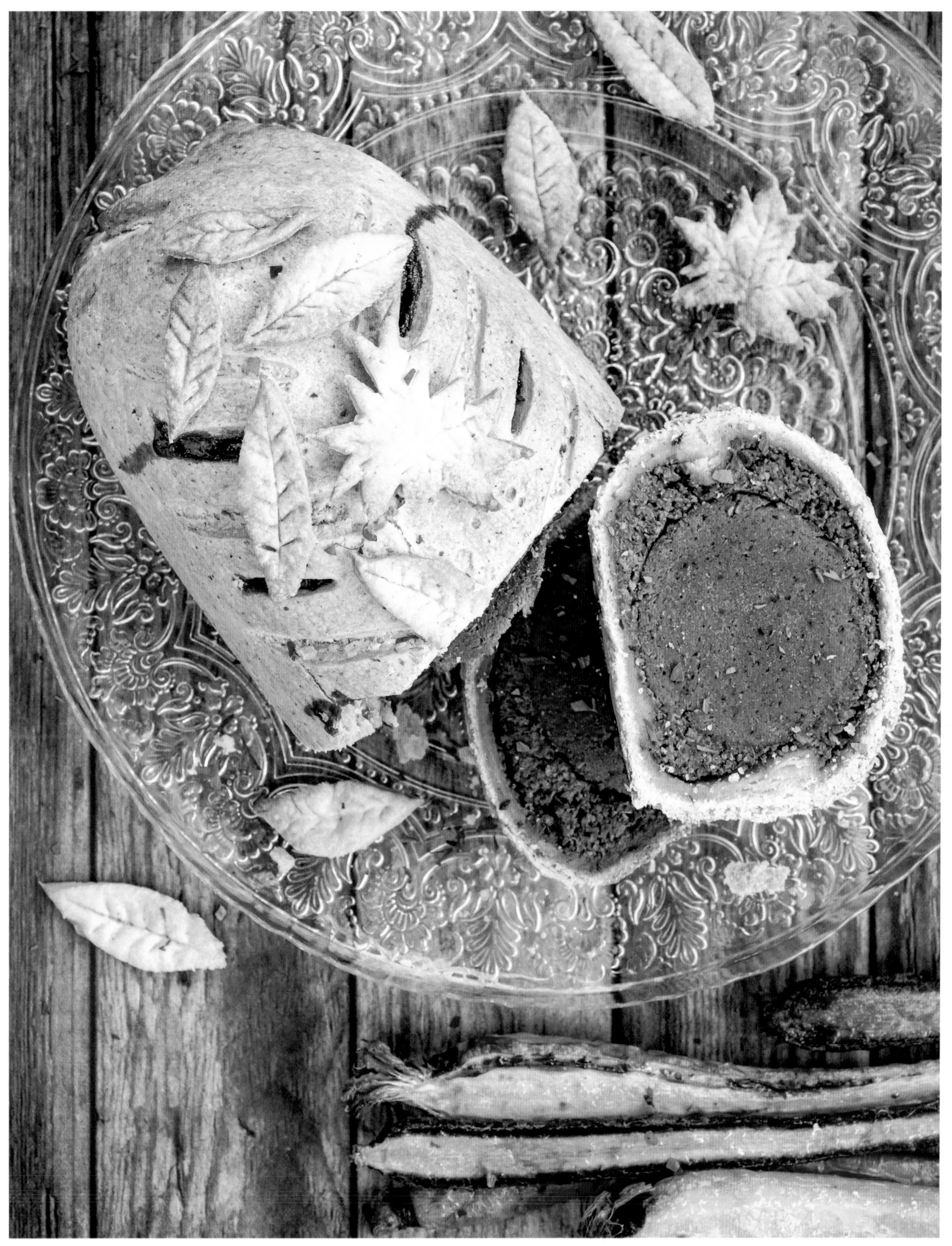

8 Time for the second rolling. Remove the dough from the fridge and roll it into a 16 by 6-inch (40 by 15 cm) rectangle again. Repeat step 6, folding the dough into thirds again. Wrap in plastic and place in the freezer again for 15 minutes. Clean and dry the work surface and lightly flour it again.

9 Last turn! Roll the dough into a 16 by 6-inch (40 by 15 cm) rectangle. Fold into thirds again. Wrap in plastic and place in the fridge until ready to use. You can store it this way for up to 3 days.

ROAST BE'EF

FOR THE SIMMERING LIQUID:

- 10 cups (2.4 L) Beefy Broth (page 302) or prepared vegetable broth
- ½ cup (120 ml) tamari or soy sauce
- 8 bay leaves
- 2 tablespoons beet powder

FOR THE ROAST BE'EF:

- 1 (15-ounce/430 g) can lentils or 1½ cups cooked lentils
- 3 tablespoons olive oil
- 3 tablespoons tomato paste
- 2 tablespoons red miso
- 1 teaspoon balsamic vinegar
- 3 tablespoons nutritional yeast flakes
- 2 teaspoons sugar
- 2 tablespoons beet powder
- 1 tablespoon onion powder
- 2 teaspoons garlic powder
- 1 teaspoon paprika
- 1 teaspoon salt
- 1¾ cups (210 g) vital wheat gluten
- 1 teaspoon ground black pepper

1 Prepare the simmering liquid: Have ready a 16-inch (40 cm) piece of double-layered cheesecloth and twine. Place the broth ingredients in a large pot and bring to a simmer.

2 Prepare the be'ef: In a blender, puree the lentils, ¾ cup (180 ml) water, the olive oil, tomato paste, miso, balsamic vinegar, nutritional yeast, sugar, beet powder, onion powder, garlic powder, paprika, and salt until smooth. This will take less than a minute in a high-speed blender, and about 3 minutes in a standard blender.

3 In a large bowl, sift together the vital wheat gluten and black pepper. Make a well in the center and mix in the wet stuff from the blender. Knead for 5 minutes or so until the dough is stringy and springy.

4 Roll the dough into a loaf that's about 10 inches (25 cm) long. Wrap snuggly in the cheesecloth and tie each end in twine.

5 Make sure the broth is at a very low simmer, barely bubbling. Add the roast be'ef bundle and let it stew very gently without boiling for about 15 minutes. When the skin is set, place the lid ajar for steam to escape and low boil for about 45 more minutes.

6 Turn off the heat and let the seitan cool completely in the broth before continuing with the recipe. If using within 3 days, store and refrigerate submerged in broth in a tightly sealed container.

PORTOBELLA YUBA ROAST

Serves 4 to 6

This layered, savory roast is a feast of texture and also just a regular old feast. It's inspired by roast duck, in the spirit of the Chinese Buddhists who first proclaimed that many thin sheets of tofu baked together in the oven could approximate a bird. The yuba works like a skin, and you will definitely need a steak knife to get a satisfying slice, straight through the yuba and the tender portobello. The portobellos are treated in a unique way—roasted to "meaty perfection" and then flattened so that you have all this stratified texture. This isn't the roast for the kid's table; it's high art, haute cuisine, if you will. Mirin heightens the flavor with its sweet, distinct aroma. It's a fermented rice wine, similar to sake, that adds depth to anything it's cooked with, while also providing a thick, glazy texture. Just like a conventional roast, the left-overs are possibly even better than the first serving. Try to hide some away from your guests to enjoy slices pan-fried and sandwiched between toasted sourdough bread the next day.

FOR THE ROAST:

- 3 large sheets (10 by 16 inches/25 by 40 cm) dried yuba

FOR THE GRAVY:

- 1 cup thinly sliced shallots
- 6 cloves garlic, minced
- 6 bay leaves
- 3 tablespoons chopped fresh thyme
- 1 teaspoon ground black pepper
- 2 tablespoons olive oil
- Pinch salt
- 3 tablespoons mirin
- 2 tablespoons red miso
- 3 tablespoons cornstarch
- 1 quart cold vegetable broth, prepared, or Chick'n Broth (page 299)

FOR THE PORTOBELLAS:

- 4 large portobella caps
- 2 tablespoons olive oil
- 1 teaspoon salt
- ½ teaspoon black pepper

1. Soak the yuba sheets in warm water to rehydrate. Use a large frying pan for this, because it's wide enough to fit the sheets. Let them soak for about 30 minutes to 1 hour, flipping them around every now and again until soft and pliable.

2. Now begin the gravy. Preheat a large pan over medium heat. Sauté the shallots, garlic, bay leaves, thyme, and black pepper in olive oil with a pinch of salt, until the shallots are translucent, about 10 minutes. Deglaze the pan with the mirin. Cook for about 5 more minutes. Add the miso and toss it with the shallot mixture until the miso is dissolved.

3. In a mixing bowl, combine the cornstarch with 1 cup of broth and mix until it forms a slurry. Add the remaining broth and stir. Now slowly add the broth to the pan, stirring as you go. Cook for about 15 minutes, until thick-ened, stirring often. Let cool in the pan while preparing everything else.

CONTINUED →

4 Roast the portobello caps. Line a baking sheet with parchment. Preheat the oven to 425°F (220°C). Place portobello caps right-side up on the baking sheet. Drizzle with half of the olive oil and sprinkle with half the salt and pepper. Rub all over. Flip the bellas and drizzle with the remaining oil and sprinkle with remaining salt and pepper. Rub again.

5 Place bellas in oven. Roast for 20 minutes. Flatten them with a flexible spatula to squeeze out some juices. Flip and roast 10 to 15 minutes more. They should be tender and still juicy. Remove from oven and let them rest until they are cool enough to handle.

6 Once cool, slice the portobellos on a bias about ¼ inch thick.

ASSEMBLE THE ROAST:

1 First of all, we are gonna get messy, but don't worry, it will all work out in the end. Reduce the oven heat to 350°F (175°C). Line a rimmed baking sheet with parchment and arrange horizontally in front of you. Have ready four 14-inch (35 cm) strands of cooking twine soaked in water.

2 Remove the yuba from the water and give each sheet a lil' squeeze. Pat them dry with a paper towel.

3 Dip a piece of yuba in the gravy and get it good and covered. Lay the sheet on the parchment. Arrange two of the sliced bellas diagonally across the middle of the yuba sheet, leaving 2 inches (5 cm) of space on the top and bottom and 4 inches (10 cm) on the side. Pour ½ cup of gravy over the bellas.

4 Dip another sheet of yuba in the gravy and layer over the bellas. Arrange the remaining bella slices diagonally, leaving space on top and sides. Pour ½ cup of gravy over the bellas.

5 Time to roll! Fold the sides of the yuba toward the middle, then roll tight like a burrito. Move it off to the side a bit. It's OK if it's messy; you'll clean it up with the last sheet.

6 Take the last sheet of yuba and slather it in gravy. Place on the baking sheet, then take your yuba burrito and place it vertically on the right side of the sheet. Now roll like a Tootsie Roll. Secure both ends with twine. Wrap two pieces of twine around the waist.

7 Slather with extra gravy. Bake for 30 minutes, until nicely browned. Remove from the oven and let cool for about 20 minutes before slicing and serving.

TUNA STEAKS WITH LEMON AND CAPERS

Everything you want in a tuna steak: flaky, a li'l fishy, meaty, and, of course, pink. These steaks appear fancy but are some of the easiest fake meat to make. Silken tofu is frozen, thawed, and pressed. There's no special technique involved; you just get beautiful flaky fillets that create a gorgeous display when served on a beautiful white platter. This is also a great recipe for other fish-centric dishes, like sushi or Niçoise (page 67). And if you're going super casual, it's completely divine in a sandwich.

- 2 (14-ounce/400 g) packages extra-firm tofu (the vacuum-packed kind, like Mori-Nu)

FOR THE MARINADE:

- ¼ cup (60 ml) fresh lemon juice
- 1 cup (240 ml) vegetable broth
- ¼ cup (60 ml) olive oil
- 2 teaspoons kelp granules
- 2 teaspoons beet powder
- 1 teaspoon salt

FOR THE LEMON CAPER SAUCE:

- 2 cups (230 g) thinly sliced shallots
- 2 tablespoons olive oil
- Salt to taste
- 6 cloves garlic, minced
- 3 tablespoons nutritional yeast flakes
- ½ cup (120 ml) dry white wine
- 2 cups (475 ml) vegetable broth
- ¼ cup capers, with brine
- 2 tablespoons lemon juice
- Several dashes freshly ground black pepper

FOR SERVING:

- 4 cups arugula
- 1 lemon, thinly sliced
- 2 tablespoons chopped fresh parsley
- Freshly ground black pepper

1 Remove the tofu from its package, following the package instructions. Be careful when doing so to keep the blocks together in one piece, but they should just slide right out.

2 Now we will press the tofu. Gently place each block of tofu onto its own layer of 3 paper towels and wrap. Place a kitchen towel on the counter and line up the wrapped tofu on it. Place another kitchen towel over it to cover.

3 Place a cutting board on top of the tofu and weigh it down with a few heavy books to press the water out for about an hour.

4 While the tofu is pressing, make the marinade. In a mixing bowl, whisk together the lemon juice, vegetable broth, olive oil, kelp granules, beet powder, and salt.

5 Unwrap the tofu and then slice each into two slabs, so you have two large rectangles.

6 Transfer the marinade to a 9 by 9-inch (23 by 23 cm) baking dish or Tupperware. If you don't have that size, a large mixing bowl will work. Dredge the tofu in the marinade for about 2 hours, flipping halfway through.

7 Time to cook the tofu! Preheat a cast-iron pan over medium-low heat. Spray the pan with cooking spray and sear the tuna steaks for 2 to 3 minutes on each side, pressing with a spatula as you cook. The steaks should look flaky, but you can make them even flakier-looking by pressing down and lightly pulling the flat part of the spatula across the tuna steak. Keep warm in the pan until ready to serve.

CONTINUED →

MAKE THE LEMON CAPER SAUCE:

1. Preheat a large skillet over medium-high heat. Sauté the shallots in oil with a pinch of salt for 7 to 10 minutes, until lightly browned. Add garlic and sauté until fragrant, 30 seconds or so.
2. Add the nutritional yeast and toss to coat, flipping the shallots for about 1 minute, as the nutritional yeast toasts. Immediately add the wine to deglaze then raise the heat to bring to a rolling boil. Let boil and reduce for about 3 minutes.
3. Add the vegetable broth, capers and brine, lemon juice, and black pepper. Lower the heat to medium and cook for about 5 more minutes to reduce a little more. Taste for salt.

ASSEMBLE:

1. Place the arugula on the bottom of a serving platter. Put the hot tuna steaks on top. Pour sauce all over. Garnish with lemon, parsley, and fresh black pepper.

TURKI POT PIE

Makes one 9-inch (23 cm) pie

Dig your fork through the flaky crust and into a creamy base laced with nostalgic fall flavors. It will make you feel like a kid again! Unless you are already a kid, in which case, keep it up. These have a top AND bottom crust because how disappointing is it to run out of crust? I make the crust edges super thick, because again, it's all about the crust. You'll brush it with mayo for a total glow-up that glazes and browns beautifully. Cut cute little shapes out to decorate the top. I love to use hearts for every occasion, but leaves are pretty standard to be like, "Hey, in case you haven't noticed it's autumn." And if it's not autumn, and you are serving pot pie in the middle of summer, I have nothing but respect for you.

- 1 cup (120 g) unroasted cashews
- 2 cups (480 ml) Chick'n Broth (page 299) or prepared vegetable broth
- Double-Trouble Crust (recipe follows)
- ½ recipe Roast Turki (page 20)
- 3 tablespoons olive oil
- 1 teaspoon salt, plus a pinch
- 1 medium yellow onion, cut into medium dice
- 1 medium carrot, peeled and cut into small dice
- A big handful green beans, sliced into ½-inch (12 mm) pieces (to equal 1 cup)
- 3 ribs celery, thinly sliced
- 3 tablespoons chopped fresh thyme
- 2 teaspoons poultry seasoning, prepared or homemade (page 89)
- 1 teaspoon dry-rubbed sage
- ½ teaspoon ground black pepper

FOR GLAZING:

- 2 tablespoons vegan mayo, store-bought or homemade (page 309)
- 2 tablespoons unsweetened soy milk

FOR GARNISH:

- A few teaspoons chopped fresh parsley

1 Place the cashews and broth in a high-speed blender and puree until completely smooth, pausing to scrape down the sides with a rubber spatula to make sure you get everything. If you don't have a high-speed blender, see "Let's Get Nuts" on page 11.

2 Preheat the oven to 425°F (220°C). Roll out the pie crusts about 2 inches (5 cm) bigger than the deep-dish pie pan you are using. Line the pan with the bottom crust and chill the top crust in the refrigerator until ready to use.

3 Using a chef's knife, "shave" the turki roast into ⅛-inch-thick oblong slivers. They can vary in length from ¾ inch to 1½ inches (1 cm to 2.5 cm); see photo on page 21.

4 Preheat a cast-iron pan over medium heat. Sauté the turki shavings in 1 tablespoon of the oil until lightly browned, about 3 minutes, then transfer the turki to a plate.

5 In the same pan, sauté the onion, carrot, and green beans in the remaining 2 tablespoons oil with a pinch of salt until the onion is translucent and the carrot is slightly softened, about 5 minutes. Add the celery, fresh thyme, poultry seasoning, sage, pepper, and 1 teaspoon salt and sauté until the celery is softened, about 5 minutes.

6 Pour the cashew cream mixture into the pan and cook until thickened, stirring often. Add the sautéed turki to the pan and toss to coat. Let cook just until warm, giving a stir once in a while. Don't cook for too long or too high, or the cashew cream will thicken too much. Taste for salt and pepper and adjust if needed.

CONTINUED →

7 Transfer the filling to the prepared pie pan lined with the bottom crust. Take the chilled top crust out of the fridge and cut out cool shapes. Set the decorative shapes aside on a plate and refrigerate.

8 Place the top crust on the pie and crimp the edges using your thumb and forefinger. Alternatively, you can press the edges with a fork if you don't want to be fancy, or use your preferred way to crimp an edge.

9 In a coffee mug, stir together the mayo and soy milk and glaze the crust with it. The easiest way is to use your fingers to coat the top crust and edges. Reserve some of the glaze for the decorations.

10 Bake the pie for 32 to 35 minutes, until hot, bubbly, and lightly golden. When the time is almost up, glaze the cut-out shapes on both sides. Remove the pie from the oven and stick the shapes on the top of the pie. Bake for another 8 to 10 minutes, until everything is fully golden.

11 Remove from the oven. Garnish with parsley and let cool for about 30 minutes before digging in!

DOUBLE-TROUBLE CRUST

Makes two 9- to 10-inch (23 to 25 cm) crusts

A really traditional, buttery crust! Apple cider vinegar is the secret ingredient that keeps things tender and also adds a little mystery to your pie crust, prompting everyone to ask for the recipe.

- 2½ cups (315 g) all-purpose flour, chilled
- 2 tablespoons sugar
- ½ teaspoon salt
- 2 cups (1 pound/455 g) cold vegan butter
- 8 to 10 tablespoons (120 to 150 ml) ice water
- 1 tablespoon apple cider vinegar

1 In a large bowl, sift together the flour, sugar, and salt. Add half the butter in spoonfuls, cutting it into the flour with your fingers or a pastry cutter until the flour appears pebbly. Add the remaining butter the same way.

2 In a cup, mix together 4 tablespoons (60 ml) of the ice water with the apple cider vinegar. Drizzle it by the tablespoonful into the flour and butter mixture, gently mixing it after each addition. Knead the dough a few times, adding more water a little at a time until it holds together. You may only need the 4 tablespoons (60 ml) more depending on the humidity, but add up to 6 more tablespoons (90 ml) ice water in all if needed.

3 Divide the dough in two, roll each half into a ball, then press into disks. Wrap the disks in plastic wrap and chill for at least an hour before using. They may need to sit at room temperature for 20 minutes or so to warm slightly before using.

MEMBERS-ONLY MEATLOAF

- 2 bay leaves
- ¾ cup (55 g) textured vegetable protein (TVP)
- 1 cup (200 g) overcooked brown or green lentils, canned or homemade (see Hot Take)
- ½ cup (120 ml) vegetable broth
- 2 tablespoons tomato paste
- 3 tablespoons tamari or soy sauce
- 2 tablespoons olive oil
- 1 tablespoon smoked paprika
- 1½ teaspoons dried thyme
- 1 teaspoon onion powder
- 1 teaspoon garlic powder
- ½ teaspoon black pepper
- ¼ teaspoon salt
- ¾ cup grated or very finely chopped yellow onion
- ½ cup (50 g) store-bought dried breadcrumbs (see Hot Take, page 264)
- 1 cup (120 g) vital wheat gluten

Serves 6 to 8

Let's talk about the eighties. It was a time when the only thing we were allowed to eat was meatloaf. And it was specifically this kind of meatloaf: hearty and meaty, not dry but not tooooo juicy, that was delicately seasoned straight from the eighties spice rack—paprika, thyme, onion, and garlic—and finished with a smoky, sweet glaze (OK, sometimes it was just ketchup). We literally had no other spices. And although this very meal was the punchline in lots of Sunday comics, who doesn't crave the hell out of these flavors? It's amazing in a sandwich the next day. It's the perfect accompaniment for peas and mashed potatoes. And it's still as comforting as ever, which is just what we need right here and now in the 2020s.

1 In a small pot, bring 3 cups (720 ml) water to a boil with 2 bay leaves. Turn off the heat, mix in the TVP, and let it sit for about 10 minutes until soft and spongy. Pour into a fine-mesh strainer and let cool. Remove the bay leaves.

2 Preheat the oven to 350°F (175°C).

3 In a large bowl, mash the lentils into a puree, then mix in the vegetable broth. Or, if you prefer, you can simply puree the lentils with the broth in a blender, then put the mixture in the bowl. Mix in the tomato paste, tamari, and olive oil and beat until the tomato paste is incorporated. Add the smoked paprika, then rub the dried thyme between your fingers and add it along with the onion powder, garlic powder, pepper, and salt.

HOT TAKE

The lentils should be overcooked and bordering on mushy! Canned lentils that are drained will work perfectly.

CONTINUED →

FOR THE GLAZE:

- ⅓ cup (85g) tomato paste
- 3 tablespoons water
- ¼ cup (55 g) packed brown sugar
- 1 tablespoon smooth Dijon mustard
- ⅛ teaspoon ground nutmeg
- Pinch salt

HOT TAKES

This recipe is easy but does require some attention so the meatloaf cooks correctly. There's about 1 hour 20 minutes of baking time total. So just read the directions carefully when it comes to flipping. Basically, you're gonna bake for a bit, flip the loaf once, then flip it again. Then, you're gonna unwrap it and bake it for a bit. THEN you're gonna transfer it to parchment, glaze it, and bake it again. It's easy, but your eyes might GLAZE over while reading the directions.

I strongly suggest store-bought breadcrumbs here, because moisture content is going to be key. You can try homemade, but don't say I didn't warn you.

4 When the TVP is cool enough to handle, press it against the strainer to release as much moisture as possible. Add it to the bowl with the lentil mixture and mix well, mushing it up to make sure it soaks up the liquid.

5 Lightly mix in the grated onion and the breadcrumbs. Add the vital wheat gluten and use your hands to knead the mixture for about 2 minutes, then form it into a ball. You might want to wear kitchen gloves for this to keep your hands fresh and clean.

6 Line an 18-inch (46 cm) sheet of aluminum foil with parchment and spray with cooking oil. Place the ball of meatloaf in the center of the sprayed parchment and form it into an 8 by 3-inch (20 by 7.5 cm) loaf that is rectangular and as flat as you can make it on all sides. Wrap the parchment and foil around the loaf and transfer to a baking sheet.

7 OK, now comes an important part about flipping, so pay attention. Bake for 30 minutes, then flip the meatloaf upside down, so it's resting on its top, and bake for another 20 minutes. Then flip it again to the original position. This time, unwrap the loaf (but don't remove it from the pan) and bake the meatloaf for 10 more minutes, just to get it a little crusty. Do not turn off the heat.

8 While all this baking is happening, make the glaze: Simply combine all the glaze ingredients in a mug and, using a fork, vigorously mix them together. Set aside.

9 After the loaf bakes, you are going to transfer it to a new sheet of parchment paper. So place the baking sheet somewhere safe where it won't burn you or anything else (on the stovetop works for me) and lay out a kitchen towel as close as possible.

10 Use oven mitts or towels to lift the loaf in the foil onto the towel. Now line the baking sheet with parchment and spray it with cooking oil. Use a wide spatula to get the loaf onto the parchment-lined baking sheet. Pour the glaze all over the meatloaf and use the back of a spoon to make sure you get it good and coated.

11 Place the baking sheet in the oven and bake the meatloaf for another 20 minutes. Remove and let cool slightly before slicing and serving!

U'REAL PARMESAN

Serves 6

Guilty secret: Veal Parmesan was my jam in the seventies. Even if we didn't use the term "my jam" yet, I ordered it anytime we went out for Italian, and we went out for Italian a lot. These cutlets take shape with a mixture of lentils and gluten, bolstered by rich porcini AND truffles, the royalty of mushroom umami. Stretched thin to maximize surface area, each piece gets nice and crispy, laying the perfect groundwork for gobs of gooey mozz, slowly melting into the marinara and mingling in a nostalgic bite. Bring back the romance for future generations, but with compassion and, of course, lentils.

FOR THE VEGAN CUTLETS:

- 1 (15-ounce/430 g) can lentils or 1½ cups overcooked lentils
- 2 tablespoons olive oil, plus more for pan-frying
- 2 tablespoons truffle oil
- 1 cup (120 g) vital wheat gluten
- 1 tablespoon porcini powder
- 2 teaspoons onion powder
- 1 teaspoon garlic powder
- 1 cup (100 g) fine dried breadcrumbs
- ½ cup (120 ml) vegetable broth or water
- ¼ cup (60 ml) tamari or soy sauce

1 Make the cutlets: In a medium-size bowl, mash the lentils together with the olive oil until no whole ones are left and they are very mushy but not quite pureed. Use an avocado masher or a strong fork.

2 Add the truffle oil, vital wheat gluten, porcini powder, onion powder, garlic powder, breadcrumbs, broth, and tamari to the lentils. Knead together for about 3 minutes, until strings of gluten have formed.

3 Preheat a large, heavy-bottomed skillet over low-medium heat. Cast iron works best. If you have two pans and want to cook all the cutlets at once then go for it, otherwise you'll be making them in two batches.

4 Divide the cutlet dough into 2 equal pieces. Then divide each of those pieces into 4 separate pieces (so you'll have 8 pieces altogether). To form cutlets, knead each piece in your hand for a few moments and then flatten and stretch it into a roughly 6 by 4-inch (15 by 10 cm) rectangular cutlet shape. The easiest way to do this is to form a rectangle shape in your hands and then place the cutlets on a clean surface to flatten and stretch them.

CONTINUED →

FOR THE PARM:

- 1 (32-ounce) jar marinara or 4 cups (950 ml) Best Friend's Mom's Marinara (page 306)
- Olive oil, for sprinkling
- 8 balls Fresh Mozz-Shew-Rella (page 286)

FOR GARNISH:

- A handful fresh basil leaves
- Red pepper flakes to taste

5 Pour a thin layer of olive oil into the bottom of the pan, about ⅛ inch. Place the cutlets in the pan and cook on each side for 6 to 7 minutes. Cover the pan in between flips so they cook more evenly, and add more oil, if needed, when you flip the cutlets. You can also press down on the cutlets with the spatula to get proper searing. They're ready when lightly browned and firm to the touch.

6 Now let them rest for a bit and you're ready to assemble the parm!

7 Make the parm: Preheat the oven to 425°F (220°C). Place 2 cups of sauce on a parchment-lined baking sheet, in 8 dollops that will go under each cutlet. Lay a cutlet on top of each dollop. Spoon the remaining marinara over the cutlets. Flatten the mozzarella balls and place on top of each cutlet.

8 Bake for 15 minutes. Top with fresh basil and red pepper flakes to serve.

MEAT LOVERS' PINWHEEL LASAGNA

Serves 6

No one's saying there's anything wrong with classic lasagna, but that doesn't mean we can't improve it all the same. Forget all that painstaking layering and stacking; grab a noodle and start rolling instead! Each coil is stuffed with all the cheesy, meaty goodness of the original, while the additional exposed edges get every bit as crispy as the prized edge pieces. Lentil walnut meat is exactly what you want to feed someone who is craving meat but wants to use familiar ingredients, like mushrooms, nuts, and beans. Drown the whole thing in red sauce and get everyone excited for lasagna night all over again!

- 12 frilly lasagna noodles
- 2 (24-ounce) jars of marinara or 1 recipe Best Friend's Mom's Marinara (page 306)
- Mushroom Walnut Meat (recipe follows)
- 10 balls Mozz-Shew-Rella
- Fresh basil or microgreens for garnish
- Red pepper flakes to taste

FOR THE LENTIL WALNUT MEAT:

- 1 yellow onion, cut into small dice
- 2 tablespoons olive oil
- Pinch of salt
- 6 cloves garlic, minced
- ½ teaspoon dried rosemary
- ¼ teaspoon dried thyme
- ¼ teaspoon red pepper flakes
- ¼ teaspoon dried oregano
- Several dashes freshly ground black pepper
- 1 cup (120 g) chopped walnuts (pea-size pieces or smaller)
- 8 ounces (225 g) mushrooms, finely chopped
- ¼ teaspoon salt
- ½ cup (120 ml) red wine
- 1 cup (200 g) cooked brown or green lentils, drained
- ½ cup (60 g) dried breadcrumbs
- ¼ cup (60 ml) prepared marinara or Best Friend's Mom's Marinara (page 306)

1 Make the lentil-walnut meat: Preheat a large, heavy-bottomed skillet over medium heat. Sauté the onion in the olive oil with a pinch of salt until translucent, 7 to 10 minutes. Add the garlic and sauté a minute more. Add the rosemary, thyme, red pepper flakes, oregano, black pepper, and the walnuts and toss to coat. Allow the walnuts to toast for 3 minutes or so.

2 Add the mushrooms and ¼ teaspoon salt; sauté until lightly browned, about 5 minutes. Deglaze the pan with the red wine, scraping up any brown bits with a spatula, and raise the heat to reduce the liquid, about 3 minutes.

3 Add the lentils and heat through. Press them with a spatula to mash them a bit. You're not making hummus, they should just be slightly mashed. Add the breadcrumbs and marinara and let cook for about 5 minutes, stirring often, then remove from the heat to cool completely. If not using immediately, refrigerate in a tightly sealed container up to 3 days ahead.

CONTINUED →

HOT TAKES

You can absolutely double this recipe if you're feeding a crowd and have a larger casserole on hand.

The lentil walnut meat is a nice recipe in its own right, laced with herbs, red wine, and lots of meaty texture, so use it to stuff any sort of pasta (shells or cannelloni, maybe?).

PREPARE AND ASSEMBLE THE LASAGNA:

1 Preheat the oven to 350°F (175°C).

2 Bring a very large pot of salted water to a boil. Add 12 lasagna noodles (2 are safety noodles, in case one rips). Cook al dente, just until they are pliable enough to handle.

3 Drain them and carefully lay them out flat on a piece of parchment, using tongs to handle. Cover with a wet kitchen towel so they don't dry out.

4 Pour 3 cups of marinara in a 4-quart casserole and spread it out. Set aside.

5 Use a large rimmed baking sheet to roll the noodles. Remember you are just rolling 10; the extra 2 were in case one ripped. Pour about 2 cups of marinara on the lasagna noodles and dredge the noodles in sauce. Lay one out flat. Spread an additional tablespoon of sauce onto the noodle. Spread about 2 tablespoons of walnut meat on top of that. Dot the meat with mozzarella, using one ball per noodle and breaking it into small pieces.

6 Roll each noodle up into a spiral, then arrange upright in the pan next to each other. If the filling starts drooping, you can add additional meat, sauce, and cheese to the top of the spiraled noodle once it is situated.

7 Bake for 30 minutes, or until the edges are lightly browned.

8 Top with fresh basil or microgreens and sprinkle with red pepper flakes.

QUICHE LORRAIN'T II

Makes one 9-inch (23 cm) quiche

Prepare yourself for a resounding chorus of "oohs" and "aahs." This quiche is a stunner! OK, so it's pretty, but how does it taste? Classic quiche Lorraine, which I assume is named after everyone's Aunt Lorraine, features caramelized onion, Gruyère cheese, and bacon. Just imagine smoky, chewy bacon with sweet and aromatic onion, all mingling in an eggy custard with rich, cheesy bites. It is, needless to say, ridiculously decadent. We achieve that feat with tofu, cashews, chickpea flour, and that sulfuric salt, kala namak. I love to use homemade Swizz Cheese for maximum effect, but you can buy some to streamline the process instead. The bacon is the crown jewel, so it should definitely be something dramatic. I prefer the Ribbony Seitan Bacon, but the Trumpet Bacon wouldn't disappoint, either. Serve with a refreshing salad and a zesty dressing to cleanse the palate (the balsamic on page 68 or Italian herb on page 314 would do nicely). I have a Quiche Lorrain't in another book, so this one is the new and improved version based on everything I've learned since then. This one is a definite upgrade. It even tastes great cold or at room temperature.

- 14 slices Ribbony Seitan Bacon (page 171)
- 2 tablespoons olive oil
- Pinch of salt
- 3 medium yellow onions, finely diced
- ¾ cup (90 g) unroasted cashews
- ¼ cup (15 g) nutritional yeast flakes
- ¼ cup (25 g) chickpea flour
- ½ teaspoon turmeric
- 1½ teaspoons kala namak
- ¼ teaspoon ground nutmeg
- 1 (14-ounce/400 g) block extra-firm tofu
- 1 Deep-Dish Single-Pastry Crust, rolled out into pan and chilled until ready to use (recipe follows)
- ½ cup (70 g) diced Swizz Cheeze (page 294) or your favorite store-bought version, plus a few slices for the top

1 Preheat the oven to 350°F (175°C). Lightly spray a large skillet with cooking oil and preheat over medium heat. Cook 8 slices of the bacon for about 3 minutes, flipping once. Transfer to a plate so that it doesn't overcook.

2 Now, caramelize the onions. Preheat a heavy-bottomed skillet, preferably cast-iron, over low heat. Add the oil along with a pinch of salt. Cover and cook for 20 minutes or so, leaving a little gap for steam to escape and stirring occasionally, every 5 minutes or so. The onions should turn a nice, mellow amber color; don't allow them to burn, but a couple of darker spots are fine.

3 Remove the lid and turn up the heat just a bit, to a medium setting. Stir often for another 10 minutes, until the onions become darker in color and some of the moisture evaporates from the pan. Set aside to cool.

4 In a high-speed blender, add 1 cup (240 ml) water, the cashews, nutritional yeast, chickpea flour, turmeric, kala namak, and nutmeg. Blend until relatively smooth.

HOT TAKE

You need a deep-dish pie pan for this recipe. If you only have standard, shallow ones, then divide the filling between two pies.

CONTINUED →

5 Crumble the tofu into the blender and blend again until relatively smooth. Scrape down the sides and use a blender plunger as needed, because the mixture will be thick. Transfer the custard to a large bowl.

6 Dice the cooked bacon into ½-inch (12 mm) pieces and add it to the custard, along with the caramelized onions and diced cheese. Use a rubber spatula to fold the ingredients together.

7 Pour into the prepared pie crust and use a rubber spatula to smooth the top out. Bake for 20 minutes.

8 Remove from oven and add the sliced cheese to the top, just enough to cover. Return to the oven and bake for 20 more minutes.

9 Place the 6 remaining bacon slices on top of the quiche; a little overlapping is OK. Spray lightly with cooking spray. Cover with an aluminum foil tent and bake for 15 to 20 more minutes, until the cheese is melty and the crust is golden.

10 Place on a cooling rack for 30 minutes before serving. Slice and serve topped with chives.

DEEP-DISH SINGLE-PASTRY CRUST

- 2 cups all-purpose flour, chilled
- 1 tablespoon sugar
- ¼ teaspoon salt
- 1 cup (2 sticks) cold vegan butter
- 3 to 6 tablespoons (45 to 90 ml) ice water
- Chives, for garnish

1 In a large bowl, sift together the flour, sugar, and salt. Add half the butter in tablespoon-sized pieces, cutting it into the flour with your fingers or a pastry cutter until the mixture appears pebbly. Add the remaining butter in the same way.

2 Drizzle in the ice water by the tablespoonful, gently mixing it after each addition. Knead the dough a few times, adding more water until it holds together.

3 Gather the dough together into a ball, then press it into a thick disk. Wrap in plastic wrap and chill for at least 1 hour before rolling it out and lining a deep-dish pan.

OMELET
WITH LOX, FETA, AND FRESH MINT

Makes 4 omelets

Brew some coffee, roast some potatoes, and break out the mimosas! The brunch table becomes a very inviting place when it features a pile of these little packages. Slick, salty, smoky carrot lox with creamy refreshing feta is a killer combination. Add some mint for fresh, herby bites. I've been making tofu omelets for years, and this is a pared down version that takes only a few minutes to blend. You can even make the omelets up to a day in advance and gently reheat them before you serve.

1 Make the omelet: Crumble the tofu into a blender and add the nutritional yeast, olive oil, onion powder, turmeric, kala namak, and salt. Puree until smooth. Add the chickpea flour, carrageenan (if using), and the cornstarch and puree again until combined, for about 10 seconds. Make sure to scrape down the sides of the blender container so that everything is well incorporated.

2 Preheat a large skillet, preferably cast-iron, over medium-high heat. Spray it lightly with cooking spray.

3 Working in batches as needed, pour ½-cup (120 ml) measures of omelet batter into the preheated skillet. Use the back of a spoon or a rubber spatula to spread the batter out into about 6-inch (15 cm) rounds. Be gentle when spreading it out, but if any rips or holes develop, that is fine, just gently fill them in as you spread the batter. When the tops of the omelets look dry and matte, after about 3 to 5 minutes, they're ready to flip. The undersides should be flecked and browned.

4 Cook the other side for 2 minutes, until lightly browned. Keep them warm on a plate covered with foil while you make the remaining omelets.

5 Fill the omelets: Make sure the omelet is still warm. If it is not, gently reheat in a covered pan for 2 minutes. On one side of each omelet, scatter even amounts of feta, tomatoes, and mint. Fold in the carrot lox. Sprinkle with a little bit of salt. Close each omelet and serve!

HOT TAKE

The carrageenan is not totally necessary, I just figured, if you have this book, maybe you have some on hand? It makes the omelet even fluffier! But without it, no one will complain, either.

FOR THE ACTUAL OMELET:

- 1 (12-ounce/340 g) package extra-firm silken tofu (the vacuum-packed kind, like Mori-Nu)
- 2 tablespoons nutritional yeast flakes
- 2 tablespoons olive oil
- ½ teaspoon onion powder
- ½ teaspoon turmeric
- 1 teaspoon kala namak
- ½ cup (45 g) chickpea flour
- 1 teaspoon carageenan (optional; see Hot Take)
- 1 tablespoon cornstarch

FOR THE OMELET FILLING:

- 1½ cups vegan feta, store-bought or homemade (page 290)
- 2 cups (380 g) cherry tomatoes
- 1 cup loosely packed fresh mint leaves
- ½ recipe Everybody's Doin' It Carrot Lox
- ½ teaspoon salt

FULLY LOADED NACHOS

Serves 6 to 8

FOR THE CHIPS:

- 1 large (15-ounce) bag taqueria-style chips
- ½ recipe MVP Meat (page 305)
- Pico de Gallo (page 313)
- Guacamole (page 313)
- Hot sauce, for serving
- ½ cup fresh cilantro, for garnish

FOR THE QUESO:

- 1 cup vegetable broth
- 1 cup whole unroasted cashews
- 1 roasted red pepper, chopped
- 1 tablespoon red miso
- ¼ cup nutritional yeast flakes
- ¼ teaspoon turmeric
- 2 teaspoons chili powder
- 1 tablespoon fresh lemon juice
- Salt to taste

Hear me out! Nachos are a centerpiece, not just an appetizer or drunken munchies. They are a glorious vision, controlled chaos, oozing with cheese, lousy with meat, covered in pico, and dolloped with guac. Even when they're sloppy and messy, they're a vision of beauty, and nothing could be more inviting! To ensure nacho harmony when serving a crowd, spread the chips out on a larger tray for more even topping distribution. But, it's a rule, don't eat all the fully loaded ones and leave everyone else with, like, just chips.

MAKE THE QUESO:

1. Place all ingredients in a high-speed blender in the order listed. Puree until completely smooth, about 1½ minutes, scraping down the sides with a rubber spatula. Taste for salt.
2. Transfer to a small pot and warm over low-medium heat until thickened, about 7 minutes.

ASSEMBLE:

1. Ladle a small amount of queso on the bottom of a large serving tray, just to get the chips not to slide around.
2. Spread out the chips on the tray. Ladle queso all over the chips. Scatter on the meat. Top with pico. Dollop with big scoops of guacamole. Top with cilantro and serve with hot sauce.

THE NON-DAIRY DIARIES

We live in a blessed time where melty, shreddy vegan cheeses line the supermarket shelves. Vegan ranch flows down aisle 6 like a waterfall. So by all means, if you just want to pick up a package of mozz, et cetera, to use in these recipes, I'm not mad at you. But in case you want to take the leap from fake meat to fake dairy, here you go. It is by no means an exhaustive list of vegan dairy, just the ones I use most often.

Most of the recipes are nut based; just picture a little cashew with black patches saying "Moo!" and you've got yourself a vegan pasture.

I do want to mention that there are companies and vegan cheese makers who are going the distance, using fermenting techniques from traditional cheese-making. This is not that. What I do is take ingredients already packed with fermented goodness, or otherwise umami bombs, and blend them. If you'd like to look more into vegan cheese-making, I highly recommend books by Miyoko Schinner and Karen McAthy.

FUN WITH MOLDS

A silicon cheese mold is ideal for square blocks of cheese. Check that the silicon is food-grade, and around 4 inches (10 cm) wide for these recipes. You can often find these molds at craft stores for use in soap-making, but please refrain from showering with your cheese. See the Prove-Me-Wrong Provolone (page 292) for an example.

But buying special equipment is not totally necessary! You can use any smooth vessel as a mold that can hold 3 cups (720 ml) of liquid. I use a round Pyrex container, but of course any shape will work. Always lightly spray with cooking oil so that the cheese slides out nice and easy. See the Green Gorgonzola (page 289) for an example.

If you want to really DIY it, you can use an empty 25-ounce can. This will give you nice, round slices, perfect for deli sandwiches. So empty those diced tomatoes and get ready for cheese town. Again, make sure to spray with cooking oil, and make sure there is no rust or jagged edges on the can.

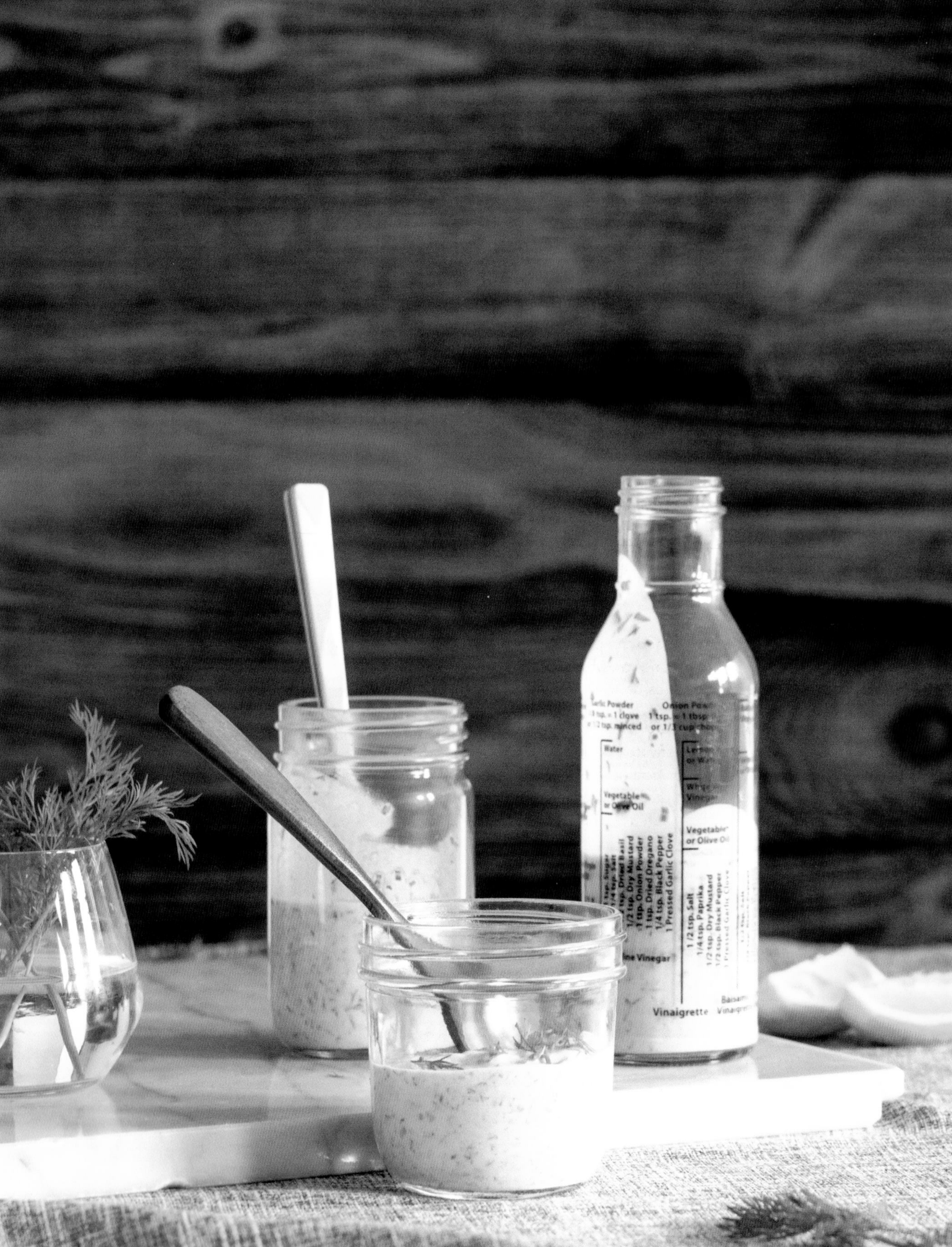

Water
Vegetable
or Olive Oil
1/2 tsp. Dry Mustard
1 tsp. Onion Powder
1 tsp. Dried Oregano
1/4 tsp. Black Pepper
1 Pressed Garlic Clove
Vegetable
or Olive Oil
1/2 tsp. Salt
1/4 tsp. Paprika
1/2 tsp. Dry Mustard
1/2 tsp. Black Pepper
Vinaigrette

RESCUE RANCH DRESSING

Makes about 1 cup (240 ml)

If we replaced all the dairy ranch dressing on earth with vegan ranch dressing, we would reverse the climate crisis and save millions of lives. It's a fact, look it up. But I'm not here to preach, I'm here to give you a creamy, herby, zesty dressing that you will want on hand at all times. You don't need any tips on what to do with ranch dressing; you will naturally dip anything and everything in it. Wings, obviously. But being in Nebraska, I've seen people take this dressing in some weird directions. Pizza? OK. Nachos? You do you. Except that one person who dipped samosas in it. What were you thinking?

Don't miss the variations listed at the bottom! There's a ranch for every occasion.

- **2 tablespoons finely chopped fresh parsley**
- **2 tablespoons finely chopped fresh dill**
- **2 tablespoons finely chopped fresh chives**
- **1½ teaspoons onion powder**
- **½ teaspoon garlic powder**
- **¼ teaspoon ground black pepper**
- **½ teaspoon salt, plus more if needed**
- **2 tablespoons fresh lemon juice**
- **¾ cup (180 ml) vegan mayo, prepared or homemade (page 309)**

1 In a small mixing bowl, add the parsley, dill, chives, onion powder, garlic powder, black pepper, and salt. Drizzle in the lemon juice and give it a stir. Let sit for about 5 minutes, soaking up the flavors and wilting the herbs.

2 Add the mayo and stir well. Depending on the kind of mayo you used, you may need to add a little water to thin it out. Do this by the tablespoon until the consistency seems correct, thick but pourable. Taste again for salt and seasoning. The flavors enhance as it sits, so it's even better the next day! Seal in an airtight container and refrigerate for up to 5 days.

VARIATIONS:

1 Avocado ranch: Mash a ripe avocado into a puree, along with an additional teaspoon lemon juice. Stir into the finished ranch dressing until well combined. This will only keep for a day or so, because avocado likes to brown, so use as quickly as possible.

2 Chipotle ranch: Stir in 3 tablespoons of the adobo sauce from a can of chipotles. Smoky! Spicy!

CREAM CHEEZE DREAMZ

Makes 2 cups (460 g)

- 2 teaspoons apple cider vinegar
- 1 teaspoon fresh lemon juice
- 1½ cups (180 g) whole unroasted cashews
- 1 teaspoon salt
- 2 tablespoons refined coconut oil, melted
- ½ teaspoon onion powder

Brooklynites know the joy of the bagel shop case, with, like, ten different vegan cream cheeses lined up behind the glass. Will they accidentally give you dairy cream cheese? That's just part of the excitement. Now you can re-create that joy at home! Whether you're in need of a smear for your bagel or a base for your dip, this is the DIY cream cheese of your dreams. Just a few simple ingredients create a tangy spread that will make you want to purchase one of those weird-shaped spready knives. It needs at least 8 hours to chill and for the flavors to marry, so plan accordingly. Try one of the variations below.

1 Add ½ cup (120 ml) water, the vinegar, lemon juice, cashews, salt, coconut oil, and onion powder to the blender. Blend until smooth, adding additional water by the tablespoon as needed until it blends easily. You shouldn't need to add more than 2 or 3. Scrape down the sides to make sure you get everything.

2 Transfer to a storage container and seal tightly. Place in the refrigerator to set for at least 8 hours before using.

VARIATIONS:

1 Lox: Fold in ½ cup (60 g) chopped Carrot Lox (page 84).

2 Bacon: Fold in ½ cup (85 g) chopped Ribbony Seitan Bacon (page 171).

3 Fresh Herb and Garlic: Sauté 6 cloves minced garlic in 2 tablespoons olive oil. Let cool and fold in, along with ½ cup (25 g) chopped fresh dill and ¼ cup (11 g) chopped fresh chives.

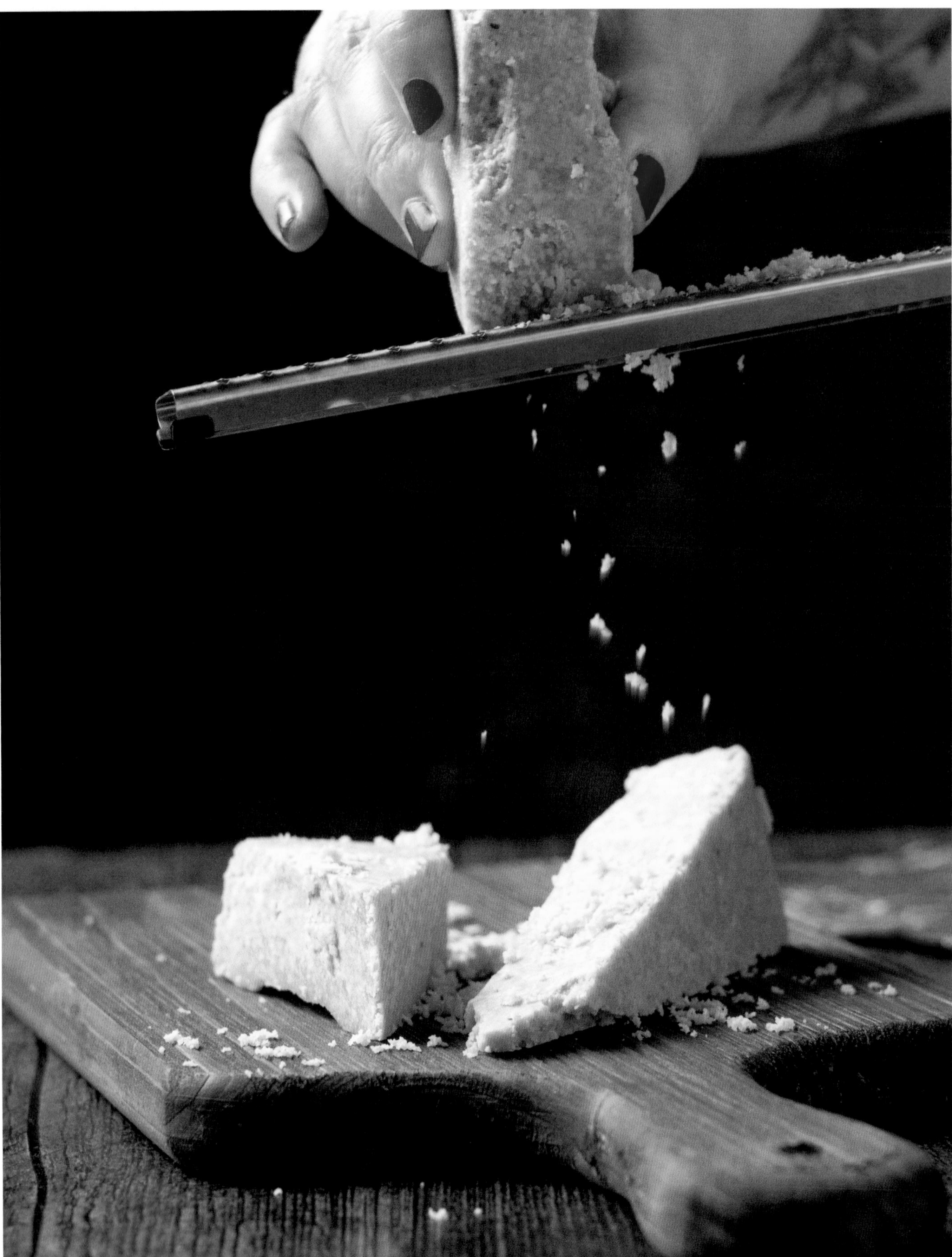

IT'S GREAT PARMESAN

Makes 2 cups (200 g) grated

Great! A vegan Parmesan that you can grate. For when you want romantic snowflakes of cheese cresting the mountaintops of your pastas and salads. Credit where credit is due: We got the idea to add agar-agar from Evi, a food creator in Germany who blogs at GreenEvi.com. It works like a charm.

- 3 tablespoons refined coconut oil, melted
- 1 teaspoon agar powder
- 1½ cups unroasted cashew pieces
- 3 tablespoons nutritional yeast flakes
- 1 teaspoon apple cider vinegar
- 1 tablespoon mellow white miso
- ¾ teaspoon salt
- ½ teaspoon onion powder
- ¼ teaspoon garlic powder

1 Combine the coconut oil and agar-agar in a small saucepan. Cook over low heat, whisking constantly for 5 minutes. Set aside.

2 Pulse the cashew pieces in a small food processor until finely ground. Pour in the melted coconut oil mixture and add the nutritional yeast, vinegar, miso, salt, onion powder, and garlic powder. Pulse until combined. Should be a dough-like consistency.

3 Transfer the mixture to a cheese form or a little bowl. Wrap in plastic and refrigerate for 4 hours to set before grating.

HOT TAKE

To get a long triangular shape, like you see in the pic, set the Parmesan in a 3-cup rectangular Pyrex. Once it's set, slice in half on a diagonal in one swoop with a chef's knife. Wrap each triangle with plastic wrap to store. But don't be afraid to set it in a circular mold; circles are cool, too.

FRESH MOZZ-SHEW-RELLA

Makes 1 dozen balls

- 2 teaspoons agar powder
- 1¼ cups (150 g) whole unroasted cashews
- 2 tablespoons refined coconut oil, melted
- 1 tablespoon apple cider vinegar
- 1 tablespoon fresh lemon juice
- 2 tablespoons nutritional yeast flakes
- 1 teaspoon onion powder
- 1½ teaspoons salt, plus more for brine
- 3 tablespoons tapioca starch

"You eat with your eyes first." Well, your eyes are about to feast. Yes, these mozzarella balls are creamy, tangy, and rich. But they are also absolutely beautiful, floating in brine, looking straight out of an Italian deli. "But how can I, who has never achieved anything in my life, make these?" you might wonder. And the answer isn't years of study in a cheese cave. It's an ice cream scoop, a high-speed blender, and some ice water. This method was perfected by Miyoko Schinner, of Miyoko's cheese fame.

1. In a large coffee mug or glass measuring cup, mix the agar powder into 2 cups (480 ml) water and let sit for about 30 minutes.
2. In a high-speed blender, blend the cashews, coconut oil, apple cider vinegar, lemon juice, nutritional yeast, onion powder, salt, and tapioca with agar and water mixture until completely smooth, about 2 minutes. Scrape down the sides of the blender with a rubber spatula to make sure you get everything.
3. Transfer to a saucepot. Heat over medium and cook, stirring often with a rubber spatula, until the cheese mixture is thick and glossy and pulling away from the sides of the pot, about 10 minutes.
4. Fill a 6-quart (5.7 liter) pot or bowl halfway with water and add about 15 ice cubes. Salt it well so it tastes like seawater. This is the brine for the mozzarella.
5. Use an ice cream scoop to scoop a cheese ball into the ice water. Dip the ice cream scooper all the way into the ice water to release the ball. It will firm up and start setting right away. Continue until all the mixture is used.
6. Cover the container, refrigerate, and let the cheese set for at least an hour. It's ready to use!

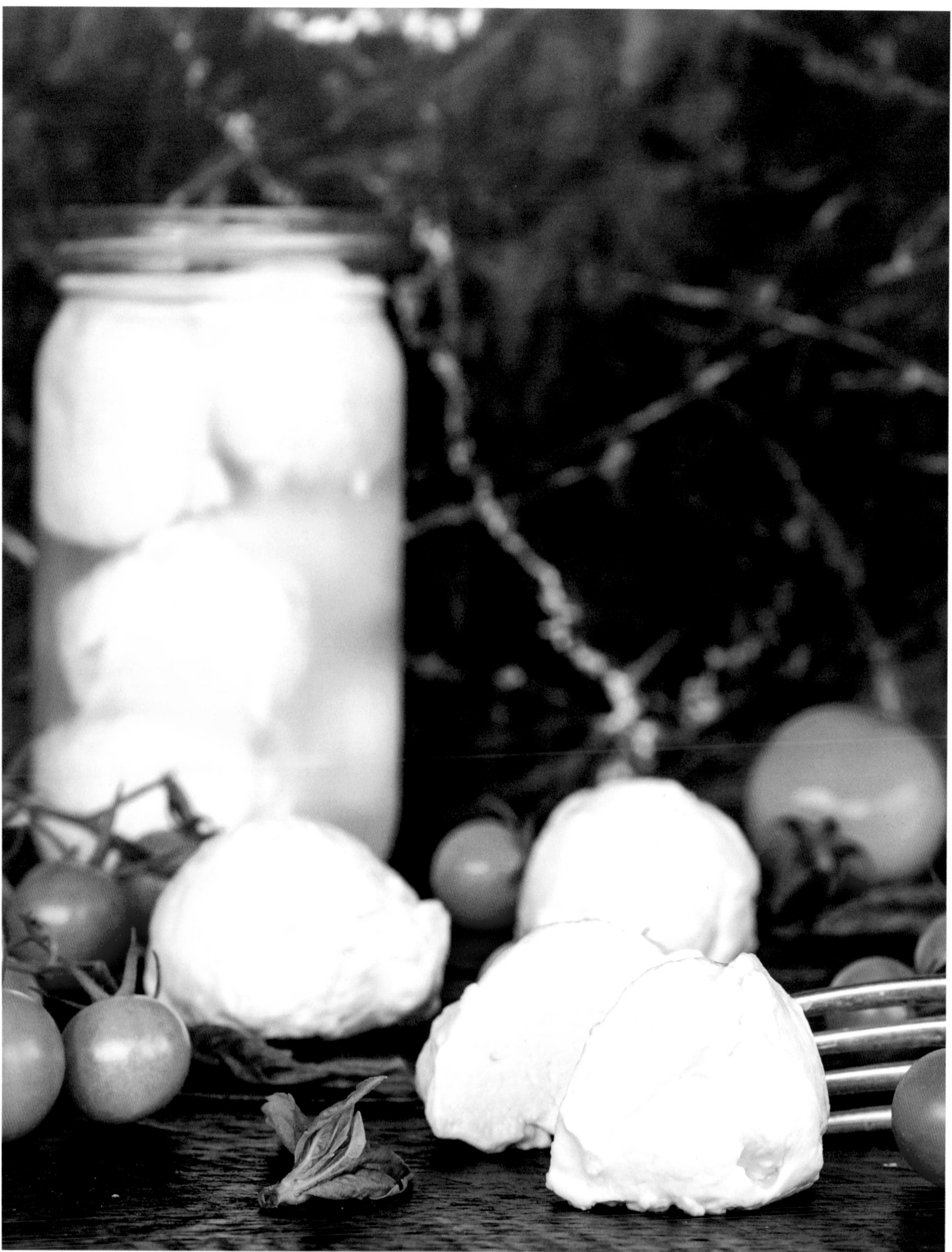

GREEN GORGONZOLA CHEEZE

Makes 3 cups (405 g)

Pepitas are unsung heroes. Although their texture never gets as smooth as cashews when blended, it works to their benefit in a crumbly cheese like this. They also have a yummy ripe flavor and a cool pale-green color that pops when crumbled over salad, or anything, for that matter.

- 1½ cups (100 g) raw pepitas
- 4 cloves minced garlic
- 2 teaspoons olive oil
- 2 tablespoons nutritional yeast flakes
- 1 tablespoon mellow white miso
- 1 teaspoon onion powder
- 1 tablespoon apple cider vinegar
- 2 tablespoons refined coconut oil, melted
- 1¼ teaspoon salt
- 2 teaspoons kappa carrageenan

1 Place the pepitas in a saucepan and submerge in just enough water to soak. Bring to a boil then simmer for 30 minutes to soften the pepitas. Drain and let cool completely.

2 Preheat a small pan over low heat. Sauté the garlic in the olive oil low and slow for about 2 minutes, until lightly golden and fragrant.

3 In a high-speed blender, blend the cooled pepitas, sautéed garlic, 1½ cups (360 ml) water, the nutritional yeast, miso, onion powder, apple cider vinegar, coconut oil, and salt until smooth. This could take as long as 3 minutes, even with a high-speed blender, so give the motor a rest every once in a while.

4 The blender will heat the pepita mixture, so let it cool a bit, just until it's not warm to the touch, that way it won't activate the carrageenan yet. Place in the fridge to cool if you like. Then add the carrageenan and blend for 20 more seconds.

5 Transfer the cheese mixture to a saucepan. Cook over low heat for 8 to 10 minutes, stirring constantly. Alternate between a whisk and a rubber spatula so you can scrape the sides and bottom corners of the pot. The mixture will get thick and begin pulling away from the sides. You'll know it's done when it's glossy and holding its shape as you stir it.

6 Immediately pour into a lightly greased 3-cup (720 ml) mold (see "Fun with Molds," page 279) and smooth the top with a spatula. Let cool for 30 minutes at room temperature. Cover and refrigerate for at least 4 hours to set. It tastes best the next day, and even better the day after that!

FAUX FETA

- 4 cloves garlic, minced
- 1 tablespoon olive oil
- 1⅓ cups (140 g) slivered almonds
- ⅓ cup (75 ml) oat milk
- ⅓ cup (75 ml) sauerkraut juice (from a jar of sauerkraut)
- 1 teaspoon salt
- 1 tablespoon plus 1 teaspoon kappa carrageenan

HOT TAKE

This feta also makes a wonderful cheeseball for charcuterie or a cheese plate. Form the feta into golf-ball sizes, then roll them in chopped nuts or herbs. This recipe will make about 8 balls.

Makes about 2 cups (300 g)

Tangy feta is ready to crumble! Use it on pastas, in salads, or in omelets, or just spread it onto some crackers. Wherever you need a tangy, cheesy bite.

1 Preheat a small pan over very low heat. Sauté the garlic clove in the oil until fragrant, being careful not to burn, about 30 seconds. Add immediately to a high-speed blender.

2 To the blender, add the almonds, oat milk, sauerkraut juice, and salt and blend until completely smooth. This could take up to 3 minutes. Scrape down the side with a rubber spatula every 30 seconds or so.

3 Turn the blender off and let it cool for a few minutes, just until it's not steamy from the blending. Add kappa carrageenan and blend for another 30 seconds just to incorporate.

4 Transfer cheese mix to a saucepan. Cook over low heat for 8 to 10 minutes, stirring with a rubber spatula constantly. It will get thick and begin pulling away from the sides. You'll know it's done because it's glossy and holding its shape as you stir it.

5 Pour into a lightly greased 3-cup (720 ml) mold (see Fun with Molds, page 279) immediately and smooth the top with a spatula. Cool 30 minutes at room temp. Cover and refrigerate for at least 4 hours. Now it's ready to crumble!

HERBED FETA BALLS: Roll in ½ cup each finely chopped dill, chives, and parsley.

CHOPPED NUT BALLS: Roll in 1 cup finely chopped toasted walnuts or pistachios. Sprinkle with a little flaky sea salt.

NUTTY RICOTTA

- 1 cup (120 g) whole unroasted cashews
- 1 cup (110 g) slivered almonds
- 1 tablespoon onion powder
- 2 tablespoons olive oil
- 2 tablespoons fresh lemon juice
- ¼ teaspoon salt

Makes about 3 cups (735 g)

A low-maintenance vegan cheese that requires no weirdo ingredients. How refreshing! Use it in lasagna (obviously) or any stuffed pasta. You can also dollop it on pizzas or enjoy it as a burger topping.

1 In a food processor fitted with a metal blade, combine the cashews, almonds, onion powder, ½ cup (120 ml) water, olive oil, lemon juice, and salt. Blend on high speed until it resembles ricotta. Transfer to a storage container and refrigerate for an hour or so, where it will thicken a little bit.

OH SO QUESO

Makes about 2 cups (480 ml) crumbled

- 1 cup (240 ml) vegetable broth
- 1 cup (120 g) whole unroasted cashews
- 1 roasted red pepper, chopped
- 1 tablespoon red miso
- ¼ cup (15 g) nutritional yeast flakes
- ¼ teaspoon ground turmeric
- 2 teaspoons chili powder
- 1 tablespoon fresh lemon juice
- ½ teaspoon salt, plus more if needed

Cashew queso is smooth, creamy, and satisfying! A melty cheese sauce that pours like a dream over nachos, burgers, and fries. This is a mild cheese, but if you want spicy, add cayenne. Start with ¼ teaspoon and go from there.

1 In a high-speed blender, combine the vegetable broth, cashews, roasted pepper, miso, nutritional yeast, turmeric, chili powder, lemon juice, and salt. Puree until completely smooth, about 1½ minutes, scraping down the sides with a rubber spatula. Taste for salt.

2 Transfer to a small pot and warm over medium-low heat until thickened, about 7 minutes. It's ready to use! If using later, let cool and store in a covered container. Warm up in a pot before using.

SHREDDY CHEDDY

Makes about 2 cups (230 g)

- 1½ cups (180 g) whole unroasted cashews
- 3 tablespoons nutritional yeast flakes
- ¼ teaspoon ground turmeric
- 1 tablespoon tomato paste
- 1 tablespoon red miso
- 1 teaspoon onion powder
- 1 tablespoon apple cider vinegar
- 1¼ teaspoons salt
- 2 tablespoons refined coconut oil, melted
- 2 tablespoons tapioca starch
- 2½ teaspoons kappa carrageenan

This cheddar shreds! Over chili or a casserole, it adds that inviting cheesy hue to all it touches. The method is much the same as for the Prove-Me-Wrong Provolone (page 292). It slices, too, so don't hesitate to use it on a cheese plate, on a burger, or in sandwiches. And grilled cheese, here you come!

1 In a high-speed blender, combine 1½ cups (360 ml) water with the cashews, nutritional yeast, turmeric, tomato paste, miso, onion powder, apple cider vinegar, and salt. Blend for a minute or so, until completely smooth. Use a rubber spatula to scrape down the sides every 20 seconds to make sure everything is incorporated. Add the coconut oil and blend again for 20 seconds. Let the mixture cool down a bit so that the carrageenan won't activate right away. Two minutes in the refrigerator should do it.

2 Add the tapioca and carrageenan and blend for 20 seconds to combine.

3 Pour the mixture into a 2-quart (2 liter) saucepan and bring to a simmer over medium heat. Stir vigorously, alternating between a whisk and a rubber spatula, making sure to scrape the bottom of the pan so the cheese mixture doesn't burn. Once it reaches a rapid boil, lower the heat to medium low and cook for about 10 minutes, until it's glossy, thick, and pulling away from the sides of the pot.

4 Pour into a mold (see Fun with Molds, page 279). Let set at room temperature for 20 minutes, then wrap in plastic and refrigerate for at least 4 hours before using.

PROVE-ME-WRONG PROVOLONE

- ¼ cup (60 ml) fresh lemon juice
- ½ cup (60 g) whole unroasted cashews
- 3 tablespoons tahini
- 2 tablespoons nutritional yeast flakes
- 1 tablespoon mellow white miso
- 3 tablespoons refined coconut oil, melted
- 1½ teaspoons salt
- 2 tablespoons plus 1 teaspoon tapioca starch
- 4½ teaspoons kappa carrageenan

Makes 1 pound (140 g)

A light cheese with a mild but tangy flavor that slices beautifully for cold sandwiches and melts like a dream when the need for a grilled cheese strikes. Use it in the Spicy Italian Roast Be'ef Subs (page 53), or draped, warm and melty, over a burger. I recommend a 1-quart (about 1 liter) square silicone container for square slices, but it also looks really cool in circles if you pour it into a few coffee mugs to set.

1 In a high-speed blender, combine 1¾ cups (420 ml) water with the lemon juice, cashews, tahini, nutritional yeast, miso, coconut oil, and salt. Blend for a minute or so, until completely smooth. Use a rubber spatula to scrape down the sides every 20 seconds to make sure everything is incorporated. Add the tapioca and carrageenan and blend for 20 seconds, just until combined.

2 Pour the mixture into a 2-quart (2 liter) saucepan and bring to a simmer over medium heat. Stir vigorously and often with a strong whisk, making sure to scrape the bottom of the pan so the cheese mixture doesn't burn. Once it reaches a rapid boil, lower the heat to medium-low and cook for about 10 minutes, until it's glossy, thick, and pulling away from the sides of the pot.

3 Pour into a lightly greased 1-quart (about 1 liter) silicone mold or plastic storage container (see Fun with Molds, page 279). Let set at room temperature for 20 minutes, then seal and refrigerate for at least 4 hours before using.

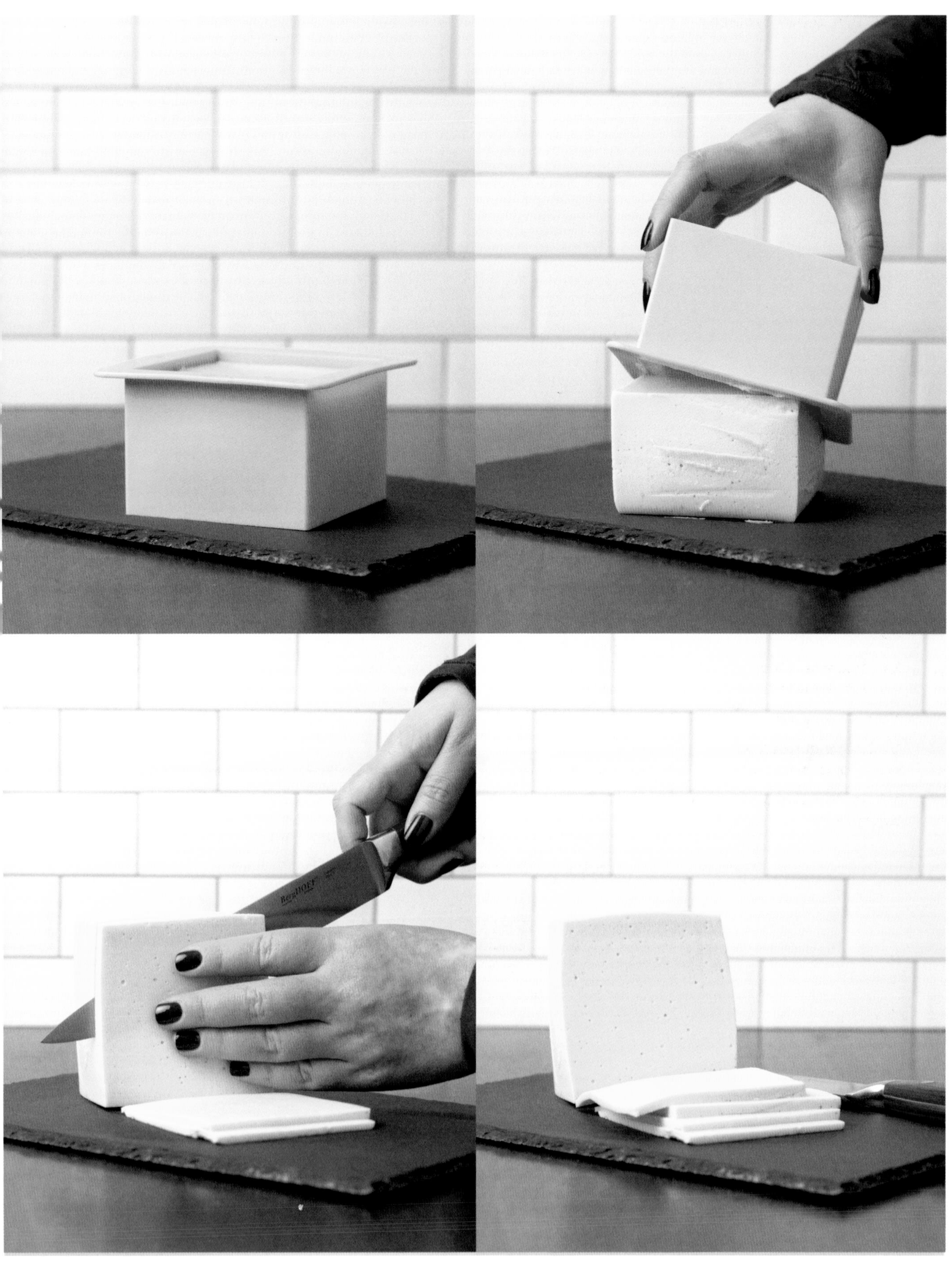
BergHOFF

SWIZZ CHEEZE

Makes about 1 pound (455 g)

- ½ cup (120 ml) sauerkraut juice (from a jar of sauerkraut)
- ½ cup (60 g) whole unroasted cashews
- 2 tablespoons nutritional yeast flakes
- 1 tablespoon tahini
- 2 teaspoons truffle oil
- 1 tablespoon olive oil
- 1 tablespoon chickpea miso
- 1½ teaspoons salt
- 2 tablespoons plus 1 teaspoon tapioca starch
- 4½ teaspoons kappa carrageenan

Somehow I discovered that sauerkraut juice plus truffle oil plus a little miso equals Swiss cheese. I don't know—my taste buds sometimes know things before I do! This is the perfect cheese for Hot Pastrami Sandwiches (page 25), but it's also wonderful melted on roasted veggies like broccoli and cauliflower. I found little Swiss cheese molds online—they look so cute on a cheese plate—so try to find some. Otherwise, just use the same method as for Prove-Me-Wrong Provolone.

1 In a high-speed blender, combine 1½ cups (360 ml) water with the sauerkraut juice, cashews, nutritional yeast, tahini, truffle oil, miso, and salt. Blend for a minute or so, until completely smooth. Use a rubber spatula to scrape down the sides every 20 seconds to make sure everything is incorporated.

2 Add the tapioca and carrageenan and blend for 20 seconds.

3 Pour the mixture into a 2-quart (2 liter) saucepan and bring to a simmer over medium heat. Stir vigorously and often with a strong whisk, making sure to scrape the bottom of the pan so the cheese mixture doesn't burn. Once it reaches a rapid boil, lower the heat to medium low and cook for about 10 minutes, until it's glossy, thick, and pulling away from the sides of the pot.

4 Pour into a mold (see Fun with Molds, page 279). Let set at room temperature for 20 minutes, then wrap in plastic and refrigerate for at least 4 hours before using.

STAPLES AND CONDIMENTS

A hodgepodge of recipes maybe, but we use them all throughout the book! Every time I say "store-bought or homemade" you can flip right to this section. Some you'll use a lot, like the mayo, which is my actual religion. Some are a special-occasion treat, but nice to have anyway, just in case the urge to DIY takes hold.

THE MOTHER BROTHS

These are my "mother broths." The three main ones I live by: Chick'n, Beefy, and Seafood (I call it Bay Broth, for my hometown, Sheepshead Bay). But why make your own broth? There are so many varieties available in the supermarket these days, that simmering can seem like a hassle. And maybe, compared to simply grabbing some off a shelf, it is. But creating your own scratch-made broth has many benefits. Not everything should be overlooked in the name of convenience! My top three reasons for making your own broth:

1) TASTE

Taste is a great place to start. Plenty of pre-made broths taste anywhere from "just fine" to "pretty darn good." But homemade is fresher, more aromatic, and endlessly customizable to your taste. Make it as salty as you like, add different veggies, more or less garlic, and on and on.

2) USE SCRAPS

I know that you occasionally have an onion lying around, beginning to sprout. Or a few carrots just languishing in the fridge. And how about those sad little celery stalks that will probably wither away eventually? That is (almost) all you need to make this vegetable broth. I also leave the skins on everything—onions, garlic, carrots—for color and convenience. No peeling necessary!

3) AROMATHERAPY

There is a definite difference between being in a home that has a veggie broth simmering on the stovetop, its gentle aroma filling your senses . . . and being in a home that has bubkes. But honestly, the process of making the broth will improve your mood drastically. From the scent to the sense of accomplishment when sipping the finished product, the therapeutic benefits are unbeatable.

The biggest drawback I've encountered is that one Passover, I spent the day making a metric tonne of broth for the matzoh balls. Once it had cooled on the stovetop, my mom threw it out, thinking it was garbage. What the hell, Mom?

OK, so moms tossing out your creation aside, I'm assuming you're now completely on board. Find a relaxing time, when you have plans to read or watch a movie or troll the internet or whatever, and then get brothing!

Note: I prefer to use cheesecloth to strain the broth, because that means you can squeeze the boiled veggies and get every bit of flavor, while still having a nice, translucent broth. But if you don't have it/don't want it, then don't worry! Just use a fine-mesh colander, and let the veggies drain over a pot.

CHICK'N BROTH

Makes about 4 quarts (3.8 liters)

A lighter, herby broth that still packs lots of flavor.

- 2 tablespoons olive oil with a pinch of salt
- 1 large yellow onion, roughly chopped, skin on
- 6 cloves garlic, smashed
- 2 large leeks, chopped into 2-inch (5 cm) pieces, cleaned
- 2 large carrots, not peeled, roughly chopped
- 4 ribs celery, chopped into 2-inch (5 cm) pieces
- ½ bunch parsley
- ½ bunch fresh dill
- ¼ ounce fresh thyme, stems and all
- ¼ ounce fresh rosemary, stems and all
- 2 teaspoons black peppercorns
- 3 tablespoons nutritional yeast flakes
- Salt to taste

1. Preheat a 12-quart (11.4 liter) stockpot over medium-high heat. Sauté the onion, garlic, and leeks in the oil with a pinch of salt for about 5 minutes, just to get a little caramelization going.
2. Add the carrots, celery, parsley, dill, thyme, rosemary, peppercorns, and nutritional yeast and give a stir. Add 8 quarts (7.5 liters) water. Cover the pot and bring to a boil. Once boiling, leave the lid slightly ajar so that steam can escape, lower the heat a bit, and simmer for 1½ hours to reduce by about half. Stir occasionally.
3. Turn off the heat and let cool in the pot, just until it's not steaming. Now is the time to taste for salt. Start with a teaspoon and go from there, adding pinches until it's just right.
4. Place another large pot in the sink. It should be big enough to manage 4 quarts (3.8 liters) broth. Position a handled strainer over the empty pot and make sure it's secure (i.e., it won't fall in when the vegetables are being strained). Line the strainer with a few layers of cheesecloth with plenty of overhang.
5. Pour in the vegetables and broth and leave them in the strainer to drain for about 20 minutes.
6. Once cool enough to handle, bunch up the cheesecloth and squeeze, so that the vegetables release as much moisture and flavor as possible.
7. Taste for salt again, and now your broth is ready to use! Freeze in tightly sealed containers for up to 3 months, if not using within the week.

BAY BROTH

BEEFY BROTH
CHICK'N BROTH

BEEFY BROTH

Makes about 4 quarts (3.8 liters)

Dried porcini mushrooms, red miso, and tomato paste help create a rich, savory broth that adds flavor and nuance to any meaty dish.

- 4 large yellow onions roughly chopped, skin on
- 8 cloves garlic, smashed
- 2 tablespoons olive oil with a pinch of salt
- 4 large carrots, roughly chopped
- 2 large parsnips, roughly chopped
- 3 ribs celery, chopped into 2-inch (5 cm) pieces
- 8 bay leaves
- 3 tablespoons nutritional yeast
- 1 ounce dried porcini mushrooms
- 1 tablespoon black peppercorns
- 2 tablespoons red miso
- 2 tablespoons tomato paste
- Salt to taste

1 Preheat a 12-quart (11.4 liter) stockpot over medium-high heat. Sauté the onion and garlic in the oil with a pinch of salt for about 5 minutes, just to get a little caramelization going.

2 Add the carrots, parsnips, celery, bay leaves, nutritional yeast, mushrooms, and peppercorns and give a stir. Add 8 quarts (7.5 liters) water. Cover the pot and bring to a boil. Once boiling, mix in the miso and tomato paste. Leave the lid slightly ajar so that steam can escape, lower the heat a bit, and simmer for 1½ hours, to reduce by about half. Stir occasionally.

3 Turn off the heat and let cool in the pot, just until it's not steaming. Now is the time to taste for salt. Start with a teaspoon and go from there, adding pinches until it's just right.

4 Place a separate large pot in the sink. It should be big enough to manage 4 quarts (3.8 liters) broth. Position a handled strainer over the empty pot and make sure it's secure (i.e., it won't fall in when the vegetables are being strained). Line the strainer with a few layers of cheesecloth with plenty of overhang.

5 Pour in the vegetables and broth and leave them in the strainer to drain for about 20 minutes.

6 Once cool enough to handle, bunch up the cheesecloth and squeeze, so that the vegetables release as much moisture and flavor as possible.

7 Taste for salt again, and now your broth is ready to use! Freeze in tightly sealed containers for up to 3 months, if not using within the week.

BAY BROTH

Makes 4 quarts (3.8 liters)

A taste of the sea! Red onions, tomato, and umeboshi create a broth with a pink blush that tastes like a fresh ocean breeze. Umeboshi is a fermented plum paste that adds to the seafood flavor with its briny tanginess.

- 2 tablespoons olive oil with a pinch salt
- 4 large red onions
- 6 cloves garlic, smashed
- 4 ribs celery, sliced into 2-inch (5 cm) pieces
- 4 carrots, rough chopped
- 4 average-size tomatoes, cut into rough wedges
- 1 bunch dill
- 2 sheets nori, cut in half
- 1 tablespoon pink peppercorns
- 3 tablespoons umeboshi paste
- Salt to taste

1 Preheat a 12-quart (11.4 liter) stockpot over medium-high heat. Sauté the onion and garlic in the oil with a pinch of salt for about 5 minutes, just to get a little caramelization going.

2 Add the celery, carrots, tomatoes, dill, nori, and peppercorns and give a stir. Add 8 quarts (7.5 liters) water. Cover the pot and bring to a boil. Once boiling, mix in the umeboshi paste. Leave the lid slightly ajar so that steam can escape, lower the heat a bit, and simmer for 1½ hours, to reduce by about half. Stir occasionally.

3 Turn off the heat and let cool in the pot, just until it's not steaming. Now is the time to taste for salt. Start with a teaspoon and go from there, adding pinches until it's just right.

4 Place a separate large pot in the sink. It should be big enough to manage 4 quarts (3.8 liters) broth. Position a handled strainer over the empty pot and make sure it's secure (i.e., it won't fall in when the vegetables are being strained). Line the strainer with a few layers of cheesecloth with plenty of overhang.

5 Pour in the vegetables and broth and leave them in the strainer to drain for about 20 minutes.

6 Once cool enough to handle, bunch up the cheesecloth and squeeze, so that the vegetables release as much moisture and flavor as possible.

7 Taste for salt again, and now your broth is ready to use! Freeze in tightly sealed containers for up to 3 months, if not using within the week.

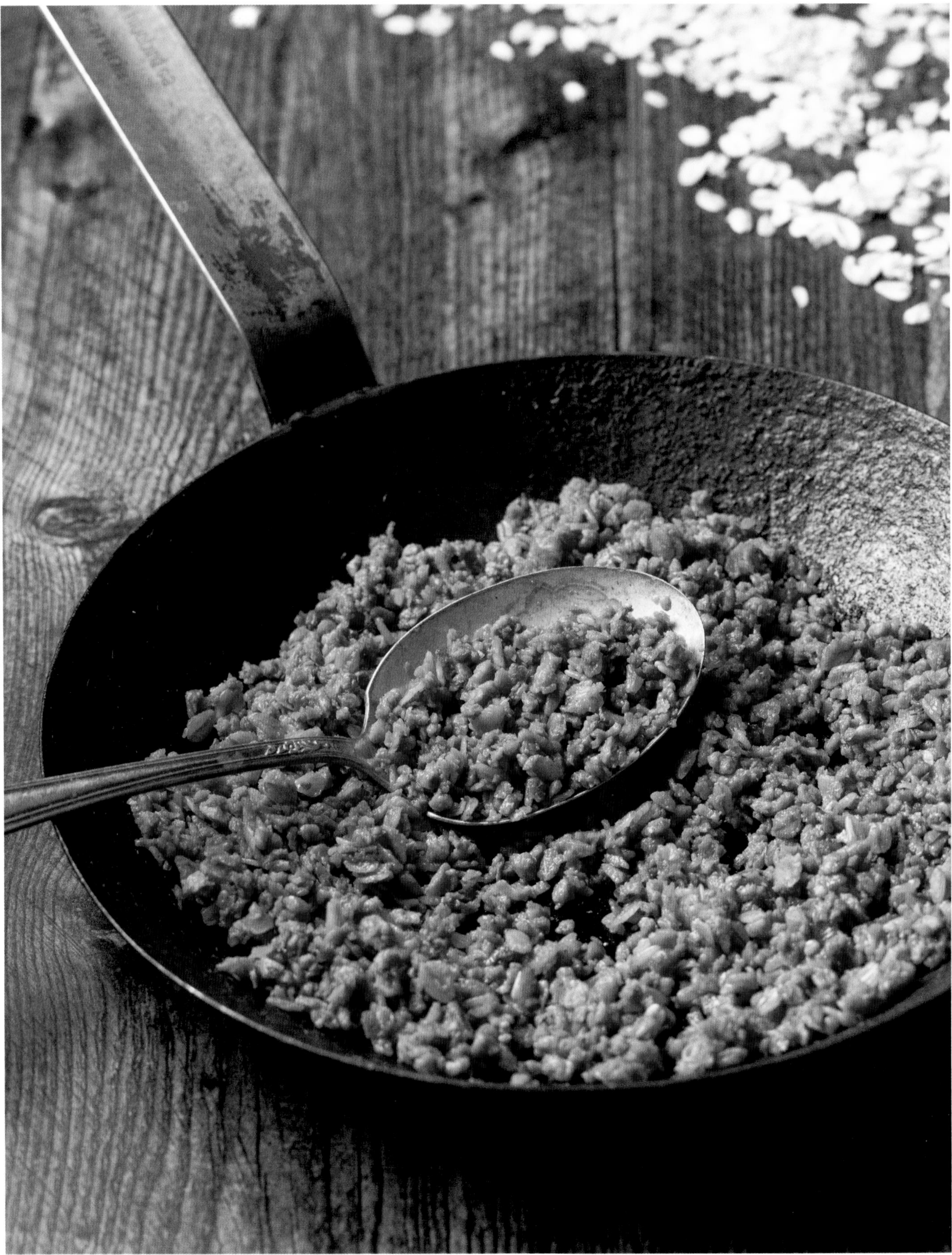

MVP MEAT

Makes about 4 cups

TVP is the MVP here! Add some rolled oats and you get an all-purpose ground meat base that is so versatile and (drumroll please) gluten-free. You can spice it up any which way in recipes that call for ground beef. The flavor is neutral, the texture is spot on, and even as-is it's completely, totally, groundbreakingly ground meat-y.

- 1½ cups (105 g) textured vegetable protein (TVP)
- 1 tablespoon apple cider vinegar
- 1 tablespoon tamari
- 3 tablespoons red miso
- ½ cup (45 g) old-fashioned rolled oats (see Hot Take)
- 2 tablespoons nutritional yeast flakes
- 1 teaspoon onion powder
- ½ teaspoon garlic powder
- ½ teaspoon ground yellow mustard powder
- 2 tablespoons olive oil

1. Place TVP in 6 cups (1.4 liters) water with the apple cider vinegar and tamari. Bring to a boil, then lower heat and simmer for 15 minutes. Strain through a fine mesh strainer and let cool completely. Once cool, press the TVP against the strainer to get out any excess moisture.
2. Transfer the cooked and drained TVP to a mixing bowl. Add the miso and mix with your hands to incorporate the miso into the TVP.
3. Add the oats, nutritional yeast, onion powder, garlic powder, and mustard. Mix again with your hands, really smushing aggressively to get the flavor in there and break down the oats a little.
4. To cook, preheat a large non-stick skillet (preferably cast-iron) over medium. Cook the mixture in oil for about 15 minutes, stirring often, until lightly browned. Use cooking spray or additional drizzles of oil if needed to keep it from sticking.

HOT TAKE

Use certified gluten-free oats to make this gluten-free if you need it to be. If you don't need gluten-free and just want some tasty meat, then don't worry about it.

VEGAN FOR MY HONEE

- 2 cups (480 ml) pure apple juice
- 2 licorice tea bags
- 2 echinacea tea bags
- 1 cup (240 ml) light agave syrup
- 2 tablespoons fresh lemon juice

Makes 2½ cups (600 ml)

Apple juice infused with licorice and echinacea makes a convincing honey when combined with thick, sweet agave. It's as easy as brewing a cuppa tea (and then dumping way too much sweetener in it).

1 In a 2-quart (2 liter) pot, bring the apple juice to a boil. Once boiling, add the licorice and echinacea tea bags. Turn the heat off and let cool and steep for 30 minutes.

2 Remove the tea bags. Add the agave syrup and lemon juice. Bring to a low boil and cook for about 30 minutes, stirring often with a rubber spatula, until the mixture is thickened and dripping from the spatula like honey. Let cool until not steaming. It will thicken more as it sits.

3 Transfer to a container, seal, and refrigerate for up to a month.

BEST FRIEND'S MOM'S MARINARA

- 1 small yellow onion, very finely chopped
- 2 tablespoons olive oil
- 8 cloves garlic, minced
- 1 tablespoon granulated sugar
- 1 teaspoon dried thyme
- 1½ teaspoons dried oregano
- ½ teaspoon crushed red pepper flakes (optional, if you like a little heat)
- Fresh black pepper
- 2 (24-ounce/720 ml) cans crushed tomatoes
- 1½ teaspoons salt, plus more as needed
- 1 cup (30 g) lightly packed fresh basil leaves

Makes about 6 cups (1.4 liters)

Growing up, I spent most of the time at my best friend's house, eating all her food. Her mom made the best marinara, and this is as close as I can get.

1 Preheat a 4-quart (3.8 liter) pot over medium-low heat. Sauté the onion in the oil for 5 to 7 minutes, until lightly browned. Add the garlic and sauté until fragrant, about 30 seconds. Add the sugar and cook for about 1 minute, until the sugar is dissolved and coating all the onions. Mix in the thyme, oregano, red pepper flakes (if using), and fresh black pepper.

2 Add the tomatoes and salt and stir everything together, deglazing the pan by scraping the bottom with a wooden spoon. Cover the pot, leaving a little gap for steam to escape, and cook for 30 minutes.

3 Tear the basil leaves into pieces and stir into the marinara. Cook for 10 minutes more. Taste for salt and seasoning. Let it rest for 20 minutes or so before using, if possible, to let the flavors develop.

VEGAN FOR
MY HONEE

HOMEMADE VEGAN MAYO

Makes 1½ cups (360 ml)

I am a mayo person through and through. There are plenty of decadent and delicious vegan brands out there, but this is one thing I prefer to make myself. It doesn't take long at all and it makes everything it touches so homey and special.

1 Combine the milk and ground flax in a blender. Blend on high speed until the flax meal is barely noticeable and the mixture is frothy, about 1 minute.

2 Add the sugar, dry mustard, onion powder, kala namak, vinegar, and lemon juice, blending for a few seconds to combine.

3 Mix the oils together in a measuring cup. With the blender running, use the hole at the top to stream in a tablespoon at a time, blending for about 30 seconds after each addition (if using a high-powered blender like Vitamix, 5 to 10 secs should do it). You should notice it thickening by the halfway point. By the time you've incorporated three-fourths of the oil, it should be spreadable. And with the last addition, you should have a thick mayo. If it seems watery, keep blending.

4 Transfer to a glass storage container, seal tightly, and refrigerate for a few hours; it will thicken even further. The flavors will also mellow out a bit. Use within a week.

VARIATIONS:

1 Roasted garlic: Add ¼ cup mashed roasted garlic to 1 cup (240 ml) mayo.

2 Pesto: Add ¼ cup pesto to 1 cup (240 ml) mayo.

HOT TAKES

The other important thing to remember is that the oil needs to be added little by little. A lot of mayo recipes say to stream it in slowly but all at once, and I don't think that is quite necessary. Just add it a tablespoon or two at a time, blend for a while, then add more.

HOT TAKES

Depending on the strength of your blender, your times may differ. The important thing is to pay attention to consistency through each step. I use a Breville, which I love and recommend! But no matter your machine, you have to get the flaxseeds good and blended, so that the flecks are barely noticeable. That activates their gloopy properties and will also make your mayo prettier.

The taste of this mayo is very strong at first; the vinegar and salt mellow out over time, so don't adjust straight from the blender. Let it chill for at least a few hours before deciding on any tweaking you'd like to do for next time.

- ½ cup (120 ml) unsweetened soy milk
- 1½ tablespoons ground golden flaxseeds
- 2 teaspoons sugar
- 1 teaspoon ground dry mustard
- 1 teaspoon onion powder
- ½ teaspoon kala namak
- 1 tablespoon white wine vinegar
- 1 tablespoon fresh lemon juice
- ½ cup (120 ml) olive oil
- ½ cup (120 ml) safflower oil

MUSTARD THAT TASTES LIKE IT CAME FROM THE STORE

- ⅓ cup (96 g) mustard seeds
- ⅓ cup (96 g) brown mustard seeds
- ½ cup (55 g) mustard powder
- ½ cup (120 ml) dry white wine
- ⅓ cup (75 ml) champagne vinegar
- 2½ teaspoons salt
- ½ teaspoon ground turmeric
- 1 teaspoon sugar

Makes a lot of mustard

All mustard is good, right? I haven't had a bad one. So why make your own? It just tastes like it came from the store. Why not do something cool like knit or learn calligraphy or even make pickles, that would be worth it? Anyway, I can't save you. If you're going to waste your life making mustard, I'd rather you use my recipe than something random off the internet. So here's my recipe called Mustard That Tastes Like It Came from the Store. I guess you could also call it Champagne Mustard if you want to be fancy, but everyone will just think it's from the store, so do what you want.

1 In a blender, grind up the mustard seeds, leaving some kinda whole. That's how everyone will know that it's mustard.

2 In a cool glass jar, mix the ground mustard seeds with the mustard powder, wine, ¾ cup (180 ml) water, champagne vinegar, salt, turmeric, and sugar. Cover and place in the fridge. The next day you will have mustard.

JIMMY CARTER TARTAR SAUCE

- 1 cup (140 ml) vegan mayo
- ⅓ cup finely chopped dill pickles
- ¼ cup (35 g) minced yellow onion
- 2 tablespoons fresh chopped dill
- 1 tablespoon fresh chopped parsley
- 1 tablespoon fresh lemon juice
- 1 teaspoon whole grain Dijon mustard
- 2 tablespoons chopped capers
- Fresh black pepper

Makes 1½ cups (350 ml)

Does Jimmy Carter like tartar sauce? I have no idea. So why is it called this? Because it rhymes, silly. And I try to mention Jimmy Carter as much as possible.

1 Mix everything together in a bowl. Ta-da!

PICKLED RED ONIONS

Makes about 3 cups (440 g)

These are the simplest pickles in the world, but you will want to add them to everything. Their pretty pink glow and fragrant acidity lend a touch of class to curries, sandwiches, and salads. I use small red onions so that they can be sliced into rings that make pretty swirls once they are pickled and soft.

- ¾ cup (180 ml) white wine vinegar
- ¼ cup (35 g) granulated sugar
- ½ teaspoon salt
- 2 small red onions, sliced into rings

1 Mix together the vinegar, sugar, and salt in a bowl. Add the onions, making sure the individual rings aren't stuck together. Let sit for about an hour, giving the rings a toss once in a while. They'll be ready in an hour but are even better and more malleable if you make them a day ahead. Store in a tightly sealed container.

VARIATIONS:

1 Pickled Cherry Tomatoes: Use cherry tomatoes cut in half instead of the onions. Add 2 teaspoons minced ginger and 2 tablespoons fresh chopped cilantro.

HOT DOG ONIONS

Makes about 2 cups (295 g)

- 2 tablespoons olive oil
- 3 medium yellow onions (tennis ball size), quartered and sliced
- ½ cup (120 ml) ketchup
- 1½ tablespoons brown sugar
- 1½ teaspoons smooth Dijon mustard
- 1½ teaspoons chili powder
- 1 teaspoon salt

1 Heat the oil in a large, heavy-bottomed pan over medium-low heat. Sauté the onions in the oil for about 25 minutes, until they start to caramelize, stirring often. Turn the heat up to medium high and stir for about 5 minutes, so the onions darken a bit.

2 Add the ketchup, brown sugar, mustard, chili powder, and salt. Lower heat to medium low and cook for about 20 minutes. Serve hot.

SUPER SIMPLE SLAW

- 4 cups (380 g) shredded red cabbage (about ½ head)
- ½ cup (120 ml) red wine vinegar
- 2 tablespoons agave syrup
- 2 tablespoons olive oil
- 1 teaspoon salt

Makes 4 cups

For when you already have a lot going on but you need a little crunch, color, and acid and you need it NOW. The longer the cabbage has to wilt, the deeper the flavors will penetrate, but it's not a big deal if you don't have the time for that.

1 After slicing the cabbage, let it stand at room temperature to wilt for as long as you can. If it's an hour, wonderful! If it's 10 minutes, no worries.

2 Add all the other ingredients and mix. Voilà!

PINEAPPLE SALSA

- 2 cups diced fresh pineapple
- 1½ cups (285 g) cherry tomatoes, quartered
- ½ cup fresh chopped cilantro, leaves and tender stems
- 1 small red onion, finely chopped
- 3 tablespoons fresh lime juice
- Small pinch salt

Makes about 4 cups

Fresh, fragrant, and fruity is the name of the game! I keep this salsa cool to serve on spicy stuff, but if you want to spice it up add a pinch of cayenne or a finely chopped jalapeño. Fresh pineapple is a must here! Don't try canned or frozen. You can definitely buy it chopped for you, but one pineapple will be enough for this recipe if you want to put in the work.

1 Mix all ingredients together in a mixing bowl. Use gloved hands to toss it for about a minute, releasing the juices and getting the flavors to marry. Keep refrigerated in a sealed container until ready to use.

GUACAMOLE

Makes 3 cups (670 g)

- ½ medium-size red onion, finely chopped
- ½ medium-size vine-ripened tomato, seeded and chopped
- 1 average-size jalapeño, seeded and minced
- 2 tablespoons finely chopped fresh cilantro
- 1 clove garlic, minced
- 2 tablespoons fresh lime juice
- ¾ teaspoon salt, plus more as needed
- 3 avocados

It's guacamole! Need I say more? No. Put it on everything.

1. In a medium-size bowl, stir together the onion, tomato, jalapeño, cilantro, garlic, lime juice, and salt. Use a wooden spoon to mash it all together a bit to get the juices flowing.
2. Halve the avocados, remove the seed from each, and scoop the flesh into the bowl. Use an avocado masher or fork to get it all mashed up together.
3. Taste for salt and seasoning. If not serving right away, transfer to a storage container, place a wet paper towel directly on top of the guac to keep it from browning, seal the container tightly, and refrigerate. Use within a few hours.

PICO DE GALLO

Makes about 3 cups (440 g)

- 1 pound (455 g) vine-ripened tomatoes, cut into small dice
- ½ cup (20 g) chopped fresh cilantro
- 1 small white onion, finely chopped
- 2 jalapeños, seeded and finely chopped
- 1 tablespoon fresh lime juice
- ½ teaspoon salt, plus more as needed
- Freshly ground black pepper

This pico is as simple as it gets, but that's the beauty of pico! I like to remove all the seeds from the peppers so I can add more fruity pepper flavor without increasing the heat.

1. Place the chopped tomatoes in a colander and let rest in the sink for 20 minutes or so, to drain them a little bit. Give the colander a shake every now and again. You don't want to lose all of the liquid, but you don't want watery pico, either.
2. Transfer the tomatoes to a bowl and toss them with the cilantro, onion, jalapeños, lime juice, salt, and pepper. Taste for salt and seasoning. Let the pico sit for at least half an hour before serving so that the flavors can marry. Keep refrigerated in a tightly sealed container until ready to use.

FRESH HERB VINAIGRETTE

- 1 clove garlic
- ¼ cup (11 g) chopped chives
- ¼ cup (10 g) loosely packed chopped fresh basil leaves
- 3 tablespoons fresh lemon juice
- 2 tablespoons nutritional yeast flakes
- 1 teaspoon granulated sugar
- 1 teaspoon salt
- ½ teaspoon ground black pepper
- ½ cup (120 ml) olive oil

Makes 1¼ cups (300 ml)

Basic is best with this vinaigrette. It's fresh and zippy and takes just a few pulses. Use a small blender (like a Magic Bullet or smoothie blender) for best results, because it's not enough liquid for a regular blender, unless you double it. But go ahead and do that—I promise you will go through it.

1 In a small blender, pulse the garlic to get it chopped up. Add the remaining ingredients and pulse for 20 seconds. It should be relatively smooth but with some texture from the herbs.

ITALIAN HERB DRESSING

- 1 clove garlic
- ½ cup (120 ml) extra-virgin olive oil
- ¼ cup (60 ml) red wine vinegar
- 2 tablespoons nutritional yeast flakes
- 2 teaspoons stone ground mustard
- 1 teaspoon granulated sugar
- 1 teaspoon onion powder
- ½ teaspoon dried oregano
- ½ teaspoon dried thyme
- ½ teaspoon dried basil
- ½ teaspoon red pepper flakes
- ¾ teaspoon salt

Makes ¾ cup (180 ml)

The zippiest, zingiest dressing in town! Make it in a little blender (like a Magic Bullet or smoothie blender) for best results.

1 Place the garlic clove in a blender and pulse to get it chopped up.

2 Add the olive oil, vinegar, nutritional yeast, mustard, sugar, onion powder, oregano, thyme, basil, red pepper flakes, and salt. Blend to combine, keeping small flakes of herbs visible. It's ready!

ACKNOWLEDGMENTS

First of all, thank you to all the vegan chefs who came before me (or during me). I certainly didn't invent seitan turkey, but I did use all the available information to create the best recipes I could! I try as much as possible to give credit where it's due, but just in case I missed anything, THANK YOU to everyone who has ever twisted wheat gluten, removed the "e" from "chicken," and aimed for the stars.

Now, specific thank-yous:

Chef Liam Smith for helping to develop many of these with me, laughing, crying, and—well, that's about it.

Justin Limoges for working with my totally normal schedule to get the photos done.

Gina Juarez for cleaning up my messes, running to the store for one anise seed at a time, and being part of my Dangerous Nights Crew (we went out for wings once).

Hannah Kaminsky for recipe testing, proofreading, and a little ghost-writing, shh.

Lacey Siomos for inventing chickwheat and being so supportive always.

Jessica Joyce Urban for styling and gossiping with me.

Josh Stern for doing a dish or two.

Sarah Kubersky for the constant support and encouragement.

Cheyenne Boccia for holding down the fort in Brooklyn while I wreaked havoc in Omaha.

Paul Kepple and Alex Bruce at Headcase Design for the doodles.

Marc Gerald, my agent with the mostest.

Heesang Lee, Lisa Silverman, and Sarah Masterson Hally for doing stuff at Abrams to make this cookbook come together.

And, last but most important, Holly Dolce, my editor, for making *Fake Meat* a reality with absolutely no hiccups at all whatsoever.

INDEX

Note: Page numbers in italics indicate photos.